KIELER GEOGRAPHISCHE SCHRIFTEN

Herausgegeben vom Geographischen Institut der Universität Kiel
durch C. Corves, F. Dünckmann, R. Duttmann, R. Hassink,
W. Hoppe, N. Oppelt, A.Vafeidis und R. Wehrhahn

Schriftleitung: P. Sinuraya

Band 128

KAIHUAI LIAO

Debordering and Rebordering Processes in Suburban Guangzhou, China

KIEL 2016

IM SELBSTVERLAG DES GEOGRAPHISCHEN INSTITUTS
DER UNIVERSITÄT KIEL
ISSN 0723 – 9874
ISBN 978-3-923887-70-5

Bibliographische Information der Deutschen Nationalbibliothek
Die Deutsche Nationalbibliothek verzeichnet diese Publikation in der
Deutschen Nationalbibliografie; detaillierte bibliografische Daten sind
im Internet unter http://dnb.dnb.de abrufbar

ISBN 978-3-923887-70-5

Die vorliegende Arbeit entspricht im Wesentlichen der von der Mathematisch-Naturwissenschaftlichen
Fakultät der Christian-Albrechts-Universität zu Kiel im Jahre 2015 angenommenen gleichlautenden
Dissertation.

The cover photo shows a row of street vendors set up outside the
fence of Asian Games Town, a newly built gated community in
suburban Guangzhou.

Photo: Kaihuai Liao

Alle Rechte vorbehalten

Acknowledgements

I am very grateful to my supervisors, Prof. Rainer Wehrhahn and Prof. Werner Breitung, for providing insightful guidance and continuous support and encouragement throughout my doctoral studies. They have my immense gratitude for guiding me to the study of this topic, responding my questions, and pushing me to think hard and deep about the research.

I thank my master supervisor Prof. Li Lixun, at Sun Yat-sen University, for encouraging me to pursue a PhD in Germany in the first place. I also thank Prof. Zhang Hong'ou, at Guangzhou Institute of Geography, for supporting me in completing my PhD.

I would like to thank Prof. Robert Hassink and Prof. Florian Dünckmann for their constructive comments during the symposium at Department of Geography at University of Kiel.

I thank my PhD colleagues in the Urban and Population Geography group at the University of Kiel, Dr. Anna Lena Bercht, Dr. Angelo Gilles, Dr. Dominik Haubrich, Dr. Frederick Massmann, Dr. Corinna Hölzl, Monika Höller, Zine-Eddine Hathat, Michael Helten, Jesko Mühlenberend, Sören Weißermel, Jan Dohnke, Sergei Melcher, Petra Sinuraya, Tobias Laufenberg, Juliane Kasten, and Niklas Matti Heintz for constructive discussion and kind support. I also thank my friends in Kiel for sharing laughter and joyfulness with me.

I would like to thank the many people who helped me to finish the empirical work in Guangzhou and the interviewees who shared their inspiring stories. They must remain anonymous, but I would like to express my particular gratitude to them.

I am thankful to the German Research Foundation (DFG, No. BR 3546/2-1), the China Scholarship Council (CSC) and the National Natural Science Foundation of China (NSFC, No. 41171123) for providing the financial support.

I would like to dedicate this thesis to my wife and my parents. Without their unconditional love and endless support, I would never have been able to complete this monograph.

Kiel, April 2016   Kaihuai Liao

Contents

Acknowledgements	I
Table of contents	III
List of figures	VII
List of tables	VIII
List of abbreviations	IX
Summary	XI
Zusammenfassung (German summary)	XIII

1	**Introduction: focus and relevance**	**1**
1.1	Research focus: residential borderland	1
1.2	Research objectives and structure	3
2	**The state of the art: borders and residential borderland in China**	**5**
2.1	Borders and borderland	5
2.2	Border studies review	7
2.2.1	Classical border studies	7
2.2.2	Border studies renaissance	8
2.2.3	Gaps in border studies	11
2.3	Research on gated communities and urban villages	13
2.3.1	Gated communities	13
2.3.2	Urban villages	17
2.3.3	Synthesis research on gated communities and urban villages	18
2.4	Summary	19
3	**Theoretical framework**	**21**
3.1	The social construction of borders and borderland	21
3.1.1	Structuration theory	21
3.1.2	The impact of structuration theory on national borders research	22
3.2	Debordering and rebordering processes	23
3.2.1	Debordering and rebordering	23
3.2.2	Functional dimension	27
3.2.3	Symbolic dimension	27
3.2.4	Social network dimension	28
3.3	Agency and structural conditions	29
3.3.1	The agency and structure at the micro level	30
3.3.2	The structural conditions and contextual dynamics	31
3.4	Structuration theory, borders and gated communities	32

4	**Methodology and methods**	**33**
4.1	Research design	33
4.2	Methods	37
4.2.1	Semi-structured interviews	37
4.2.2	Observation by following	39
4.2.3	Second-hand data sources	41
4.3	Data collection	42
4.3.1	Research phase I: conceptualization	42
4.3.2	Research phase II and III: experiential and inferential analyses	42
4.3.3	Research phase IV: synthesis and conclusion	43
4.4	Methods of analysis	43
4.4.1	Transcription	43
4.4.2	Coding	43
4.2.3	The analysis of the data collected from observation	45
5	**The national and urban conditions of bordering**	**47**
5.1	The dual land use system and its impacts	47
5.1.1	The setting of the contemporary land use system	47
5.1.2	The production of residential borderlands	48
5.2	The hukou system	51
5.2.1	The creation of hukou system	51
5.2.2	The reform of hukou System	52
5.2.3	Entitlements of agricultural versus non-agricultural hukou holders	53
5.2.4	The impact of hukou system on the border	53
5.3	Housing reform and its impacts	56
5.3.1	A brief review of the process of housing reform	56
5.3.2	The social spatial impacts of housing reform	56
5.4	Socio-spatial transformation and urbanization	57
5.4.1	Socio-spatial transformation	57
5.4.2	Urbanization	58
5.5	The city of Guangzhou and its southern district Panyu	59
5.5.1	The research region of Guangzhou and Panyu	59
5.5.2	Suburbanization as a context of residential borderland development	61
5.5.2.1	Urbanization in two cities (1978-1990)	63
5.5.2.2	Initial and early stage of suburbanization (1990-2000)	64
5.5.2.3	Rapid development and mature stage (after 2000)	64
5.5.3	The policy of "converting villages to communities"	65
5.6	Summary	66

6	**Residential borderlands in Panyu in Guangzhou**	**69**
6.1	Residential borderlands in Panyu: spatial distribution	69
6.2	Three typical residential borderlands	72
6.2.1	Three types of residential borderlands	72
6.2.2	Profile of three corresponding residential borderlands	73
6.2.3	Coding gated community residents' activities in neighboring village areas	75
6.2.4	The general features of flows of insiders across the border in residential borderland	78
6.3	Summary	80

7	**Urban debordering and rebordering processes**	**81**
7.1	The physical border and socio-demographic and economic differences between two contiguous enclaves	81
7.1.1	The creation of Clifford Estate: historical perspective	81
7.1.2	The constitution of the border	83
7.1.3	Socio-demographic and socio-economic differences between two enclaves	84
7.2	Functional debordering process and permeability	88
7.2.1	Functional debordering process	88
7.2.2	Changes to the contact zone over time	90
7.2.3	Flows of gated community residents to the neighboring village	93
7.2.4	Flows of vicinity outsiders across the border of the gated community	95
7.3	Functional rebordering	95
7.3.1	Enhanced barrier effect	95
7.3.2	Differentiation of places of consumption	97
7.4	Symbolic debordering	98
7.4.1	The collective identity in Clifford Estate	98
7.4.2	Symbolic debordering: a sense of belonging	99
7.5	Symbolic rebordering	101
7.5.1	Seeking a sense of security	101
7.5.2	Ordering and othering	105
7.5.3	Border for whom? The invisible border in Zhongyi Village	108
7.5.3.1	Security in Zhongyi Village	108
7.5.3.2	The ordering process in Zhongyi Village	110
7.5.3.3	The othering process in Zhongyi Village	112
7.6	Social networks in residential borderland	114
7.6.1	Different types of social relationships between insiders and outsiders	114
7.6.1.1	Economic connections improved weak social ties	114
7.6.1.2	Strong social ties across the border	116

7.6.1.3	Different social circles	117
7.6.1.4	The decline in social contacts	119
7.6.2	Neighborhood relationships among insiders	120
7.6.3	The transformation of social networks in residential borderland	121
7.6.3.1	Types of social networks in the 1980s	121
7.6.3.2	Types of social networks in the 1990s	122
7.6.3.3	Types of social networks after 2000	122
7.7	Actions of the developer and government	124
7.7.1	Actions of the developer	124
7.7.2	Actions of local government	125
7.8	Summary	128
8	**Synthesis: understanding debordering and rebordering processes in residential borderland**	**131**
8.1	Debordering and rebordering processes in residential borderland	131
8.2	The role of structures: contextual and institutional factors	134
8.2.1	The role of social transformation	134
8.2.2	The role of institution	135
8.2.3	The role of urbanization and suburbanization	137
8.3	The role of actors: position, preference and motivation	137
8.3.1	The role of residents' positions	137
8.3.2	The role of residents' preference	138
8.3.3	The role of local government and developers	139
9	**Final conclusion**	**141**
9.1	Empirical findings	141
9.2	Theoretical contributions and future perspectives	143
10	**References**	**147**
Appendix		**163**

List of figures

Figure 1:	Research framework of residential borderland	29
Figure 2:	A visualization of the selection strategy for a single typical case	35
Figure 3:	A visualization of the general research design	36
Figure 4:	The application of content analysis	44
Figure 5:	The process of land expropriation and the creation of residential borders	49
Figure 6:	Comparison of the average GDP growth of Guangzhou versus the national average in different periods	59
Figure 7:	The location of Panyu district	60
Figure 8:	The population development of Panyu district	65
Figure 9:	The identified gated communities and the village residential areas	70
Figure 10:	The landscape of residential borderland in Panyu	71
Figure 11:	A model of three types of residential borderland	72
Figure 12:	Three residential borderlands: Shunde Country Garden, Clifford Estate and Jinxiu Garden	73
Figure 13:	The main entrances and pedestrian gates of the gated communities	76
Figure 14:	The architectural environment inside Clifford Estate	82
Figure 15:	The living environment in Zhongyi Village	83
Figure 16:	Population age structures for Clifford Estate and Zhongyi Village	84
Figure 17:	Population education levels for Clifford Estate and Zhongyi Village	85
Figure 18:	Hukou structure of residents of Clifford Estate and Zhongyi Village	86
Figure 19:	Housing conditions in Clifford Estate and Zhongyi Village	86
Figure 20:	Rental level in Clifford Estate and Zhongyi Village	87
Figure 21:	The dynamic processes of bordering between Clifford Estate and Zhongyi Village	88
Figure 22:	The contact zone between Clifford Estate and Zhongyi Village	89
Figure 23:	The key nodes of flows in the contact zone	90
Figure 24:	Changes over time to the area around a pedestrian crossing at Zhongping road	91
Figure 25:	Changes over time along a commercial alley in Zhongyi Village that leads to the Zhongyi Food Market	91
Figure 26:	Daily flows of residents returning home on the sidewalk after visiting the Zhongyi Food Market	92
Figure 27:	Flows of gated community residents to the neighboring area	93
Figure 28:	Age structure of gated community residents who visit the neighboring vicinity	96
Figure 29:	Screenshot of a website promoting a property in Clifford Estate	100
Figure 30:	Living space inside the gated community	106
Figure 31:	Recreational space for Zhongyi residents	111

Figure 32: Two migrants processing accessories in a village park 117
Figure 33: Transformation of social networks in residential borderlands 123
Figure 34: Village planning of Zhongyi 127
Figure 35: The performance of debordering and rebordering and their agential and structural factors 132

List of tables

Table 1:	Interviews at Clifford Estate area	38
Table 2:	The record table of observation by following (sample list)	40
Table 3:	Major constituent groupings of agricultural and non-agricultural populations by hukou status and location	51
Table 4:	The main welfare differences between non-agricultural and agricultural hukou holders in a host city	54
Table 5:	Conditions and features of residential suburbanization in Guangzhou	62
Table 6:	The profile of three residential borderlands	74
Table 7:	Statistical results of the collected data from observation by following	79
Table 8:	Financial revenue and expenditures of Zhongyi Village (2011)	109
Table 9:	Debordering and rebordering processes in residential borderland	128

List of abbreviations

A	Answer
CCTV	Closed Circuit Television
CNY	Chinese Yuan
CPMLC	Clifford Property Management Limited Company
COEs	Collective Owned Enterprises
CSNIC	Chinese Standard of National Industry Classification
DFG	German Research Foundation
EU	European Union
FDI	Foreign Direct Investment
GDP	Gross Domestic Product
IC	Identity Card
LAL	Land Administration Law
NAFTA	North American Free Trade Area
NAICS	North American Industry Classification System
NDA	No Data Available
Q	Question
SEZ	Special Economic Zone
SOEs	State-owned Enterprises
SNLS	Second National Land Survey
SNPC	Sixth National Population Census
USSR	Union of Soviet Socialist Republics

Summary

This study analyzes the processes of debordering and rebordering at the scale of neighborhood borders using a residential area in suburban of Guangzhou, China, as a case study area. The vicinity of a gated community and an urban village leads to the formation of a residential borderland in which, through the processes of debordering and rebordering, borders become on the one hand more permeable but, on the other hand, more rigid.

The dynamics of bordering processes have been examined substantially at national borders; however, not much attention has been paid to how exactly borders work at the scale of the neighborhood. What kinds of bordering processes occur at this level? How and why do they happen? The answers to these questions are little known to us and require more empirical study and theoretical explanation. This study takes Anthony Giddens' structuration theory, which emphasizes the duality of agency and structure, together with the theoretical concepts of national borders from political geography, which include borders as processes and as social construction, to develop a theoretical framework for analyzing borders at a neighborhood scale. The theoretical framework stresses the processes of debordering and rebordering, which are socially constructed through the interaction between agency and structure.

The empirical research focuses on the phenomenon of residential borderland, which is defined as the residential area consisting of two contiguous urban enclaves: a gated community and an (urban) village. Special attention is paid to the city of Guangzhou in China, which has experienced rapid economic development and urbanization in the post-reform period. In the context of suburbanization, many of these residential borderlands have emerged in suburban Guangzhou. Clifford Estate, a gated community, and its neighboring urban village, Zhongyi, are selected as a typical residential borderland for an in-depth case study.

The applied qualitative research methods include semi-structured interviews and observation by following. The collected data include 69 qualitative interviews and 481 data collections through observation by following. Applying the theoretical approach to the case study, three dimensions – functional, symbolic, and social networks – of debordering and rebordering processes in suburban Guangzhou are analyzed. The results demonstrate that residential borders are becoming more permeable as flows of people increase from the gated community to the neighboring village area. At the same time, however, the borders still divide the city through rebordering processes of seeking a sense of security and of ordering and othering. This study also demonstrates how the various actors shape the processes of debordering and rebordering and how these processes are embedded in the urban spatial reconfiguration of Guangzhou. Border theory, as derived from the scale of national borders, is extended to the micro-scale of borders at the neighborhood level.

The study demonstrates that the constructed theoretical framework is beneficial to our understanding of urban conditions and dynamics.

Zusammenfassung

Die vorliegende Arbeit analysiert Prozesse des debordering und rebordering auf der Nachbarschaftsebene am Beispiel eines Wohngebiets in der Stadt Guangzhou (China). Aus der Nachbarschaft einer Gated Community und einem urbanen Dorf entsteht ein residential borderland, in dem sich aufgrund von debordering und rebordering Prozesse Grenzen einerseits auflösen und andererseits verstetigen.

Die Dynamiken von Grenzentstehungsprozessen auf der Nationalstaatsebene wurden bisher in ausreichendem Maße untersucht, wohingegen der Frage, wie sich Grenzen auf der Nachbarschaftsebene auswirken, wenig Aufmerksamkeit beigemessen wurde. Welche Art von Grenzentstehungsprozessen findet auf dieser Ebene statt? Wie und warum finden diese Prozesse statt? Die Antworten auf diese Fragen sind bislang noch sehr begrenzt, so dass ein Bedarf an umfassenderen empirischen Studien und theoretischen Erklärungen besteht. Diese Arbeit setzt sich sowohl mit der Strukturationstheorie nach Anthony Giddens, in der die Dualität von Handlung und Struktur hervorgehoben wird, als auch mit dem politisch-geographischen Konzept der Nationalen Grenzen, in dem Grenzen als Prozess und als soziales Konstrukt verstanden werden, auseinander, um ein individuelles theoretisches Konzept zu entwickeln, das die Analyse von Grenzen auf der Nachbarschaftsebene ermöglicht. Dieser theoretische Rahmen hebt das debordering und rebordering als sozial konstruierte Prozesse zwischen Struktur und Handlung hervor.

In der empirischen Untersuchung wird der Fokus auf das Phänomen des residential borderland gelegt, das als ein Wohngebiet definiert wird, welches aus zwei aneinandergrenzenden urbanen Enklaven – einer Gated Community und einem (urbanen) Dorf – besteht. Dabei wird die Stadt Guangzhou, die im Anschluss an die chinesische Öffnungs- und Reformpolitik der 1970er Jahre durch ein dynamisches Wirtschaftswachstum und eine intensive Urbanisierung geprägt ist, in den Blick genommen. Im Kontext der voranschreitenden Suburbanisierung bildeten sich zahlreiche dieser residential borderlands am Stadtrand Guangzhous heraus. Clifford Estate, eine Gated Community und das benachbarte urbane Dorf Zhongyi wurden als typisches residential borderland und somit als Fallbeispiel für die in dieser Arbeit erfolgende empirische Analyse ausgesucht.

Methodisch wurden bei der qualitativ ausgerichteten Arbeit sowohl halbstrukturierte Interviews als auch Methoden der nicht-teilnehmenden Beobachtung eingesetzt. Insgesamt wurden 69 Interviews und 481 Beobachtungsprotokolle ausgewertet. Anhand des eigenen konzipierten theoretischen Ansatzes wurden unter der besonderen Berücksichtigung dreier Aspekte – funktionale, symbolische und soziale Netzwerke – Prozesse des deborderings und reborderings im suburbanen Guangzhou analysiert.

Die Ergebnisse zeigen, dass residential borderlands aufgrund der zunehmenden Fluktuation und alltäglichen Austauschbeziehungen zwischen der Gated Community und dem benachbarten urbanen Dorf durchlässiger werden. Gleichzeitig wird die Stadt immer noch von Grenzen getrennt, die durch von dem Wunsch nach Sicherheit sowie von Handlungen des orderings und otherings ausgehenden Prozessen des rebordering konstruiert werden. Weiterhin wird in dieser Arbeit deutlich herausgearbeitet, wie die unterschiedlichen Akteure die debordering und rebordering Prozesse beeinflussen und inwieweit diese Prozesse in die stadträumliche Umgestaltung Guangzhous eingebettet sind. Mit dieser Arbeit wird die Grenzforschung dahingehend ergänzt, dass der bisher auf die nationale Ebene bezogene theoretische Rahmen auf die Mikroebene der Nachbarschaft erweitert wird. Letztendlich wird gezeigt, dass mit dem erarbeiteten theoretischen Konzept ein besseres Verständnis von städtischen Strukturen und Dynamiken gewonnen werden kann.

1 Introduction: focus and relevance

1.1 Research focus: residential borderland

"Although the spatiality of borders has undergone shifts in recent decades, it is nevertheless still important to consider the place of borders in border studies, i.e. where do we look for evidence of bordering practices and what are the impacts on particular places?" (JOHNSON, et al. 2011, p. 62).

"[T]he fractal exopolis is [...] increasingly becoming a carceral city, a city of insular cells and walls, obsessed with maintaining the boundaries between we and they, the insider and the Other, the familiar and the stranger, the resident and the alien." (SOJA 2005, p. 43).

In a world full of borders, about 300 interstate land boundaries and more than 40 sea boundaries have existed since the modern national system was set up in the 1980s (PAASI 2009b). Despite some pending regional disputes over national boundaries, most are stabilized and fixed institutionally. In the era of globalization, people, goods, ideas, and information are crossing borders more easily. The proposition of a "borderless world" is inspiring all those who pursue free movement and exchange. The number of borders is seemingly shrinking in terms of the formation of different economic and politic unions such as the European Union (EU) or the North American Free Trade Area (NAFTA). However, the thesis that the number of borders is shrinking is hard to validate if we consider borders at the urban scale.

Borders are actually burgeoning at the urban scale with regard to different urban enclaves. Endless borders appear when we look at the spatial scale of the city. The gaps between social groups, the physical barriers to flows of people, and the wired fences and walls of gated communities all constitute borders. The internal borders have separated the cities into different compartments. Particularly gated communities, as globally emergent phenomenon, have become the most remarkable borders in the cities. Compared with national borders, the borders in cities are perhaps more important since people might live out their lives without traversing national borders but experience urban borders every day. With regard to the daily mobility of people within their microenvironments, perceived borders take on a much more important role (NEWMAN 2003a).

Since the early 1990s, border studies have been enriched largely by substantial work from geography and other disciplines. In the context of diffusive study of borders, the question has arisen in border studies: Where is the border? (JOHNSON, et al. 2011). Cities, as assemblages of borders, should become an arena for border studies. The neighborhood borders of gated communities, displaying the most dramatic dividing lines in cities and bearing many similarities with national borders, are a good object of study to find evidence of bordering processes and practices. Nevertheless, in the academic discourse of border studies in political geography, the research centers on national borders but pays limited attention to the borders on an urban scale. Specifically, the study of the processes of "bordering" is wanting not only of a theory (NEWMAN 2003a) but also of sufficient empirical research. Concerning borders at the micro-scale, questions of the nature of bordering processes and of how they are shaped by different actors in the cities have not been fully explored thus far.

Urban borders are also a topic within urban studies. While border studies in political geography mainly focus on national borders and have neglected borders at the scale of cities and neighborhoods, urban studies research on borders, couched in terms of segregation, enclave urbanism, splintering urbanism, and the divided city, has not distinctly addressed borders. The result has been a gap between border studies and urban studies. In urban studies, some scholars have recently noticed the value and importance of neighborhood scalar borders and have advocated for a shift in focus to urban borderlands (IOSSIFOVA 2013; 2015). The socio-spatial structure of Chinese cities has been characterized as filled with patchworked enclaves (WISSINK, et al. 2012) and enclave urbanism (BREITUNG 2012), that is, with a juxtaposition of gated communities, urban villages, and work-unit compounds. However, research has centered mainly on the territory of each enclave and on interpreting the drawing of borders in the city. It has paid insufficient attention to the processes of debordering and rebordering and the way they play out there. The dynamics and changes of neighborhood borders have not been fully explored or interpreted theoretically. This study attempts to respond to this need by focusing on the border in residential borderland. Residential borderland is defined as residential area with two contiguous but distinct urban enclaves: a gated community and an urban village.

This study explores and theorizes upon the processes of debordering and rebordering in suburban Guangzhou. GIDDENS' structuration theory (1984) emphasizes the duality of agency and structure as well as the theoretical concepts of national borders; stress is placed upon a view of borders as processes and as social construction. The present study develops a theoretical framework for analyzing bordering processes at a neighborhood scale. Thus constituted, the theoretical framework regards processes of debordering and rebordering as an outcome of the interaction of agency and structure. Empirically, the processes of debordering and rebordering are explored in three dimensions: a functional dimension, a symbolic dimension and a social network dimension.

The city of Guangzhou in China, which has experienced rapid economic development and urbanization in the post-reform period, was selected as the research region. The empirical research focuses especially on Panyu district, which is a main suburbanization zone in Guangzhou. Within the context of suburbanization, numerous residential borderlands have emerged in Panyu district. In order to explore bordering processes in great detail, a typical residential borderland was selected for in-depth case study. It consists of a gated community named Clifford Estate and its neighboring urban village, Zhongyi Village.

1.2 Research objectives and structure

This study seeks to contribute to social theory debate by developing a theoretical framework based on structuration theory and national border theory. The aim is to expand our knowledge around the concept of bordering processes and provide an alternative perspective for understanding urban conditions.

Hence, the key research question of this study is:
How can we theoretically and empirically understand and explain the processes of debordering and rebordering in suburban Guangzhou, China?

In order to approach the main research question, it is divided into three sub-research questions:

1. What kind of debordering processes and rebordering processes occur in residential borderlands?
2. How do the actors shape the processes of debordering and rebordering in suburban Guangzhou?
3. Why, and under what structural and contextual conditions, do the debordering and rebordering processes take place?

The thesis contains nine chapters:
Chapter 1 provides a brief introduction of the study, including its research focus, research questions, and objectives. Chapter 2 first introduces the relevant concepts of borders, borderland, and residential borderland. Second, border studies in political geography as well as research into gated communities and urban villages from the perspective of urban studies are reviewed. This chapter identifies that there is a need to focus on the processes of debordering and rebordering at the neighborhood scale. Because the dynamics of bordering processes have been examined substantially in the context of national borders, however, not much attention has been paid to how exactly borders work at the neighborhood scale.

Based on structuration theory emphasizing the duality of agency and structure, and based on the theoretical conceptions of national borders which address them as processes of bordering, debordering and rebordering, and social construction, Chapter 3 develops a theoretical framework for analyzing debordering and rebordering processes at the border on a neighborhood scale. The theoretical construct adopts an agency-structure approach to analyze the processes of debordering and rebordering in functional, symbolic and social network dimensions.

Chapter 4 introduces methodology and methods. The research design and qualitative methods – semi-structured interviews and observation by following – are presented. The process of data collection and data analysis methods are introduced as well.

Chapter 5 introduces the structural conditions and contextual dynamics within which the residential borderland comes into being and within which the processes of bordering, debordering and rebordering are embedded. The first section introduces the institutional reforms, which include land reform, the household registration (in Chinese: *hukou*) system reform, and housing reform. The second section presents the background of social transformation and urbanization. The third section explores urban conditions in Guangzhou, focusing on suburbanization and urban policy.

The empirical findings are presented in Chapters 6 and 7. In Chapter 6, the spatial distribution of residential borderland in Panyu district of Guangzhou is explored. Three types of residential borderland are identified, and the flow of people across the borders from the gated community into the neighboring village is addressed. In Chapter 7, three dimensions of debordering and rebordering processes in residential borderland are explored. Functional debordering indicates that there are vigorous flows of people across the residential borders between the gated community and its adjacent village and a commercialization of the contact zone. Accompanying these, however, is a functional rebordering process consisting of an enhanced barrier effect and differentiation of places of consumption. Symbolic debordering indicates that the gated community residents have generated a sense of belonging to the places in vicinity village area. It is accompanied by a symbolic rebordering process that involves the quest for a sense of security, ordering, and othering. An invisible border of institutional exclusion in the urban village is examined. Finally, there is a social network dimension of the border indicating that some intimate social ties permeate the border, but mainly the insiders and the vicinity outsiders live in different social circles.

Chapter 8 synthesizes the theoretical framework and the empirical results. Impacts of debordering and rebordering processes are interpreted from both structural and agency dimensions. Chapter 9 draws the conclusions, including the empirical findings and theoretic contributions, and looks ahead to future research.

2 The state of the art: borders and residential borderland in China

2.1 Borders and borderland

Generally speaking, a border is equivalent to a boundary, and the terms can be used interchangeably in border studies. Traditionally, it is taken for granted that borders are state boundaries, i.e., the lines defining the spatial extent of jurisdiction and sovereignty of state territories (MINGHI 1963; PRESCOTT 1987). The understanding of borders has shifted from that of static, physical outcomes of political and social processes along walls, rivers and mountains to one that encompasses processes and institutions through which lines of separation and difference are created and perpetuated (NEWMAN 2006b; PARKER, et al. 2009). The border is in an inchoate state (JONES 2009), shedding light on a space for change. The word "borders" is understood in terms of bordering as "the human practices that constitute and represent differences in space" (VAN HOUTUM 2005, p. 672). As NEWMAN (2003b, p. 15) argues, "[i]t is the process of bordering, rather than the border line per se, that has universal significance in the ordering of society". A border may be generated, perpetuated, or in some cases eventually disappear. These processes are historical contingencies (NEWMAN and PAASI 1998). Borders do not exist prior to political decisions but only obtain their social meanings as a result of political processes and their legitimization of borders (STETTER 2008).

The term of borders is defined from multiple angles. ANDERSON (1996) defines borders as an institution determined by politics and managed and controlled by legislation. BRUNET-JAILLY (2011, pp. 1-3) argues that borders, "as territorial markers and functional-fluid vectors of demarcation, may be transforming or evolving" and are created through "the continual interactions and intersections between the actions of people (agency) within the constraints and limits placed by contextual and structural factors (structure)". A border denotes the ownership and sovereignty of space and introduces order (VAN HOUTUM and VAN NAERSSEN 2002). PAASI (1999, p. 669) argues that borders are important "institutions and ideological symbols that produce and reproduce in social practice and discourses". In a word, from the social constructivist perspective, the understanding of borders is no longer limited to physical lines of national separation but extends to socially constructed borders as well as to the "border" as a process.

The borders concept is concomitantly related to the terms "frontier" and "borderland". It is of great help to distinguish the borderland from the frontier. The frontier means the outer or leading edge of the hinterland (KRISTOF 1959). It normally has a connotation of peripheral geographical location. The "borderland" instead emphasizes the socio-spatial impacts of a border which might exist anywhere. This is because borderland not only appears at the periphery but also in the city center; it moves beyond the geographical limitation of "center – periphery". ALVAREZ (1995, p. 448) defines borderland as "a region and set of practices defined and determined by [a] border that are characterized by conflict and contradiction, [and are] material and ideational". NEWMAN (2006b, p. 150) advances the notion that "borderland" is a transitional space referring to "the region or area in relative close proximity to the border within which the dynamics of change and daily life practices were affected by the very presence of the border." Thus "borderland" refers to a transitional space where processes of separation and marginalization as well as those of integration and communication may both play out simultaneously.

The juxtaposition of different urban enclaves in Chinese gated communities, urban villages (or migrant enclaves), and work-unit compounds (in Chinese: *danwei*) has been called "enclave urbanism" (BREITUNG 2012; HE 2013). Conspicuous residential borders in Chinese cities give residential borderland some significance in border studies and urban studies. The residential borderland is a residential area comprising both sides of the border in which people's daily life practices are affected by the very existence of the residential border. In other words, two (or more) contiguous residential enclaves contribute to a residential borderland.

There are many kinds of residential borderlands between contiguous enclaves. Because gated communities in suburban areas of Chinese cities are built mostly on land expropriated from villages, juxtaposition of a gated community and a neighboring village has emerged pervasively in Chinese cities. The scope of this research is limited to the residential borderlands which include two asymmetric but adjacent enclaves: a gated community and its neighboring (urban) village. The gated community named Clifford Estate (or "CE") and its neighboring urban village, named Zhongyi ("Zhongyi" or "Zhongyi Village"), were chosen as the research object for a case study. The selected residential borderland is located in the Panyu district of Guangzhou. With the construction of Clifford Estate, the whole area of Zhongyi became separated into two enclaves forming a typical residential borderland.

The municipal government of the city of Guangzhou officially identified 139 villages as urban villages. The official number of urban villages only reflects an area encompassing the five central districts of Guangzhou. It excludes the suburban area even though a substantial number of urban villages exist there as well. A common misunderstanding would be that only those villages in the city proper are identified as urban villages. In fact, some villages in the peri-urban area also should be deemed urban villages because their agricultural land was expropriated for urban construction during the rapid urbanization process. One result is that the villagers do not engage in agricultural activities anymore. Because a great number of migrants have gathered in such villages, they have become migrant enclaves. WANG, et al. (2010) illustrate that rural migrants tend to concentrate in peri-urban areas. Because of the rapid urbanization and expansion of Guangzhou, Zhongyi Village has gradually been encircled by newly-built residential buildings and become an enclave for rural-to-urban migrants. Although Zhongyi Village lies on the outskirts of the city of Guangzhou, it is actually an urban village,[1] as distinguished from other villages on the city fringe where most villagers still engage in agricultural work.

2.2 Border studies review

Border studies experienced a classical research phase until the end of the 1960s but fell into obscurity during the 1970s. After the fall of the "Iron Curtain" between East and West in 1989 and the collapse of the Soviet Union in 1991, many border research institutes were set up and many relevant publications began appearing. Border studies have undergone a renaissance since then.

2.2.1 Classical border studies

The signing of the Peace of Westphalia at the end of the Thirty Years' War laid a foundation for the framework of the modern state system. After the Second World War, the colonial countries successively gained their independence, which contributed to the constitution of the contemporary modern state system. Based on that historical development, border studies have become a sub-discipline of political geography. As MINGHI (1963, p. 407) writes, borders "are perhaps the most palpable political geographic phenomena". The content of the traditional research included three main aspects.

First, border studies as a field initially concentrated on descriptions of demarcation, allocation and change, disputes, and historical process around national borders (PRESCOTT 1965). Second, according various dimensions such as genesis, morphology, features, and time phases, borders have been classified into various categories and typologies (JONES 1943; 1959; MINGHI 1963; PRESCOTT 1987). The distinction of natural versus artificial borders has garnered a large body research mainly concentrated on the analysis of the virtues and morality of borders from a military perspective (LYDE 1915; HOLDICH 1916). The result was overemphasis of disputes and location changes during phases of war or military occupation rather than during phases of peace (MINGHI 1963). However, social constructivism in the post-modern period let to the abandonment of the view that "borders are natural". Scholars then claimed that all borders are man-made. The effect of this shift has been that contemporary researchers pay scant attention to the morality and virtues of borders. The shifted approach "thereby risks throwing away the baby with the bathwater" (VAN HOUTUM 2005, p. 676) .

Third, ever since the late classical research stage of the discipline, border studies have moved from descriptive analysis to a functional approach. The focus shifted to grasping

---

1 The village has been officially identified recently as "urban village" by the local government of the Panyu district based on the policy set forth in The Guidelines of Village Planning of Guangzhou City (广州市村庄规划编制指引) issued by the government of Guangzhou in 2013.

the function of the border at different times and in different phases (BOGGS 1940; HARTSHORNE 1950; MINGHI 1963). KRISTOF (1959) argued that the frontier, as the outer edge or forefront of the hinterland, is outer-oriented while the border which defines the scope of the central authority is inner-oriented. SPYKMAN (1942) pointed out that the frontier is a key area to understanding the relationships between states. JONES (1959) asserted that cross-border organizations should have the function of alleviating tensions across borders.

Traditional approaches include mapping, classification, and a functional approach (KOLOSSOV 2005). The traditional research phase developed a foundation for the border studies renaissance in the post-modern era. However, the ontological cognition of the border as a static outcome of political and social process during this phase was static, decisive, and limited (NEWMAN 2006b). This is one of the most important reasons why border studies stagnated during the 1970s.

2.2.2 Border studies renaissance

There are both realistic and theoretical reasons for the renaissance of border studies. On one hand, the ambivalence – and the puzzle – presented by globalization has attracted renewed scholarly attention to border studies (LECHEVALIER and WIELGOHS 2013). After the fall of Berlin Wall and the end of the Cold War, the process of globalization accelerated immensely. Goods, ideas, people, and capital could all flow more easily across national borders. The barrier effect of state borders became increasingly weakened and even disappeared gradually. New spaces for economic, political, and cultural cooperation such as the European Union, the North American Free Trade Area etc. are being created. Globalization purists posit a theory of a "borderless world" (OHMAE 1990) or "de-territorialization" (OHMAE 1995; CANEY 2005). They argue that national and regional borders are becoming meaningless or even dying. On the other hand, borders are porous in uncertain ways. For instance, perceived or real economic competition, international migration, multiculturalism, and terrorism all reactivate the processes of state exclusion. Thinking in terms of theory, postmodern development in social science has promoted the development of border studies. Postmodern social theories have had a profound influence on border research. One example is TAYLOR's world systems theory, which deals with the interdependence and connectivity of space and scale; another is GIDDENS' structuration theory, which stresses the initiative of agency under the constraints of structure; and yet another is FOUCAULT's (and his followers') post-modern view of social discourse and the social construction of space (KOLOSSOV 2005, p. 613). In the post-modern period, borders have attracted substantial research attention.

There is a remarkable multidisciplinary study of borders. Beginning in the mid-1990s, border studies began to attract the attention of scholars in multiple disciplines including geography, sociology, political science, anthropology, and international law. Such scholars have strived to coin common or shared terminologies (NEWMAN 2006a). NEWMAN and PAASI (1998) identify four interdisciplinary themes in border studies. The first is the postmodern discussion of de-territorialization and re-territorialization under the impact of globalization. The second theme is the debate over the role of the border in creating "Us" and "Others" and in constituting socio-spatial identities. A third theme is the concern for border narratives or discourses that unfold during processes of national socialization: the theory that borders are embedded not only in compartmental landscapes of social power, control, and governance but also in the "literary landscape". Fourth, attention has been paid recently to the construction of borders at different scales.

In scale-oriented border studies the predominant view of scale involves an areal concept ("scale as size"), a hierarchical concept ("scale as level"), and a relational concept (HOWITT 1998). Remarkably, the notion of scale figures into a great deal of border literature. Borders are constituted at a number of different spatial scales from global to national, regional, local and even to microscales of social-spatial activity (NEWMAN 2006b). Scale is of great importance in the processes of border construction. Borders of difference and separation operate at different scales (NEWMAN and PAASI 1998). The study of borders has continually extended itself to different scales. Borders have been studied substantially in terms of national and regional levels in political and regional geography.

On one hand, research into state borders has extended its scope from state and regional levels to a supranational level. Scholars have noticed that there is a "territorial trap" limiting the researcher's view of state borders such that borders to them appear as fixed, physical containers of modern society and as fixed dividing lines between inside and outside (AGNEW 1994). Much effort in borders research has been devoted to avoiding this territorial trap and to constructing alternative concepts. Society should extend beyond territory through the notion of a network society within a "space of flows" rather than a "space of place" (CASTELLS 1996). Herein would lie the possibility of constituting a cosmopolitan society (BECK 2000).

On the other hand, borders research has been shifting its attention from the national scale to the internal, regional, municipal, and even neighborhood scales (LUNDÉN and ZALAMANS 2001). The importance of state borders is undoubted and well-studied; but at the same time microscale borders have received increasing attention. To the extent that they determine people's daily life practices, microscale borders have a greater impact than the national boundaries. The reason is that most people have not crossed a national border even once in their lives (ALVAREZ 1995; NEWMAN 2006b) but cross urban borders all the time.

There are various kinds of borders in the city including commercial borders, political borders, and residential borders. However, borders researchers seem to overlook borders in the city. Urban studies have explored social and economic segregation, administrative boundaries, urban design, and other urban features. Each topic does relate to borders, but the research typically does not make explicit reference to the term "borders" (BREITUNG 2011). Research into urban borders in urban geography studies has been increasing recently. KARAMAN and ISLAM (2012) argue that the urban border represents an inherent contradiction between people's pursuit of "the right to the city" and the right to be different. IOSSIFOVA (2009) focuses on blurring residential boundaries in the city of Shanghai. JIRÓN (2010) researches the performance of mobile borders in the city. BREITUNG (2011) proposes five interrelated approaches along political, physical, socio-spatial, psychological, and functional dimensions to explain intra-urban borders.

Affected by postmodern social theories, many different approaches to borders studies have emerged. Among these are world systems and territorial identities, geopolitical approaches, borders as social representations, eco-political approaches etc. (KOLOSSOV 2005). VAN HOUTUM (2000), reviewing approaches to borders in European geography studies, identifies three strands of thinking about national border studies in the post-modern era: the functional approach, the governance approach, and the people approach. First, as one of the most popular traditional approaches, the functional approach still attracts modern scholars' attention. On the hypothesis that space is a homogenous, physical, abstract concept, borders constitute barriers to free movement of people, goods, capital, and other elements and cause discontinuity and increasing marginal transaction costs. Second, globalization has resulted in ever-deepening international and regional cooperation. Thus a second strand of border and borderland studies today is a governance perspective. It refers to the management of border regions and cross-border cooperation in the context of regulation of international migration and other trans-border flows. Typically, policies and strategies of cooperation as well as economic, political, social, and cultural dissimilarities that prohibit cross-border integration between the regions are analyzed and evaluated. The third strand of debate about borders is the people approach. Its focus lies on borders as an indispensable part of social and individual life. Taking the people approach is to analyze the viewpoints and behaviors of individuals or social groups who participate in crossing or constructing borders, with focus on production and reproduction of borders as well as impacts on social-spatial identities. From this standpoint, borders are socially and politically constructed. Border studies are shifting to substantial theoretical debates. However, a lack of a general border theory still hampers progress. Theoretical reflections on the border began in the late 1980s. There have been two strands of theoretical assertion since then. Some scholars argue that it is impossible to form a general theory in border studies. They are influenced by the theory of PRESCOTT (1987), for whom "borders are unique". PRESCOTT states that every border is unique, and that it is very difficult or even impossible to abstract a general or all-encompassing theory of borders. BALIBAR (1998) coins a "borders are everywhere" view. PAASI (2009) argues further that borders are a part of the "discourse landscape" of social power. For instance, borders are present not only in the national ideological and physical landscapes, but also in places such as airports. In order to theorize about borders, both generality and particularity as well as certitude and contingency should receive adequate consideration. Therefore, a general border theory would run contrary to the inherently diverse, complex nature of borders and "would seem in many ways unattainable, and perhaps even undesirable" (PAASI 2011, p. 27).

On the contrary, many scholars have strived to constitute a border theory. To name a few, ANDERSON and O'DOWD (1999) argue that territoriality, globalization, and phases of historical change are three dimensions by which to analyze state borders and border regions. BRUNET-JAILLY (2005) posits a four-pronged theory of national borderland study, which includes multilevel governance, market flows, local political clout, and local cultural dimensions. Some scholars classify these four analytical dimensions into two forces – agency and structure – and put them into practice (CHEN 2009; BANERJEE and CHEN 2013). NEWMAN (2006b) constructs a research agenda for border studies based on four dimensions or theoretical paradigms: demarcation, perpetuation, permeability, and transition space. ALBERT and BROCK (1996) as well as STETTER (2005) and SENDHARDT (2013) distinguish three types of borders by which they interpret the process of debordering and rebordering. This last direction is reserved for a more detailed discussion in the theoretical chapter (see Chapter 3.2). There is no contradiction between the first strand and the second strand because each border is unique; to theorize upon a single border is both possible and meaningful.

2.2.3 Gaps in border studies

In the appraisal of MINGHI (1963), border studies were in their infancy at the classical research stage. Although border studies have undergone a renaissance since the early of 1990s and a large number of publications on related topics have emerged, border studies are still far from maturity. Compared with other social disciplines, border studies remain in their infancy over fifty years later. The most important difference between classical border studies and postmodern border studies is that the former focused mainly on empirical analysis of specific cases or on problem-solving-oriented studies. The postmodern phase has scrutinized and theorized upon borders based on empirical data within social and political contexts including those of states, nations, territorialities, identities, and ethnicities (AGNEW 1996). VILA (2003) observed that the focus of U.S. border studies had shifted gradually from its emphasis on empirical research to literary criticism and theoretical constructions. However, these proclaimed border theories are all either too general or too specific.

Theories arrange themselves on a continuum according to the width of explanatory power. At one pole is a grand border theory. Some of the postmodern social theories cited at the beginning of this section (such as TAYLOR's world system theory, GIDDENS' structuration theory, discourse and social construction of space etc.) have had far-reaching influence on border studies. They are metatheories that aspire to validity for all borders. For border studies, however, they are too general. In U.S. border studies, the research themes have moved from the U.S.-Mexico border to broader themes in which the border is developed into a metaphor to "represent any situation where limits are involved" (VILA 2003, p. 307). Both the spatial and not-spatial limits are thus regarded as borders: "borders among countries, borders among ethnicities within the United States, borders between genders, borders among disciplines, and the like" (VILA 2003, pp. 307–308). This shift has led to theoretical claims homogenizing different experiences as well as different borders and to theories that are too general to explain the political, economic and social borders. The claims are usually monolithic and detached from the context. Some Mexican border scholars on the other side of the border complain that these theories bear little resemblance to their experience of borders (VILA 2003).

At the other pole of the theoretical continuum are too specific claims that are difficult to validate in other social and spatial dimensions of the border. ACKLESON (2003) pointed out that many theoretical assertions about the U.S.-Mexico border lacked immersion in broader social theories, especially when the theory related to change. PAASI (2009) has criticized much border research in Europe for putting forward no more than a context-bound theoretical framework based on broader economic, cultural and political context rather a general border theory. The reason for the limitation is that a context-bound explanation lacks immersion in a broader social theory.

At the center of the continuum reside such ontological theses as "every border is unique", "borders are everywhere", "borders as processes", "borders as social construction" etc. Each thesis can be seen as a general theoretical conception covering all the spatial and social borders. These ontological assertions improve our understanding of what a border is. However, they cannot fully explain the related phenomena of identity, territory, sovereignty, and security.

NEWMAN (2003a), addressing the national political border, argues for an understanding of borders as processes of "bordering" rather than as the static outcome of social and spatial processes. A theory by which to understand this process "requires an integration of the different types and scales of boundaries into a hierarchical system in which the relative impact of these lines on people, groups, and nations can be conceptualized as a single process" (NEWMAN 2003a, p. 134). However, the theoretical framework to understand this process is poorly supported by empirical evidence, especially with respect to borders on a neighborhood scale.

SAYER (1992, p. 58) asserts two ways of evaluating a theory: in terms of its conceptual consistency and of its empirical adequacy. Conceptual invariance refers to "open categories that are general enough to be used in various contexts but which can be reflected and re-developed to study boundary-producing practices/discourses in different contexts" (PAASI 2009, p. 224). Hence, to build a theory of bordering appeals to various empirical studies in different social and political contexts and at different scales of borders. The examination in a concrete context would allow us to create new theoretical insights. Borders at neighborhood scale are at least as important and in most cases even more important than national borders. This research therefore aims to study the neighborhood border of gated communities to examine the conceptualization of bordering and to expand the concept by immersion in a broader social theory of structuration theory. A more detailed explanation synthesizing the conceptualization of bordering, structuration theory, and gated communities unfolds in Chapter 3.

2.3 Research on gated communities and urban villages

Urban studies have recently devoted much attention to the topics of "enclave urbanism" (BREITUNG 2012; DOUGLASS, et al. 2012; HE 2013), "splintering urbanism" (GRAHAM and MARVIN 2001; COY 2006), and the "divided city" (FAINSTEIN, et al. 1992; VAN KEMPEN 2007). These concepts are highly relevant to segregation, which is one of the consequences of the practices involved in these urbanisms. Residential borderland, as a phenomenon, is a spatial representation of enclave urbanism. Residential borderland comes in association with two different, but adjacent, enclaves: gated communities and urban villages (or migrant enclaves). Hence, this section reviews the research on gated communities and urban villages.

2.3.1 Gated communities

Gated communities, as a worldwide phenomenon, have proliferated in countries throughout most of the world including the United States and Canada in North America, England and Portugal in Europe, Argentina and Brazil in South America, China and Indonesia in Asia, and South Africa and Ghana in Africa. BLAKELY and SNYDER (1997b) defined gated communities in a general way, as residential areas to which access is restricted by virtue of walls, fences, or other barriers and whose public spaces are normally private. ATKINSON and BLANDY (2005) refine the definition by pointing to the "legal agreements" as pivotal features. Legal agreements provide common norms of conduct for residents and define the duty to collectively manage the community. Enclosed residential roads are depicted as part of the general character of a gated community from the perspective of urban planning and design (GRANT 2005). Hence, gated communities are those communities that represent restricted access physically in terms of walls and fences as well as institutionally through innovations on the social contract involving collective management in a community.

The fences and walls of gated communities have become remarkable borders in cities. SASSEN (2013) regards gated communities as an emergent frontier-space function and as hardwired bordering inside cities; accordingly

> "the uses that global corporate capital makes of 'our' cities are part of that hard bordering. The common assertion that we are a far less bordered world than 30 years ago only holds if we consider the traditional borders of the interstate system, and then only for the cross border flow of capital, information and particular population groups." (SASSEN 2013, p. 1).

Thus while state borders are receding against the backdrop of globalization and of increasing flows across those borders, borders are burgeoning in the cities.

There is a long-standing history of enclosure in Chinese cities. The Forbidden City in Beijing, the traditional courtyard houses represented by the Qiao Family Manor in Shanxi province in the pre-1949 era, and the Maoist-era walled "work-unit compounds" all have involved walls and fences (WHEATLEY 1971; HENG 1999; KNAPP 2000). However, in most research, gated communities in China refer to the "sealed residential quarters" (in Chinese: *fengbi xiaoqu*) (MIAO 2003) which arose after the housing reform started in 1978. The housing reform aimed at transforming the state-welfare housing system into a market-oriented system of housing provision. Gated communities have increased dramatically in the post-reform period as almost all newly-built commercial housing has taken the form of walled, gated complexes.

Contemporary Chinese cities contain many small and medium-sized gated projects, but huge gated complexes and the "foreign gated community" have also emerged under the processes of globalization and local institutional reform (WU and WEBBER 2004; WANG and LAU 2008). WEHRHAHN (2003, cited in WEHRHAHN and RAPOSO 2006) coined the phrase "pseudo-gated communities" to describe gated neighborhoods in Madrid and Lisbon to which access is not legally controlled. That is, the neighborhoods were built as gated and walled estates that retained public spaces such as streets and green space. The public was free to enter but encountered symbols of gating such as gates, signs, barriers and security guards indicating a private atmosphere and restriction of entrance. A survey of Shanghai shows that a large number of gated communities are actually a sort of "pseudo" or "faked" gated community displaying the symbols of gating while not being strictly closed (YIP 2012).

The reasons for the proliferation of gating phenomena can be interpreted from structural and agency dimensions. Globalization of economies and the withdraw of the interventionist state from providing basic services against the backdrop of neo-liberalism are understood as structural forces (GLASZE 2005; XU and YANG 2008; ROITMAN 2010). Residents, local governments, developers, and urban planners are conceived of as initiating agents. The most frequently-mentioned causes on the demand-side are: 1) the "discourse of fear" theory, which highlights the residents' need for a sense of security in the city (DAVIS 1992; BLAKELY and SNYDER 1997a; LOW 2001; LOW 2003); 2) a "club realm of consumption" theory that explains the people's pursuit of optimized utility of private amenities and services (WEBSTER 2002); 3) the struggle to sustain property values (GOIX and VESSELINOV 2013); and finally 4) market preferences.

On the supply-side, one explanation holds that that local governments seek to grow their tax bases and foster urban growth (MCKENZIE 2005) but fail to supply an efficient quantity of collective goods and services for residents (WEBSTER 2001; FOLDVARY 2006). However, neither the quantity nor quality of collective goods and services is sufficient in China because the government is unable to fulfill residents' needs equally well with respect to affordability by different social groups. In this connection developers see positive implications of gated communities as they are better able to market projects to potential buyers and maintain profits with higher densities in face of the rising land cost (MCKENZIE 1994; 2005).

The proliferation of gated communities in China has been explained along two lines of thinking. Some researchers place the gated communities into a global context and explain them based on theories formed in the context of Western countries. WU (2005) employs the "club realm" theory, while MIAO (2003) adopts the "fear of crime" theory. Other scholars approach the problem in the local social, economic, political, and historical context. Gated communities are designed to represent prestige, a high quality of life and exclusive consumption (POW and KONG 2007) through aesthetics and packaging-based strategies. These strategies nomally transplant the architectural styles of Europe or North America or appeal to traditional Chinese culture of the pre-1949 era (GIROIR 2006; WU 2010). HUANG (2006) highlights the impacts of the cultural continuity of Chinese collectivism and strong political control of the state, while POW (2007a; 2007b) considers the "moral order" between urban and rural areas as well as increasing household autonomy and personal freedoms as an escape from the central control of the authoritarian state. XU and YANG (2009) argue that gated communities have ingrained, historical roots in urban design. BREITUNG (2012) differentiates functions of gated borders, which represent ideas of security, a sense of belonging, the symbolic meaning of prestige and status, and private production of the "good life" in China. HE (2013) points to local institutional arrangements as a fundamental factor.

Scholars intensely debate the consequences of gated communities. One of the key debates is about the negative social impacts of gated communities. Most studies argue that gated communities create exclusionary spaces, restrict freedom of movement, increase urban segregation, and exacerbate social divides (CALDEIRA 1996; BLAKELY and SNYDER 1997b;

CALDEIRA 2000; LOW 2003; ROITMAN 2005; LEMANSKI 2006; VESSELINOV 2008; GOTTDIENER and HUTCHISON 2010; VESSELINOV 2012). LOW (2001) argues that there is a constant, self-reinforcing cycle between gated communities and social segregation. An obsession with security arises through the discourse about urban crime and leads to the need for gatedness, while gatedness itself results in mistrust of and unfamiliarity with outsiders which in turn feed back into the sense of insecurity. GOIX (2005) points out with respect to the form of public-private partnership in providing urban infrastructure that gated communities are a valuable source of revenue because the cost of suburbanization is paid by the developers and housing purchasers; such has increased urban segregation in southern California. Some research in the Chinese literature argues that gatedness has increased the degree of social segregation there as well (SONG and ZHU 2009; LIU and LI 2010).

However, the Chinese public does not view gates and walls as a serious problem; it even desires them (BREITUNG 2012). The literature lists some positive social and political effects. Compared to other neighborhood types, for instance the "work unit compound", gated enclaves exhibit higher levels of community attachment (LI, et al. 2012). Social affairs are self-managed in gated communities. The concentration of middle-class residents in the newly-formed homeowner associations of gated communities is conducive to cultivating democratic thought and facilitating public participation. Damage to property interests has led to protest in some instances (READ 2008).

Urban planning plays a pivotal role in the production and regulation of gated space. GRANT (2005) points out that although the Canadian urban planning system has developed some tools to regulate gated communities, it is still ineffective at coping with all the challenges. Planners are typically ambivalent because, although the gated communities facilitate approval of infill projects at higher densities, at the same time they conflict with paramount concerns about connectivity and social integration. In England, local municipalities have not recognized so much as the existence of these new urban development forms (ATKINSON and FLINT 2004). In Portugal, in order to abide by the local planning regulations and reduce the cost of approval, local urban planning departments have often adopted a strategy of packaging different projects into a single planning application, in the form of multiple, interconnected building planning models (CRUZ and PINHO 2009). Australia has seen cases in which decisions by local planning councils to reject gated community forms were overturned by a planning tribunal because the local government did not fully deliberate upon the long-term interests of the residents of gated communities (GOODMAN, et al. 2010). An empirical analysis of Buenos Aires has shown that planning regulations are defective as a matter of how they respond to the challenges presented by gated proliferation (THUILLIER 2005). In fact, planning authorities in most parts of the world do not have planning policies to respond effectively to these new forms of urban development; some authorities have not so much as recognized that gated phenomenon exist in their municipalities (CRUZ and PINHO 2009).

2.3.2 Urban villages

Urban villages, or "villages in the city" (in Chinese: *chengzhongcun*) are a typical phenomenon in China, and have proliferated to many cities, *e.g.*, Guangzhou, Shenzhen, Beijing, Shanghai, Harbin, and Kunming. Urban villages are villages encircled by built-up urban area whose land still belongs to a collective (ZHANG, et al. 2003; TIAN 2008; HE, et al. 2010). The term "urban village" was coined by GANS (1962, p. 4), who introduced the term to describe the adjusted urban environment where ethnic migrants try to "adapt their nonurban institutions and cultures to the urban milieu". In the late 1980s, urban villages were nominally promoted by urban planners in the United Kingdom as a means of creating a village-style, mixed-use sustainable neighborhoods in an urban context (ALDOUS 1992; FRANKLIN and TAIT 2002; MURRAY 2004). Here, the term "urban village" is differentiated from the Western urban planning concept of the same name. It is also distinct from the concept of a migrant village such as Zhejiang Village in Beijing, which is occupied by Zhejiang migrants (CHUNG 2010).

There was a vacuum of governmental governance in urban villages. Because the legal validity of urban planning did not cover rural areas for a long time – not until the Urban and Rural Planning Law was issued in 2008 – indigenous villagers, lacking such planning regulation, struggled to construct substandard housing units or extra floor space in order to maximize their benefit from rental income (SONG, et al. 2008). The rent-seeking behavior has led to high-density housing and narrow pathways that do not meet fire safety requirements at urban villages. Chaotic land-use, a dilapidated, dirty environment, high-density housing, and crime facilitation are the problems of urban villages.

Urban villages, as informal settlements, are similar to the slums or squatter settlements in Western countries but have characteristic demographic structures and land uses of their own. Urban villages are mainly inhabited by temporary rural-to-urban migrants and by indigenous villagers. The agricultural land has been expropriated, and the indigenous villagers have disengaged from agricultural activities. The village land belongs to the village collective.

A large body of Chinese-language research exists on urban villages, but much less has appeared English. Some scholars have profiled and characterized the social structure and spatial distribution of urban villages (ZHANG 2001; LIU, et al. 2010; HAO, et al. 2013). ZHANG, et al. (2003) and SONG, et al. (2008) address the social implications of urban villages as sites of affordable housing for low-income rural migrants. WU, et al. (2013) interpret the rationale of production and reproduction of informality in urban villages under the urban policies of redevelopment. TIAN (2008) analyzes the merits and problems of urban villages from the perspective of property rights, pointing out the importance of institutional reform of collective property rights in the renewal of the urban villages. HE, et al. (2010) take an institutional perspective to interpret stratification and housing differentiation in urban villages and argue that the hukou system, land use system, housing provision system, and village governance all have strong explanatory power about the formation of urban villages. CHUNG and ZHOU (2011) criticize that the urban village redevelopment policy launched by local governments has not taken the interests of the plural group into consideration.

2.3.3 Synthesis research on gated communities and urban villages

There are two synthetic approaches to studying gated communities and urban villages. One approach considers the two types of neighborhood as spatial representations of enclave urbanism from a general perspective and explains them through social, economic, and political discourses. In other words, gated communities and urban villages are considered as a form of enclave urbanism. Taking Guangzhou as an example, HE (2013) takes an historical approach to explain the evolution of gating in China and its contemporary implications. QIAN (2014) argues that enclave urbanism in China is not only a cultural continuation of Chinese tradition but also a consequence of contemporary social, economic, and political discourses.

The other approach takes a concrete perspective to analyze the probable social and economic relationships between two dissimilar enclaves based on empirical data. The related empirical question asks whether gated communities lead to an increase in social segregation or not. Some international researchers have addressed the relationship between a gated community and its poorer adjacent neighborhood. LEMANSKI (2006) surveys the attitudes and perceptions of the residents at gated communities and their neighboring areas in South Africa; in spite of spatial contiguity, they are found to be socially and functionally separate. Based on a case study in Chile, SALCEDO and TORRES (2004) conclude that gated communities and their local (poor) neighborhood are functionally integrated with each other. The poorer local residents welcome the gated community because it has brought modern transportation, water supply, and sewage treatment facilities while raising land values, while the gated community residents have a positive attitude toward their poorer neighbors such that some wanted to employ them. MANZI and BOWERS (2005) argued that, if there were no walls or fences, the gated communities could not exist as neighbors of poor communities. The spatial proximity of rich and poor neighborhoods strengthened each group's social understanding of the other. SABATINI and SALCEDO (2007) found that the gated communities are functionally and symbolically integrated into their respective neighborhoods in Santiago, Chile.

However, there is limited empirical research addressing the relationship between gated communities and neighboring villages in China. IOSSIFOVA (2015) focuses on everyday practices in urban borderland and interprets the borderland urbanism in China. FENG, et al. (2014) base an analysis of the relationship between a gated community and its neighboring vicinity in Guangzhou on home construction. They conclude that different groups employ different homemaking strategies according to their own resources.

2.4 Summary

This literary review indicates several motivations for the present research. First, review of the literature reveals a gap in the discipline. That is, despite border researchers' emphasis on multiple scales of borders, most scholars in political geography have focused on state borders and regional borders but paid little attention to borders on an urban scale, such as the residential borders within cities. Meanwhile, much research in urban studies has adopted the perspectives of enclave urbanism in general and the perspectives of concrete social impacts in detail. But such research does not explicitly address the border which is so determinative of urban structure. The microscale borders at urban and neighborhood levels bear many similarities to state borders. The general principles of national border theory can inspire an analysis of the microscale border. Although existing border theories have not emerged from study of residential borders, they employ principles and concepts, such as the notion of the border as a process involving debordering and rebordering, that are helpful in understanding and explaining the residential border. The contrary ought to hold as well: empirical research on microscale borders should provide a useful contribution to a grand border theory. Hence, the national border scholars should not only focus on state borders but also on the microscale of borders.

Second, theoretical reflection toward understanding the phenomenon of bordering is insufficient. On the one hand, the theoretical concept of "borders as processes" with aspects of bordering, debordering and rebordeing in different dimensions, as a means of understanding bordering phenomena, has limited empirical support, especially at the neighborhood scale. On the other hand, these theoretical conceptions are of important to understand what kinds of processes there are, but it cannot explain why and how these processes and dynamics happen. Hence, immersion in a broader social theory will increase the explanatory power of the theory.

Third, urban studies have focused mainly on the territory of each enclave interpreting the drawing of different borders in the city, but giving insufficient attention to the processes of debordering and rebordering. The fences and walls of gated communities, as a subsequent or even a superimposed border for the village in a residential borderland, have far-reaching influence on the villager's everyday practices. Borders not only define and reinforce the power and ownership of territory but also denote the probability of contact and relationships with the outer world. From the perspective of border and borderland, two adjacent enclaves are viewed as a whole, while the border is viewed as processes. However, there is limited empirical research considering the two adjacent enclaves as a whole research object, and focusing seldom on the processes of debordering and rebordering. Regarding two adjacent enclaves as a whole research subject, and to bridge the above-mentioned gaps, next chapter is going to develop a theoretical framework.

3 Theoretical framework

This chapter is devoted to constructing a theoretical framework for the study of debordering and rebordering processes in residential borderland. GIDDENS' structuration theory is significant in border studies and has had major impact on national borders research. It provides a useful method for understanding bordering from both agency and structural dimensions. Theoretical conceptions of national borders, including that of borders as processes and that of borders as socially constructed, are beneficial to constructing a research framework for a neighborhood border. In this chapter, the structuration theory and the theoretical conceptions of borders are merged into a research framework that helps shed light on the processes of debordering and rebordering of neighbourhood borders.

3.1 The social construction of borders and borderland

3.1.1 Structuration theory

GIDDENS (1984) advanced the structuration theory in his famous book The Constitution of Society. The book expresses the idea that social reality consists of agency and structure. GIDDENS' structuration theory arises from syncretism and eclecticism of the classical social theories, including the individualistic theories as well as the structuralistic theories (LIPPUNER and WERLEN 2009). The individualistic theories emphasize the actor's knowledge and experience as well as the ways people use them to improve the social world, while the structuralistic theories accentuate that the power of structure, super-individual institutions, and social systems shape individual action. Opposed to the classical social theories which go to either extreme, structuration theory takes a mediate position, stressing the duality of agency and structure.

Structuration theory holds that action plays out among different, interrelated agents acting under structural conditions; meanwhile structures are maintained and reproduced by the agents' actions. Action is understood as "a *durée*, a continuous flow of conduct" (GIDDENS 1984, p. 3), but not as a combination or set of "acts". Society is generated by and through social action. Action is enabled first by the agent. In GIDDENS' theory, individuals are regarded as active, knowledgeable, and reflexively monitoring agents who possess unconsciousness, practical consciousness, and discursive consciousness in their social practice (GIDDENS 1979, p. 54). Unconsciousness refers to action outside an actor's self-awareness. Practical consciousness covers what people have done but cannot verbalize. Practice consciousness, in other words, means implicit understanding of action that the actor cannot express in words. Discursive consciousness refers to the capacity of actors to give reasons for or rationalize their actions. The stratification of consciousness applies to different levels of action, including its motivation, rationalization, and reflexive monitoring. Action originates in reason or motivation, where reason is the source of the action and motivation is its promotion. When an actor has implemented an action, he or she seeks to rationalize it so that it may be recognized and followed by others. In the process, actors continuously monitor their actions and rationalize their intentions in context – the body, surroundings, and the self. If an action deviates from the actor's intention and does not generate the desired outcome, the actor has a transformative capacity to adjust his or her strategies of acting. This transformative capacity means that agency logically connects to the power to change course, i.e., the actor is able to change or influence processes or situations (GIDDENS 1984, pp. 14-15).

An agent's actions are bounded by structure. Structure is both the medium and the outcome of the (re)production of day-to-day activities. In other words, the social system affects agents' action through structure; meanwhile the structure is the very outcome of their actions. Structures consist of rules and resources. Rules and resources "draw[n] upon in the production and reproduction of social action are at the same time the means of system reproduction" (GIDDENS 1984, p. 19). Rules are generalized procedures which provide the methods or techniques of day-to-day activities. GIDDENS argues that most rules reside in practical consciousness. Rules enable agents to produce and reproduce their actions. At the same time, rules shape the action. In other words, rules play both a regulative and a constitutive role in the action.

Resources refer not to a certain state or to things such as natural resources or raw materials, but to the transformative capability of authorization and allocation. Structures exist as memory traces and are instantiated in social action and discourse. Structures are also both enabled and constrained by human agents (HAUGAARD 1997). GIDDENS distinguishes between two types of transformative capacity: authorization and allocation. Authoritative resources refer to the capacity of actors to control the social world created by humans, or to control the actors themselves. Allocation resources mean a transformative capacity of actors to steer the appropriation and use of natural resources.

The duality of agency and structure provides a theoretical method for analyzing social phenomena. DYCK and KEARNS (2006, p. 87) comment that "structuration theory intended to sensitize empirical research through emphasizing the knowledgeability of the individual agent in the reproduction of social practice, the time-space contextuality of social life, and the hermeneutic or interpretative nature of analysis". Hence, "the analysis of praxis [actions] and the analysis of structural settings can therefore be seen as two compatible concepts of social research" (LIPPUNER and WERLEN 2009, p. 41).

3.1.2 The impact of structuration theory on national borders research

Borders are socially constructed. The perspective of social constructivism has had a major impact on border-theoretical reflections. Structuration theory provides an interpretative approach to understanding the phenomenon of borders from the perspectives of agency and structure. Based on GIDDENS' structuration theory, BRUNET-JAILLY (2005) develops a theory to analyze national borderland. It posits four dimensions: policy activities of multiple levels of governments, flows of trade, local community political clout, and culture.

Structural forces are those social processes that both support as well as confine individual action. They include a) the policy activities of multiple levels of governments, which involve both general-purpose and task-specific governance. General-purpose governance refers to vertical interactions among local, provincial, and state governments, while task-specific governance refers to horizontal interactions between public and private sectors. Structural forces also include b) market forces and trade flows, which refer to flows of goods, people, and investments across boundaries. Agency force means the initiative of actors and their practices that shape social life, including c) the local political clout of borderland communities with "local level relations, local policy network, local policy communities, symbolic regime, [and] local cross border institutions" (BRUNET-JAILLY 2005, p. 645). The last type of agency force is d) the local cross-border culture encompassing the sense of belonging, food, social-economic background, and common language.

BRUNET-JAILLY argues that all four of these analytical lenses exhibit intricate interplay resulting in the emergence and integration of an economic, political and cultural borderland region. KONRAD and NICOL (2008) integrate a dimension of socially constructed and reconstructed identities into BRUNET-JAILLY's national borderland theory. According to BRUNET-JAILLY (2011, p. 3), borders are created through "the continual interactions and intersections between the actions of people (agency) within the constraints and limits placed by contextual and structural factors (structure)". This theoretical conception is useful to our understanding of urban borderland. This research adopts the agency-structure approach because is an important social theory for theorizing about urban borderland. However, the emphasis of BRUNET-JAILLY's theory lies wholly on the economic, political, and cultural integration of the national borderland. It forgets both the othering nature of the border and the borders at the scale of the city. Therefore, it is necessary to reformulate the theoretical framework for application to neighborhood borders.

3.2 Debordering and rebordering processes

3.2.1 Debordering and rebordering

The concept of bordering has been explored in the context of national borders. NEWMAN (2006b) argues that the border should be viewed as a set of processes rather than as fixed lines. Such processes create and perpetuate borders. They consist of bordering, debordering, and rebordering. Bordering is understood as the creation or demarcation of borders. However, demarcation of borders should not imply a simple understanding such as "the drawing of a line on a map or the construction of a fence in the physical landscape"

(NEWMAN 2006b, p. 148) but rather it should imply dynamic social processes. The processes of debordering and rebordering occur simultaneously over time (RUMFORD 2006). The simultaneous processes of debordering and rebordering are not contradictory. As ALBERT and BROCK (1996, p. 70) define them, "debordering processes in the world of states are understood as an increasing permeability of [territorial] borders together with a decreasing ability of states to counter this trend by attempts to shut themselves off." Rebordering, then, consists of "the demarcation phenomena as a specific reaction to the debordering processes that are actually taking their course within the framework of globalization. Viewed in this light, demarcation (re-territorialization) would be, first and foremost, a way of regulating the process of transformation, not of arresting it" (ALBERT and BROCK 1996, p. 96). Therefore, debordering and rebordering are self-regulating, circular processes governed by the power relations between agency (e.g., the migrants, the state) and structure (e.g., the trends of globalization).

In order to theorize about residential borderland, it is important to compare national borders with neighborhood borders, such as those formed by a gated community, at the micro-level. There are two major differences. First, state actors predominate in the creation and perpetuation of national borders, while the non-state actors, e.g., developers and residents, predominate in forming residential borders. Second, in people's everyday lives, the micro-level borders are much more important than national borders, for while people cross and experience urban borders every day, they might not cross a national border even once in their lifetime (ALVAREZ 1995; NEWMAN 2006b). Hence, it is necessary to zoom into the neighborhood scale to see what kinds of processes are underway at neighborhood borders and how they form.

However, there are also many similarities between national borders and neighborhood borders. One of these is the distribution of ownership and jurisdiction. NEWMAN (2003a, p. 130) argues that "[t]he functional impact of boundary on the behavioral patterns of the people who are enclosed by these lines is common to all types of boundary, regardless of the spatial scale at which the bounding process takes place". The similarities allow the general principles of national border theory to inspire analysis of the urban border. More specifically, the above-mentioned theoretical concepts of debordering and rebordering can apply to residential borders. Although neighborhood borders are not the level to which border theory abstracted at first, border theory is helpful in analyzing them, and therefore this study has chosen the national border theory as a means of understanding urban conditions and dynamics.

At the scale of neighborhood borders, debordering and rebordering are similarly related to power relations between agency and structure. That is, the dynamics of debordering and rebordering are an outcome of agency and structure. The debordering process is understood as the power to make borders softer and more permeable, while the rebordering process is understood as the power to make borders harder and more rigid. GIDDENS (1985, p. 120) claims that the state is like a power container, wherein power is understood as the power relationship between the agency and structure. Power here means the capacity of agents to negotiate with external forces and structural conditions, in particular with the conditions imposed by pre-existing borders. The borders are reconstructed and deconstructed according to the agents' ability.

In precisely the same way, debordering with respect to neighborhood borders indicates the increasing permeability of borders instantiated in part by flows of people across the borders of a gated community. It also refers to the decreasing ability of the related elites, e.g., residents, developers, and governments, to counter this trend by attempting to seclude themselves. Rebordering is a continuation of bordering processes and a response to the debordering processes unfolding within the framework of structural and contextual conditions. In other words, it is a reaction of the elites to perpetuate borders and preserve the original order.

Bordering processes have multiple dimensions. Scholars have increasingly realized that borders have such abundant and varied meanings that it is impossible to put them all into to a single, consistent definition. An aspect-seeking perspective is therefore required (BAUDER 2011). Much discussion among border researchers has addressed types of national borders (see, e.g., ANDERSON and O'DOWD 1999; DONNAN and M.WILSON 1999; ANDERSON 2001; O'DOWD 2002; ANDERSON, et al. 2003). ANDERSON (2001) distinguishes political and social borders. O'DOWD (2002) represents an understanding of borders as barriers, bridges, resources, and symbols based on European border practices. One classic classification of borders is that of HARTSHORNE (1936), who puts forward "antecedent", "subsequent", and "superimposed" borders. HARTSHORNE claims that no matter how these borders originated, spatial borders are entrenched in cultural structures in areas proximate to the border. Antecedent borders represent the existence of boundaries preceding human settlement, and in effect these later affect human life. The fences and walls of gated communities thus represent antecedent borders from the perspective of gated community residents. Subsequent boundaries emerge from existing ethnic territorial groups, while superimposed boundaries work upon existing cultural divisions. For instance, the invisible borders between indigenous villagers and rural migrants are subsequent borders. The fences and walls of gated communities in residential borderlands are superimposed borders to the indigenous villagers.

The processes of debordering and rebordering have been distinguished into different aspects (see, e.g., ALBERT and BROCK 1996; STETTER 2005; BONACKER 2007; FERRER-GALLARDO 2008; SENDHARDT 2013). FERRER-GALLARDO (2008) argues that rebordering takes in geopolitical, functional, and symbolic dimensions. STETTER (2005) and BONACKER (2007) emphasize a distinction of processes along territorial, functional, and symbolic dimensions. Territorial borders are "those that separate states or regions and serve first and foremost as a means of control, of ascribing areas of competence and demarcating jurisdictions" (SENDHARDT 2013, p. 27 cited from BONACKER 2006, p. 81). Functional borders "separate different functional systems, such as politics, law, science, economy, sports, love or the health system" (STETTER 2005, p. 5). Symbolic borders create collective identities, differentiating people into "self" and "other" (STETTER 2005, p. 5). BONACKER (2007, p. 24) argues that debordering is "the functional change of borders, the loss of importance of their territorial anchoring and – as a consequence – the decoupling of (functional) system borders and territorial borders". In this vein, the functional and symbolic borders can decouple from the territorial border. The multidimensional debate around debordering and rebordering is useful for studying residential borders. However, the analysis of debordering and rebordering at micro-scale borders should be neither isolated from the social structure and contexts nor limited to the territorial, functional, and symbolic dimensions.

With respect to the urban borders, BREITUNG (2011, pp. 57-58) distinguishes five interrelated border approaches: the physical, the political, the socio-spatial, the psychological, and the functional aspects. Political borders separate "political and administrative territoriality by different laws and jurisdictions"; socio-spatial borders "are both socio-economic and socio-cultural division lines"; psychological borders are represented in people's minds, marking territories of groups of people with different spatial identities and sense of belonging; and finally, functional borders are "as filters of flows and networks". These approaches are beneficial to intra-urban borders research. However, not all of them are important for analysis of residential borderland.

In the study of social integration, SABATINI and SALCEDO (2007) constructed a three-dimensional framework involving functional, symbolic, and community aspects to analyze social integration between a gated community and its neighborhood. Functional integration indicates the extent to which poor people are integrated into society as judged through their use of the functional means of exchange, namely power and money. Functional integration involves questions of how the poor participate in the market, implement their political rights in the democratic process, and access urban facilities and services. Symbolic integration refers to the degree of resident's attachment to the place where they live. Community integration refers to the formation of social ties between the residents of two adjacent neighborhoods. Although the authors do not characterize it distinctly as a border, the different levels of social integration between the gated community and its poorer vicinity actually represent a kind of debordering process.

Therefore, debordering and rebordering processes at a neighborhood border are analyzed from functional, symbolic and social network dimensions. At the micro-scale, based on empirical findings to be analyzed in Chapter 7, social networks, as part and parcel of residents' daily lives, are extracted as an independent dimension from the functional dimension.

3.2.2 Functional dimension

The functional dimension of borders separates different functional systems and acts as a filter of flows (STETTER 2005; BREITUNG 2011). As the classical approach in border studies, it specially attends to cross-border flows. Borders are not always completely closed. Borders act simultaneously as a barrier and a bridge. Borders resemble membranes in cells, which possess "selective permeability" and "differential filtering effects" (ANDERSON 2001). On one hand there is a barrier effect: the border becomes less permeable to some flows, such as to illegal migrants, urban crime, and so forth. On the other hand, borders become more permeable to other flows, such as those of goods, services, and capital. NEVINS (2002, p. 7) argues that state borders are devoted to "maximizing the perceived benefits of globalization while protecting against the perceived detriments of increasing transnational flows". This logic "seriously impedes the free movement and exchange of labour and is generally accepted by neo-liberals despite the fact that it contradicts their free-trade, anti-state ideology" (ANDERSON 2001, p. 30). Take for instance the state border: both the U.S.-Mexican and Spanish-Moroccan borders are quite permeable to flows of goods and capital but not very permeable to labor migration (COLEMAN 2005; FERRER-GALLARDO 2008).

With respect to neighborhood borders, functional debordering means borders become more permeable as a result of flows of residents, goods and money across borders. Functional debordering indicates the formation of spaces for common activities and constant exchange of goods and money between two enclaves. Functional rebordering impedes the free movement of people and exchanges of goods and money. Functional rebordering represents the formation or enlargement of exclusively bounded space.

3.2.3 Symbolic dimension

The symbolic dimension of borders refers to collective identities and differentiation among people into the "self" and the "other" (STETTER 2005). Borders exist not only as barriers and bridges but are heavy with symbolism (O'DOWD 2002, p. 27). The role of national borders in constructing identities has received substantial discussion in a series of academic works (see, e.g., LEIMGRUBER 1991; WILSON and DONNAN 1998; ACKLESON 1999; DONNAN and M.WILSON 1999; ALBERT, et al. 2001; MEINHOF 2002).

FERRER-GALLARDO (2008, p. 315) argues that "the demarcation of limits by means of borders enables both the formation of collective identities and the creation of others". The formation of collective identities is always associated with the strategy of place-making. Place making is a spatial strategy that "presupposes a place that can be circumscribed as one's own, and that can serve as the base from which to direct relations with an exteriority consisting of targets or threats such as clients, competitors, enemies and strangers" (VAN HOUTUM and VAN NAERSSEN 2002, p. 126).

Borders impose the order of "inside" and "outside". DIENER and HAGEN (2009) argue that borders reflect existing differences and engender new "others". The processes of homogenization within and differentiation from "outside" are each nested in the symbolism of borders (PAASI 1996). Bordering involves othering "others". Borders pursue spatial purification of a place to be demarcated as one's own against territorial ambiguity and ambivalent identities (VAN HOUTUM and VAN NAERSSEN 2002). Therefore, in the process of constructing collective identities, the spatial strategies of ordering and othering coincide.

With respect to the neighborhood borders, symbolic debordering therefore means a hybrid of collective identities and a rising sense of belonging to the residential borderland. Symbolic debordering indicates the formation of a common identity in residential borderland and the elimination of stereotypes and stigmas in the minds of residents of two enclaves. Symbolic debordering suggests the question whether residents in a gated community consider the neighboring village as a part of them. Symbolic rebordering, by contrast, means the pursuit of differences through the processes of seeking a sense of security and of ordering and othering. For instance, symbolic rebordering represents an enhancement of different collective identities in each group of residents and the persistence of stigmas and discrimination.

3.2.4 Social network dimension

A social network dimension is to be distinguished from the functional dimension. The social meanings of borders at the micro-scale are much more significant than those of national borders. Because not everyone crosses national borders to form international social ties but crosses urban borders daily, they perceive the boundary as very real. Social contacts are a part the daily life in a city. However, social network borders are the hardest borders dividing people at the individual and collective level. The neighborhood is a source of social relations, but the study of social networks should go beyond the boundary of residential neighborhood (HAZELZET and WISSINK 2012). Gated community and adjacent urban village residents both inhabit the residential borderland. The formation of social networks across borders goes beyond simple functional exchange, indicating the most open of borders (SABATINI and SALCEDO 2007). Hence, social network borders refer to lines dividing social ties between two enclaves.

Social network debordering refers to the formation of social ties across the residential borders. There are three levels of social ties in residential borderland. At the first level are weak social connections such as mutual facial recognition, greeting, or engaging in small conversations upon meeting. Occupying the second level are normal social connections such as the relationships among participants in group activities and colleagues. The third level is comprised of strong social connections from which intimate social ties form. Strong social connections mean stable social networks such as village clan networks or

Theoretical framework 29

those of friendship, kinship, and the relationships among fellow townsmen. Weak social ties can strengthen into strong social ties over time (GRANOVETTER 1973). Social network rebordering refers to the differentiation of social circles and to the atrophy of stable social ties between two enclaves.

3.3 Agency and structural conditions

The three dimensions of debordering and rebordering account for processes taking place around the neighborhood border, while structuration theory is introduced to explain how and why they happen. In other words, these theoretical conceptions of the border as process and as social construction constitute the theoretical framework. As Figure 1 shows, the processes of debordering and rebordering at the micro level are considered as actions. The actions are enabled and constrained by different actors but at the same time are embedded in the structural and contextual settings.

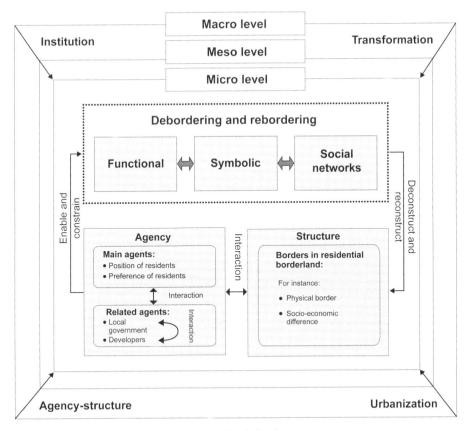

Figure 1: Research framework of residential borderland
Source: Illustration by author

3.3.1 The agency and structure at the micro level

At the micro (district) level, the pre-existing border in residential borderland gives structure while debordering and rebordering processes constitute the actions. In residential borderland the actors – the residents, local government, and developers – are engaging in bordering practices; they are practicing borders. The gated community residents are the "insiders", while residents of surrounding villages are the "vicinity outsiders".[1] The vicinity outsiders include indigenous villagers, rural migrants, and other citizens who have urban hukou. The gated community residents (or insiders) and those living outside of the gated community but nearby (or vicinity outsiders) are the main actors engaged in debordering and rebordering practices. The residents are the central focus of this study. Local government and developers as players are viewed as related actors as they either are engaged in actions of debordering and rebordering or have an indirect impact on the residents' actions. As formulated, the processes of debordering and rebordering, as actions, are enabled and constrained by different actors including the residents, the developers, and local government. The same actions meanwhile construct and reconstruct the structure.

Agency dimensions include many factors. Individual preference, individual position, and the players are three main ones. They are important factors in explaining urban spatial segregation (MADRAZO and KEMPEN 2012). As the driving force of debordering and rebordering, individual preferences, perceptions and decisions should be highlighted because they bear much interpretive power: the residents of the gated community are able to decide whether they want to go to the neighboring village area or not. The position of the individual with respect to income is an important factor in border crossings at a gated community. The related agents, including the developers and local government, are important players driving the processes of debordering and rebordering. Their incentives and values contribute to understanding the mechanisms of debordering and rebordering processes.

Residential borderland consists of many structures. In this study, however, the focus lies on two specific structural aspects: the physical border and socio-economic differences among residents. The physical border refers, according to BREITUNG's (2011) definition, to the visible lines in landscape. They consist not only of the physical structures such as fences and walls but also of the discontinuities of land-use, building style, signage etc. Urban borders always present themselves spatially in space in terms of physical edges like walls and fences. In urban design, paths, edges, districts, nodes, and landmarks are key elements of urban space as portrayed in KEVIN LYNCH's book The Image of the City. Edges are defined as "the linear elements not considered as paths: they are usually, but not

---

[1] The way these terms are used here shall be maintained throughout the work. The "insiders" refers to the residents of a gated community; while the "vicinity outsiders" refers to residents of neighboring villages.

quite always, the boundaries between two kinds of areas." (LYNCH 1960, p. 62). The tangible edges within the city are significant objectives of urban design. The fences and walls of gated communities are, obviously, one of the most dramatic urban edges. The territorial border denotes sovereignty and ownership of an area such as is often achieved by means of physical borders. Physical borders initially mark the scope of territorial ownership in the city. However, the border in residential borderland is not just a matter of walls and fences but also of socio-economic differences. The physical borders are valuable for social study because they take on social attributes as a reflection of social, economic, and political differences.

3.3.2 The structural conditions and contextual dynamics

PAASI (1999) argues that borders are produced and reproduced in social practices and discourses. In other words, borders are cultivated through both discursive landscapes and technical landscapes of control. First, borders are part of the discursive landscape of social power and control. Borders are produced "in historically contingent practices and discourses that are related to national ideologies and identities" (JOHNSON, et al. 2011, p. 63). Various forms of nationalism are embodied in the material manifestations of borders, e.g., the flags flown at international sports competitions or on national independence days. At the city level, residential borderlands are the material manifestation of enclave urbanism. Second, borders are also manifest in technical landscapes of social control and surveillance. Take for instance the surveillance technology used in airports to monitor the flows of people and goods or in gated communities to help control access. In a word, borders are produced on multiple scales of border practices and discourses.

Social, political, and economic contexts provide the ground for the creation of borders and their multiple meanings. Put another way, to understand the processes of debordering and rebordering, one should focus not only on the border area but also on broader social discourses. Processes of debordering and rebordering in residential borderland are embedded in multi-scalar, structural conditions and in contextual dynamics. The various scales of social settings are along the lines of the national, the city, and the district. As PAASI (2009a, p. 225) argues, "[i]t is useful to understand boundary-making as a part of a broader process of territory/region building or institutionalization". The dimensions of institution, transformation, urbanization, and agency-structure, being conditions existing at the city and national levels, are integrated into the theoretical framework. They are contributors to the processes of bordering, debordering and rebordering. Agency and structure exist at different scalar levels. Nevertheless, only at the micro level is agency distinguished from structure, because the agents are stakeholders who directly participate in debordering and rebordering practices. At the super-micro level, agency and structure are part of social settings. This study does not distinguish the two because they indirectly influence on the processes of debordering and rebordering.

3.4 Structuration theory, borders and gated communities

The theoretical framework is, on the one hand, guided by the theory of national borders but on the other hand it is immersed in a broad social theory: structuration theory. The theoretical conceptions of national borders which distinguish multidimensional processes of bordering are used to explain the kinds of debordering and rebordering processes found to occur at neighborhood borders. Meanwhile structuration theory is adopted to interpret how and why these processes happen. According to NEWMAN (2003a), a theory explaining the processes of bordering should consider different spatial scales at which borders exist. The border of a gated community bears many similarities to a national border. Both are spatial borders circumscribing space in terms of territory. Although the theoretical conceptions of bordering pertain to political national borders, they help understand the processes of debordering and rebordering at the neighborhood scale too. The notion of bordering discards the idea that the boundary of a gated community is a static, physical line. Rather, it is a process, that is, the line changes over time. The theoretical guidance of multiple dimensional processes of national borders demonstrates that bordering at the residential borderland be analyzed in three dimensions, or in terms of its functional, symbolic and social network aspects.

Structuration theory is a kind of metatheory that would aspire to validity for all borders, and indeed it is an epistemological position. The theory informs a method for analyzing social phenomena from both agency and structural dimensions. The processes of debordering and rebordering at different scales can be understood as an outcome of the interaction between agency and structure. Hence, structuration theory forms a basis for broadening the theoretical concepts of national borders for analysis at the micro-scale of borders.

Through the constant conversation between the elaborated theories and this study's empirical findings, the theoretical framework outlined here is filled out with detail. First, the concepts of functional debordering and rebordering, symbolic debordering and rebordering, and social network debordering and rebordering are abstracted from the empirical findings under the guideline of the theory discussed in the section 3.2. Second, Structuration theory is adopted to interpret the impact factors. Many factors drive the processes of debordering and rebordering. Factors of individual position and preference as well as the motivations of local government and developers are highlighted based on the empirical findings.

4 Methodology and methods

This chapter introduces the methodology and methods. The research employs qualitative methods. The research design is introduced in the first section, including its theoretical basis, case selection, and general design. The second section addresses the selected methods, including semi-structured interviews, observation by following, and second-hand data sources. The research process and field work are presented in the third section, which also examines the validity of the collected data. The last section presents the methods of data analysis.

4.1 Research design

The relation between theory and data is a central issue in empirical research. Theoretically informed research demonstrates that the research starts with a theory and works down, and the empirical work aims to answer the theory-driven questions through a deductive approach (HERBERT 2010). This research is based on the theory of structuration and the theoretical conceptions of border. Structuration theory provided an epistemological tool to interpret social phenomena with the agency-structure model. However, HERBERT (2010, p. 73) argues that a theoretically informed approach is idealized, and a researcher cannot follow it strictly; the best approach is to tack constantly back and forth between the theory and data. Hence, in the construction of the theoretical framework and analysis of empirical data, an inductive approach is also used. Thus the theoretical framework arises through a constant dialog between the theory and empirical data over the course of this study.

The research questions are addressed by qualitative research using methods of semi-structured interviews and observation by following. Qualitative research, as a traditional research approach, has many strengths, e.g., studying a limited number of cases in depth, describing complex phenomena in rich detail as situated and embedded in local contexts, and generating inductively a theory about a phenomenon that is tentative but also has explanatory power (JOHNSON and ONWUEGBUZIE 2004). There are several rationales for choosing qualitative research for this study:

1. Under the background of the recent "textual turn", border studies are focusing increasingly on textual interpretation and (second-hand data) analysis instead of time-consuming empirical study (PAASI 2005, pp. 668-669). Hence, substantial fieldwork on border studies is needed, especially on the neighborhood scale, where not much field work has contributed theoretically.
2. Qualitative research into residential borderland is useful to describe the complex debordering and rebordering processes in depth and to contribute to theoretical reflections.

3. In doing so, it is necessary to explore the actions of different related actors, including the residents of the gated community and its neighboring urban village as well as of local government and developers through qualitative interviews.

Another issue of research design is case selection. There are two different research strategies with respective advantages. One is a multiple cases strategy, which offers the advantage of comparison. The other is a single case strategy, which allows deep familiarity with the case area. HERBERT (2010, p. 75) argues that "deep familiarity with a single case makes it easier to move continually between theoretical propositions and empirical findings; one can revise concepts in light of ongoing research, and redirect with evolving concepts". Also, RAGIN (1992, p. 5) points out that "this feature explains why small-N qualitative research is most often at the forefront of theoretical development. When N's are large, there are few opportunities for revising a case." The purpose of qualitative research is to answer the key research questions and to explore the phenomena through in-depth surveying. Choice of strategy depends on the research questions and objectives. This study explores the processes of debordering and rebordering and seeks to understand their reasons rather than to engage in comparison. A single case study can answer research questions well, so this study adopts a single-case strategy and selects therefor a typical residential borderland located in suburban Guangzhou. It consists of a gated community named Clifford Estate together with its neighboring urban village, Zhongyi Village.

The single case area is selected based on a preliminary investigation of and comparison among three different types of gated communities (Figure 2). Afterwards one of these was selected for the in-depth case study. Among the considerable factors impacting what flows between a gated community and its neighboring village, the supply of neighborhood facilities in a gated community (its self-sufficiency or lack thereof) would be a factor strongly impacting the relationship between a gated community and its neighboring poor area. If a sufficient supply of facilities and services exists inside a suburban gated community, its residents might not need to enter the neighboring village to obtain daily necessities but rather can obtain the services or goods in the city center or inside the community. Therefore, as identified later in Chapter 6.2.1, there are three types of residential borderland based on the layout and supply model of neighborhood facilities in a gated community: a self-sufficient type, an open-oriented type, and a publically supplied type.

The choice of one typical case proceeded as follows. First, three corresponding residential borderlands (Shunde Country Garden, Clifford Estate, and Jinxiu Garden) were selected for observation in order to compare the flows of people across the respective borders. Then the residential borderland of Clifford Estate was selected as the single case area, for two reasons. First, with respect to the supply pattern of the neighborhood facilities in a gated community, Clifford Estate (an open-oriented type) occupies the middle,

Methodology and methods 35

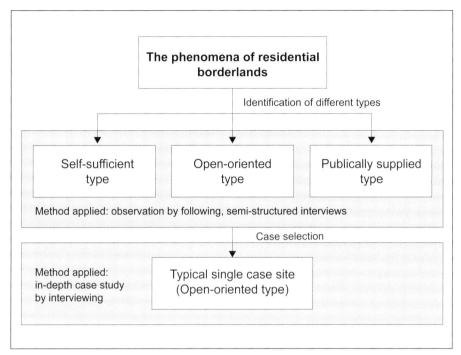

Figure 2: A visualization of the selection strategy for a single typical case
Source: Illustration by author

whereas the other two types of gated communities are at the extremes. Second, Clifford Estate is selected because it typically shows the same strong flow of residents from the gated community to its surrounding village as the other two case areas.

This study adopts qualitative research methods to explore the processes of debordering and rebordering. MAXWELL (2012) develops a useful, research-questions-oriented model for qualitative research design that includes five components: goals, a conceptual framework, research questions, methods, and validity. TEDDLIE and TASHAKKORI (2006) divide the research processes into a conceptualization stage, an experiential stage and an inferential stage; however, the whole process can involve more than one phase (or strand). The conceptualization stage includes the formulation of research purposes and questions. The experiential stage includes methodological operations, data generation, and analysis. The inferential stage is dedicated to abstract explanations and understanding, including emerging theories and explanations. In this study, the multi-phases are integrated into MAXWELL's (2012) qualitative research design model. The resulting research design includes six components: theoretical reflection, research questions, research methods, research phases, validity, and goals (Figure 3).

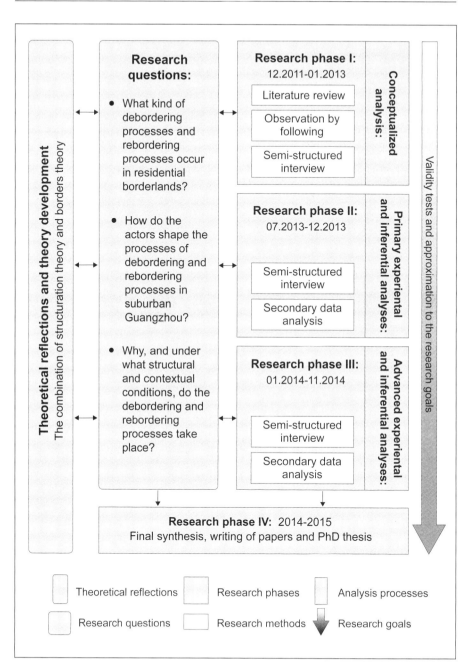

Figure 3: A visualization of the general research design
Source: Illustration by author, including ideas of MAXWELL (2012), TEDDLIE and TASHAKKO-RI

In order to obtain rich data and to secure long-term involvement in the research area, fieldwork was staggered into three rounds over three years. The research process consists of four phases. Research phase I consists of the work of conceptualization and the first round of fieldwork. In this phase, the research purpose, research questions, and theoretical framework are formulated and yield a sound basis for the second round of fieldwork. Research phase II involves the second round of fieldwork as well as the experiential and inferential analyses. This phase generated rich empirical data. Based on the collected data, the primary experiential and inferential analyses were conducted. Research phase III comprised a short period of supplementary investigation as well as advanced experiential and inferential analyses. Phase IV synthesizes the results and draws the final conclusion. In the course of research, some procedures are followed throughout each phase:

1. The empirical work and data analysis are in dialogue with theoretical reflections in each stage.
2. The validity of qualitative research is evaluated at each stage. Deviation and bias in field work are avoided to the greatest extent possible through corrections and prompt revision in subsequent empirical work.
3. The processes of each phase are guided by the research questions and objectives presented in Chapter 1.

4.2 Methods

The methods of semi-structured interviews and observation by following, as associated with some other methods, i.e. literature review and second-hand data analysis, were selected for this study. To avoid systematic biases from a single interview method, the design included a methodological triangulation. The methods of semi-structured interviews and observation by following were designed to explore the debordering and rebordering processes between a gated community and an urban village.

4.2.1 Semi-structured interviews

There is a continuum of qualitative interviews ranging from structured to unstructured (LINCOLN and GUBA 1985, p. 269). Occupying the middle of this continuum are semi-structured interviews, in which some questions are determined in advance, but open-ended questions are allowed and the conversations are conducted as interactions (DUNN 2005, p. 80). The semi-structured, in-depth interviews are organized in stages and mainly carried out in the case study area. The semi-structured interview is designed to explore the processes of debordering and rebordering.

The semi-structured interview is guided by some basic questions (see Appendix 1) but ensures open-ended questions during the interview. The target groups for interviews are

Table 1: Interviews at Clifford Estate area

Interviewee source	Informants' status	Number of interviews
Clifford Estate	Permanent residents (housing owners)	22
	Temporary residents (renters)	3
Zhongyi Village	Indigenous villagers	10
	Rural migrants (floating population)	21
Property company	Employees of Clifford Estate (guards, drivers)	3
Local government	Village cadres (group interview)	1
	Local urban planners	2
	Total	**62**

Source: Compiled by author

the residents of Clifford Estate, the residents of Zhongyi Village, the developer, and the local government (in detail, see Appendix 2). In all, 62 interviews were conducted in the Clifford Estate area (Table 1), and 15 and 2 interviews were conducted in Shunde Country Garden and Jinxiu Garden, respectively[1]. Interviews lasted between 15 and 80 minutes. All the interviews in Clifford Estate area were voice-recorded by a professional-quality recorder using an external microphone. All voices were recorded clearly enough to be transcribed. The interview of village cadres was a group interview.

Gaining access to the targeted group is a challenge for most qualitative research. The study utilized several strategies depending on the group. For interviews in the gated community in Clifford Estate, a temporary entrance card was obtained through personal contacts living inside. There is a recreational lake inside Clifford Estate at which many residents linger. Most of the first-stage interviews were done at this site. The second- and third-round interview sites were more diversified across different areas of Clifford Estate including each sub-divided residential area, the Clifford bus station area, and the Clifford commercial area. Interviewing the indigenous villagers in Zhongyi Village followed a strategy of continual visits. Although there is no entry restriction to Zhongyi Village, it was challenging to interview local villagers there, who normally refused to talk at first. Only after several regular visits did they become familiar with this study and were glad

---

1 Three of the interviews with residents became a sort of group interview in which other people got involved; however, each of these kept a main informant. In interview No. 33 for instance, with a mother and daughter resting at the side of a lake in Clifford Estate, I mainly interviewed the daughter, but her mother sometimes contributed too.

to talk. Compared to indigenous villagers, migrants were easier to interview. Giving a cigarette or small gift to informants and showing them identification proved helpful in gaining their confidence. The selected interviewees span different genders, ages, and economic statuses. In order to access to the different groups, varied interview locations were chosen.

The Clifford Estate development company declined a formal interview because it still has land under development and did not want to become the focus of research. In order to offset the weakness, informal interviews with Clifford Estate employees (including a Clifford guard, a bus driver, and a property agent) were conducted. Secondary data were collected, including news reports and website materials. The interviews with urban planners and village cadres were facilitated by a government contact. On the evening of every interview day, the recorded data were sorted and numbered, and information about each interview was briefly transcribed including features of the interviewee, the interview site, and the key contents of interview.

4.2.2 Observation by following

Participant observation is a traditional method for data collection. The researcher observes the everyday activities of insiders, seeking to uncover, make accessible, and gain a deep understanding of an aspect of meaning or a reality of human existence as viewed from the standpoint of the insiders (SPRADLEY 1980; JORGENSEN 1989). The method of participant observation is especially appropriate for exploring social phenomena about which is little known or which is to some extent obscured, as when the behavior of interest is hidden from public view (JORGENSEN 1989). As reviewed in Chapter 2.3.3, it is controversial whether gatedness exacerbates social exclusion and segregation, and empirical results differ from one social context to the next. Within China there are two voices, one holding that gated communities increase residential segregation and another that gated communities next to villages alleviate social segregation. A variety of empirical work is necessary to address this controversy. Participant observation is an appropriate method for exploring the connection between two enclaves in such circumstances.

Based on the role of researchers engaged in participant observation, GOLD (1958) put forward a participation continuum ranging from complete participant, to observer-as-participant (more participant than observer), to participant-as-observer (more observer than participant), and finally to complete observer (no participation). The method of observation by following is consistent with a participant-as-observer role of the researcher, who follows the observation objects and records their actives. A similar method was used by JIRÓN (2011) during research on mobility practices; she depicted the method as one of becoming a shadow of the observation objects.

Table 2: The record table of observation by following (sample list)

No	Record time	Number of people	Gender		With child	Approximate age			Destination	Purpose
			M	F		Youth and young adults	Middle-aged adults	Older people		
Q-1	09:01	1	1		No	0	1	0	Zhongyi Food Market	For the service of sewing clothes
Q-2	09:08	1		1	No	0	0	1	Zhongyi Food Market	Buy food
Q-3	09:13	1	1		No	0	1	0	Zhongyi Food Market	Buy food
Q-4	09:22	1		1	No	1	0	0	Greenery bakery in Zhongfu Mall	Working (an employee at bakery)
Q-5	09:25	1	1		No	0	0	1	Food market in Zhongfu Mall	Buy food
Q-6	09:30	1	1		No	0	1	0	Xinhe supermarket in Zhongfu Mall	Shopping
Q-7	09:34	1		1	No	0	0	1	Xinhe supermarket in Zhongfu Mall	Shopping
Q-8	09:38	2		2	No	2	0	0	Barber shop in Zhongfu Mall	Haircut
Q-9	09:41	1		1	No	1	0	0	Xinhe supermarket in Zhongfu Mall	Shopping
Q-10	09:45	5	2	3	No	3	0	2	Food market in Zhongfu Mall	Buy food
Q-11	09:48	2	1	1	No	2	0	0	Food market in Zhongfu Mall	Buy food
Q-12	09:53	1		1	No	0	0	1	Food market in Zhongfu Mall	Buy food
Q-13	09:55	3	2	1	No	2	0	1	Zhongyi Food Market	Buy food
Q-14	09:58	1	1		No	0	0	1	Zhongyi Food Market	Buy food
Q-15	10:05	2	1	1	No	2	0	0	Duobao housekeeping shop in Zhongyi Village	For the housekeeping service

Observation site: Clifford Estate/Zhongyi Village Date: 30/12/2012
Note: Informants are categorized into four basic age groups: child (referenced age: less than 6), youth and young adults (referenced age: 6-35 years), middle-aged adults (referenced age: 36-55), and older people (referenced age: older than 55 years). The estimated age of informants is based on the observer's judgment. Two principles have been used for the age judgment: the informants' features, including their dress, hair, facial appearance and figure; and the informants' relation to their companions if applicable, for instance, whether they are accompanied by their family members or taking care of a child.

Source: Compiled by author

The decision to adopt this strategy came in light of the fact that most of the gated communities in Panyu have at least one small, pedestrian gate to the neighboring village for the sake of convenience. A great number of gated community residents will use the small gate to visit the neighboring village on foot. Hence, observation by following is designed to ascertain why this group of gated community residents goes to the village area, where they go, and how different people perceive boundary.

Depending on the type of residential borderlands (identified in Chapter 6.2.1), one of each of the three types of gated communities has been selected for participant observation. The selected gated communities are Clifford Estate, Shunde Country Garden, and Jinxiu Garden. However, Clifford Estate is selected as the single case site for qualitative research. The inclusion of the other two sites in the design, Shunde Country Garden and Jinxiu Garden, is meant to provide contrast at the conceptualization stage, to explore the features of how persons flow from the gated community into neighboring village, and to identify the common features of the selected single case area.

Besides the author, two student assistants from the Guangzhou Institute of Geography were employed and received training in observation by following. They were asked to maintain a certain distance from their subjects. Residents of gated communities who pass through the small gate to the neighboring area are the target group for observation. Each observation was recorded in a dedicated table. The table, depicted in Table 2, recorded the time, the subject's gender and approximate age, and the destination of each trip.

The observations by following were conducted over the course of a given day, from 9 a.m. to 6 p.m., successively and on an individual basis. In total, the observation yielded 481 samples at three case sites, including 110 in Shunde Country Garden, 111 Jinxiu Garden, and 260 in Clifford Estate. The method of observation by following allows the researcher to get a first idea of the daily routines of residents moving to neighboring village area, such as where they went and what they did in the neighboring village area.

4.2.3 Second-hand data sources

Beside the data collected from the first-hand survey, second-hand data were also collected. The collected secondary data include related academic literature, the Yearbook of Statistics, news reports and website materials, the data of Sixth National Population Census (SNPC) of the People's Republic of China, land use investigation data, and text documents of urban planning and design. The second-hand data has been used to analyze the background of the development of residential borderlands as well as the structural and contextual conditions of debordering and rebordering.

4.3 Data collection

4.3.1 Research phase I: conceptualization

The research started with a review of literature on gated communities and enclave urbanism. The literature review covered the reasons for the proliferation of gated communities and the consequences of gated enclaves, and in particular the relationship between a gated community and its poor neighboring residential area. The phenomenon of a gated community abutting villages in suburban Guangzhou appeared as a compelling object for study and attracted the research attention of the author.

The first round fieldwork took place from September to December of 2012 and included observation by following at three case sites as well as semi-structured interviews. In this phase, the observation by following was done first. Then, after a certain amount of observation data was collected, the focus shifted in particular to Clifford Estate for more detailed, in-depth semi-structured interviews. In total, 34 interviews were completed in the first round. However, some interviews were also conducted in the other two gated communities. These include 15 interviews in Shunde Country Garden and two interviews in Jinxiu Garden.

Based on the results of the first round of collected data and the constant search for theoretical support, structuration theory and national borders theory entered the research's scope. The literature of national borders in political geography was scrutinized for a means of introducing the theory of borders and its perspectives into this research. Late in this phase, by way of constant dialogue between the findings from fieldwork and theory, the theoretical framework was formed.

4.3.2 Research phase II and III: experiential and inferential analyses

The second stage fieldwork investigated debordering and rebordering practices and was conducted from September until the end of October of 2013. In total, 22 in-depth interviews were done, including nine interviews with Clifford Estate residents, ten interviews with residents of Zhongyi Village, and one interview with a Clifford guard and two local urban planners, respectively. After the rich data were collected, the primary experiential and inferential analyses followed, including analysis of the processes of debordering and rebordering in functional, symbolic, and social network dimensions.

The third-stage fieldwork explored the driving forces and conditions in which debordering and rebordering are practiced. It occurred during a short period in November, 2014. Here, interviews mainly focused on the institution of the household registration system and its impacts on borders. A group interview of the Zhongyi Village committee as well as five additional semi-structured interviews of residents were completed in this stage.

The group interview was held at the office of the Zhongyi Village committee. Six village cadres and a town cadre attended the group interview. The intensive, multiple stages of fieldwork at the case study site enabled the author to go beyond the prejudiced attitudes of a small portion of the residents and record different views reflecting different social situations. A comprehensive perspective on the research area thereby took shape.

Data collection was followed by the advanced experiential and inferential analyses. The importance of the dynamics of social, economic, and political context became apparent. The focus shifted accordingly to the analysis of structural and contextual factors involved in the debordering and rebordering practices.

4.3.3 Research phase IV: synthesis and conclusion

First during this phase all data collected throughout the entirety of the research phases were evaluated, compared, and synthesized. Comparison of empirical results from semi-structured interviews and observation by following reveals a convergent outcome of triangulation. Second, based on abstraction from the empirical findings, the theoretical framework was ultimately confirmed. The empirical findings and explanation were synthesized into the theoretical framework (see Chapter 8.1). Third, conclusions were drawn and future research proposed. The last step was to compose the doctoral thesis. All photographs and informants remained anonymous during the writing of the dissertation.

4.4 Methods of analysis

4.4.1 Transcription

O'CONNELL and KOWAL (1999) describe spoken discourse as consisting of verbal features (e.g., words, word fragments), prosodic features (e.g., rhythm, intonation, pitch, volume), paralinguistic features (e.g., laughter, audible breaths, sighs), and extra-linguistic features (e.g., gestures, fidgeting, gaze), pauses, and various contextual cues. This study transcribed the main verbal information rather than all the discourse features. All verbal information was recorded as verbatim transcription. During verbatim transcription, a foot pedal mechanism was used to control playback progress of the audio recording. In order to avoid reducing the contents of interviews by way of translating the transcripts into English, the audio recordings were transcribed in Chinese on Microsoft word and analyzed in a Chinese language setting. The results of analysis were then translated into English for reporting purposes. During the transcription, important contents of interviews were marked.

4.4.2 Coding

A qualitative content analysis method was used to analyze the interview data. Qualitative content analysis examines language intensely to classify a great deal of text into an efficient set of broader categories. These categories can represent either explicit or inferred meanings (WEBER 1990). The major function of content analysis is to provide knowledge and understanding of undiscovered phenomenon (DOWNE-WAMBOLDT 1992, p. 314). Content analysis involved a three-step process: 1) data reduction, 2) data display, and 3) conclusion-drawing and verification (MILES and HUBERMAN 1994). HSIEH and SHANNON (2005) have identified three approaches to content analysis: conventional content analysis (coding categories starting from the collected data); directed content analysis (coding categories deriving directly from a theory or relevant research findings); and summative content analysis (coding categories constituted through counting and comparing keywords derived from review of literature or interests of the researcher).

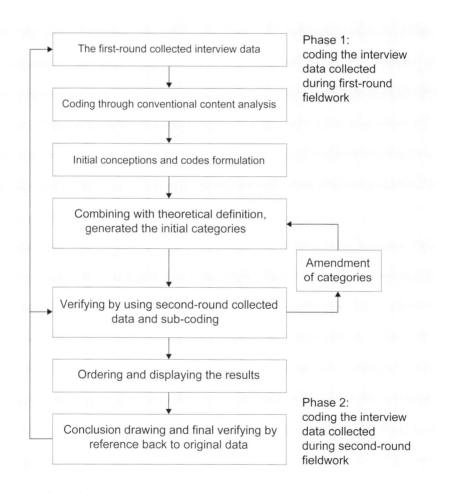

Figure 4: The application of content analysis
Source: Illustration by author

In this study, coding of the empirical data was designed to consist of two phases based on the data collected during different stages of the research. The total coding process is depicted in Figure 4. Phase 1 involved the transcription and coding of the data collected during first-stage fieldwork. The first-stage interview data were coded through conventional content analysis. The analysis was conducted stepwise by reference to the method described in HSIEH and SHANNON (2005). Initial conceptions were formed in this phase about such phenomena as flows of people, security, othering, and social ties. The initial conceptions thus formed were in dialogue with the theory, yielding categories such as the functional, symbolic, and social networks dimensions of debordering and rebordering processes.

In Phase 2, the initial categories formed during the first-round coding become the basis for the coding of the data collected during second-round fieldwork; however, the initial categories were also improved and verified in the second-round coding. Hence, the second-stage analysis of interview data became a directed content analysis. Next, the final categories were formulated, and data were organized into displays. Finally, conclusions were drawn and verified by reference back to the original data.

4.4.3 The analysis of the data collected from observation

The observation data as recorded was entered using Microsoft Office Excel software. The purpose of the activities of the gated community residents visiting the village area was coded. The short-trip purpose was coded into various broader categories (see Chapter 6.2.3). The analysis of purposes was done through a statistical analysis based on the categories. The data from three case sites were compared. The purpose was to locate similarities and differences among the sites and prove the generality of the selected single case site.

5 The national and urban conditions of bordering

China launched a policy of reform and opening up in 1978. Accompanying the process of opening up, a set of institutional reforms, including the land reform, the household registration ("hukou") system reform, and the housing reform, have been undertaken to change the centrally planned economy of Mao's period into a market-oriented economy. MADRAZO and KEMPEN (2012) argue that the influence of the state, its institutions, and of China's cultural background go a long way toward explaining China's divided cities. This chapter first explains border formation regarding the institutional reforms in China, including the land, hukou system and housing reforms. Later, the social settings of socio-spatial transformation and urbanization are introduced. Finally, the research focuses down to the urban level, exploring the urban conditions of bordering, which consist of a trend of suburbanization and policies of administrative adjustment and "converting villages to communities".

5.1 The dual land use system and its impacts

5.1.1 The setting of the contemporary land use system

The contemporary Chinese urban-rural dual land use system came about with the 1986 Land Administration Law (LAL). The LAL placed all land in the hands of the state or the village collective; there is no private land. When the People's Republic of China was established, a great deal of land was privately owned. However, under the first Constitution of China, the central government started to confiscate private land in 1954. It adopted two methods. One, privately owned housing was confiscated by the state to be leased to those in need of housing, though the owners could receive a certain amount of the rental proceeds (in Chinese: *guojia jingzhu*), and the land attached to the property was accordingly confiscated. Meanwhile private sector-owned land was confiscated as "joint state-private ownership" (in Chinese: *gongsi heying*). By the end of the 1950s, almost all urban private land had been confiscated and transferred to state ownership (ZHU 1994; LIN and HO 2005). The latest Constitution, of 1982[1], provided that all urban land belongs to state, so that private land ownership was terminated officially and legally.

However, according to the political and economic philosophy of Marxism, which aims to annihilate exploitation, land had not been considered an element of production until 1988 (ZHANG 1997b). At that time, there were three features of land use: first, urban land was allocated to a user of the land without payment; second, the land was held indefinitely; third, it was proscribed to sell, buy, or transfer the land. That land was obtained without payment resulted in inefficient use and largely wasted land resources. After the open door

---

1 There have been four constitutions in China: the 1954 Constitution, the 1975 Constitution, the 1978 Constitution, and the 1982 Constitution. The 1982 Constitution is the presently valid version; however, it has undergone four amendments, in 1988, 1993, 1999, and 2004.

policy importing the Western market mechanism into China, the original Marxist view of land as a natural resource without economic attribution was no longer applicable to economic development. The first ground-breaking experiment with the transfer of land use rights took place in 1987 in the Special Economic Zone (SEZ) of Shenzhen. Afterwards, the 1988 amendment to the 1982 Constitution officially allowed for transfer of urban land use rights (TANG 1989). The change in the land use system gave birth to the land market.

The reformed land use system has three main features. First, land use rights are distinguished from land ownership (ZHANG 1997b). Accordingly, land ownership permanently resides in the village collective and the state, while the right to use the land is leased. Therefore, a private individual or corporation can only own the right to use the land, not the land itself. The urban land use right is also time-limited: the right to use residential land is leased for 70 years; industrial, educational, cultural, health, sports, and mixed-use land for 50 years; and land for commercial, entertainment, and tourism uses is subject to the shortest lease period of 40 years. Second, the land in urban areas falls under state ownership, while rural land falls under the ownership of the village collective. Ownership of rural land falls to the village collectives, where land use rights are leased to rural households (DONG 1996; KUNG 2002). Third, the state monopolizes the supply of land (HO and SPOOR 2006). Peasants are forbidden to transfer their agricultural land use rights to non-agricultural uses or transfer their land-use rights of housing land (in Chinese: *zaijidi*) to non-agricultural hukou holders. All rural land meant for urban development is first subject to expropriation by the government into the state ownership before it can supply the land market.

5.1.2 The production of residential borderlands

Residential borderlands result from the dual land use system and the derivative dual land market. In the process depicted in Figure 5, the local government, on behalf of the state, expropriates agricultural land. The village collective obtains a certain amount of compensation for the requisitioned land, and the compensation fee is allocated to individual village households through the village collective.

Rural village land takes two basic forms: farmland and built-up land. The land requisition process provides different standards of compensation for farmland and built-up land. The LAL provides three components to the compensation fee for requisitioned farmland: the compensation fee for the land itself, a resettlement fee, and a fee for improvements or young crops on the land. The standard compensation fee for land is three to ten times the annual average agricultural output value calculated from the previous three years' average land productivity. The standard compensation fee for the resettlement is four to six times the average annual output value of the expropriated agricultural land. The standard compensation fee for improvements and young crops is prescribed by local governments

The national and urban conditions of bordering 49

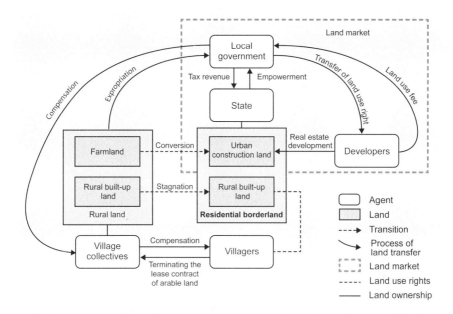

Figure 5: The process of land expropriation and the creation of residential borders
Source: Illustration by author, based on WANG and SCOTT (2008) and WANG et al. (2012)

directly. Article 47 of the LAL provides that the total compensation fee in total should not exceed fifteen times the average annual output value calculated from the preceding three years' output. However, the LAL does not clearly prescribe the standard compensation fees for the built-up land. The expropriation of built-up land involves housing demolition and resettlement of residents, and the procedure is more complicated and expensive than the expropriation of farmland. Because of this, the local government normally only expropriates the farmland, which it can do at low cost, while the built-up village land is bypassed during the process of urban expansion.

The expropriation of the farmland separated the village into two parts: the bypassed rural built-up land and the requisitioned farmland that has become urban construction land[2]. The former remains as it was while the local government places the latter into the land market for urban development. The villagers are excluded from the land market in the process and have no opportunity to share in the land value appreciation achieved by the land development projects (WANG and SCOTT 2008). The low compensation for cultiva-

---
2   The villages in Guangdong province can keep a small part of the agricultural land as economic development reservation land after land expropriation. The local policy provides for the municipalities to retain a small proportion (about 10 to 15 percent) of arable land for the village to develop secondary or tertiary industry in order to maintain the livelihood of villagers after land expropriation.

ted land has caused many conflicts between villagers and local governments (KELIANG and PROSTERMAN 2007).

China has a dual-track land use right conveyance system involving an administrative allocation method and a price mechanism that coexist in the land market (ZHANG 1997b). The price mechanism has existed since the mid-1990s, since which time the number of land conveyances under the price mechanism has grown steadily. Since 2001, the administrative allocation method no longer dominates conveyances of land use rights. Both the number of cases and the area of land whose use rights were conveyed under the price mechanism has exceeded what has taken place under the administrative allocation since then (LIN and HO 2005).

Local governments employ three approaches to leasing land under the price mechanism: negotiation, tender, and auction. The method of negotiation accounts for a large proportion of all conveyances of land use rights; for instance, 86% of land conveyances were accomplished by the method of closed-door negotiation between 1995 and 2002 (LIN and HO 2005) and more than 50% were still being accomplished this way in 2007 (WANG, et al. 2012).

The key reason why local governments zealously expropriated rural land is to obtain local extra-budgetary revenue. The tax system reform of 1994 brought about a framework of tax sharing between the state and local governments. Land revenue as an extra-budgetary fund has become one of the most important financial devices for the local government to promote urban construction and development. For the purpose of attracting foreign investment and stimulating local economic development, the local government must improve urban infrastructure. However, when the local government lacks public financing for infrastructure investment, land leasing revenues become the main financing source.

The opportunity for political promotions is one of the main forces driving local governments to stimulate economic and urban development. The central government has also made continued economic growth its central mission. Economic development goals as measured by GDP growth were prescribed in a series of Five-Year Plans. In order to achieve the development goals, an economic growth index was assigned to each local government. Hence, the growth of GDP has become one of the most important indexes for evaluating the political achievement of local governments.

In sum, the dual rural-urban land use system has, on one hand, allowed local governments to derive massive revenues from land. Local governments only expropriated farmland and excluded rural built-up land in order to maximize their profits from land expropriation, and this has prevented a renewal of built-up rural areas under a market approach and created the urban village in the city. On the other hand, the institutional reform that separated land use rights from land ownership rights has fostered the land market and a developmental real estate industry (HU and KAPLAN 2001). However, the exclusion of rural land from the land market also curbs the renewal of rural built-up land under a market approach. When requisitioned farmland is developed as commercial housing in the form of a gated community adjacent to rural built-up area, it creates a residential borderland.

5.2 The hukou system

5.2.1 The creation of hukou system

Much like the institution of *propiska* implemented in the former USSR, the hukou is residency permit tied to political and economic rights and is considered a product of the socialist economy. The hukou system was set up in 1958 and strictly enforced from 1960. It involves a register of population and households and regulates internal movements of people based on residence registration (CHENG and SELDEN 1994). There are four salient attributes of the hukou system. First, hukou determines a person's status as part of the urban or rural population and distinguishes the two. Second, hukou indicates the person's location as either local (in Chinese: *bendi*) hukou or non-local/external (in Chinese: *wailai*) hukou, and the system strictly restricts members of the rural population from migrating to urban areas (YANG 1993). As Table 3 shows, depending on hukou type and place of registration, the population can be classified into four categories: the agricultural hukou holders living in urban areas, agricultural hukou holders living in rural areas, non-agricultural holders living in urban areas, and non-agricultural hukou holders living in rural areas (CHAN 2009).

Table 3: Major constituent groupings of agricultural and non-agricultural populations by hukou status and location

Hukou location	Agricultural hukou	Non-agricultural hukou
Urban areas	**A** Rural migrant workers Farm workers Dependents	**C** Urban workers State cadres and professionals Dependents
Rural areas	**B** Rural (industrial) workers* Farmers Dependents	**D** State farm workers** State cadres and professionals Dependents of above
* In township and village enterprises ** In state-run agricultural enterprises		

Source: CHAN (2009, p. 202).

Third, hukou defines a person's entitlements with respect to land-use rights and state-provided welfare. Only non-agricultural hukou holders are eligible for state-provided welfare, while only agricultural hukou holders are eligible to profit economically from the village collective and to own housing land. Fourth, hukou has a descendible feature: wherever a child is born, he or she will inherit his or her parents' hukou status.

The basic function of hukou is to create a registry of the population for purposes of statistics, tax collection, and conscription. However, hukou defines eligibility for state-provided welfare, limits population migration, and restricts the status transfer from rural to urban hukou. It has been met by many social criticisms.

5.2.2 The reform of hukou system

In the wake of reforms and opening-up, rapid industrialization required massive labor in the city. The way hukou restricts the rural population from migrating to the city is not suitable for economic development. Hence, in order to make up for the gap between labor and demand in cities, many measures have been implemented to make the hukou system more flexible (ZHANG 2012a). Two approaches have relaxed hukou restrictions. One has been a loosening of the restriction on transfers from agricultural to non-agricultural hukou, through a policy called *nongzhuanfei* (in Chinese). Nongzhuanfei encompasses the status transfers from B to D, A to C, and B to C in Table 3. The following are hukou transfer pathways from agricultural to non-agricultural hukou: 1) *Zhaosheng*: recruited for enrollment in an institution of higher-education; 2) *Zhaogong*: recruited as a permanent employee by a state-owned enterprise; 3) *Zhengdi*: displaced due to state-initiated land expropriation; 4) *Zhaogang*: promoted to administrative positions; 5) *Qianyi*: relocated because of family crises; 6) *Canjun*: joining the army and demobilized to cities; 7) Other: deemed to belong to special categories (CHAN 2009).

The other approach is to relax migration controls to enable and facilitate the rural population migrating to the city. Many special types of residential registration have been introduced: 1) The "self-supplied township hukou" (in Chinese: *zili kouliang* hukou); 2) "temporary residential permit" (in Chinese: *zanzhuzheng*); and 3) the "blue-stamp hukou" (in Chinese: *lanyin* hukou). The temporary residential permit was first invented by the city of Shenzhen in 1984 and then adopted by other cities. However, it was terminated in 2014. The temporary residential permit was issued to migrants with legitimate jobs or businesses in the city. The blue-stamp hukou was first implemented by the local government between 1992 and 2000 and issued to investors, buyers of property, and professionals in order to attract capital and a well-educated population (TAO 2008).

The policy of *nongzhuanfei* is designed to transfer rural hukou into non-agricultural hukou with full entitlement to state-provided welfare; however, compared to the huge floating population (see below at Chapter 5.4.2), the hukou transfer index in the city is scarce. The relaxation of rural-to-urban migration is only to facilitate the rural population migrating into the city rather than to provide an entitlement to state-provided welfare. In 2004 a new measure was introduced in some cities called the point system. The hukou point system provides talented migrants the chance to apply for urban hukou by accumulating points. However, ZHANG (2012b) criticizes that the point system is a strategy to include a selected minority while excluding the majority of migrants.

5.2.3 Entitlements of agricultural versus non-agricultural hukou holders

Hukou is a strictly institutional barrier for people seeking to settle in a host city. The hukou system as a residence registration system would not be different from the registration permit in the western part of the country but for the fact that the hukou system also defines an entitlement to state-provided welfare. Based on hukou status, different groups of people are eligible for distinct welfare (Table 4). Urban hukou holders have a broad scope of entitlement to state-provided welfare that includes education, health care, social security, employment, housing etc. Rural hukou holders on the other hand have the collective's land use rights and the right to have a second child, provided that the parents both hold rural hukou and the first child is a girl. The state welfare system is designed based on the hukou system such that migrants that lack local urban hukou cannot share public services (e.g., free education, health care, and pensions) the same way registered residents can. Rural hukou holders who are not eligible for state welfare are therefore akin to inferior or second-class citizens in the city (CHAN and BUCKINGHAM 2008).

5.2.4 The impact of hukou system on the border

Hukou as an institution plays a prominent role in explaining how residential borderland comes into being. In the pre-reform era, China strictly implemented the hukou institution and restricted the population's movement both from rural to urban dwelling and among different cities. In the post-reform era, the hukou institution was relaxed to facilitate internal movements, which spurred a massive rural migration to urban areas. However, after the migrants arrived in the city, most of them were unable to transfer their rural hukou into an urban hukou. This group of people is called the floating population, who without local urban hukou are excluded from the state welfare system. State-subsidized housing excluded the rural migrants on one hand; and on the other hand, they could not afford commodity housing. They therefore were forced into urban low rent areas, creating migrant enclaves in urban areas (SHEN 2002; LIU and WU 2006). Thus the hukou system as a legal institution affects people's lives to such an extent that it forms the core of the residential border, dividing inhabitants into urban versus rural, permanent versus temporary, and indigenous versus migrating.

Table 4: The main welfare differences between non-agricultural and agricultural hukou holders in a host city

	State (city)-provided welfare	Non-agricultural hukou — Local urban hukou holder	Agricultural hukou — Local agricultural hukou (local villagers)	Agricultural hukou — Non-local agricultural hukou (Rural-to-urban migrants)
Employment	Employment services (i.e. job vacancy information, policy consultation, vocational guidance and vocational recommendation)	Yes	If any, paid by village collective	Yes (2006)*
	re-employment assistance	Yes	If any, paid by village collective	No
	Training allowance	Yes	If any, paid by village collective	No
Social	Local-urban-hukou-based or contribution-based social insurance	Yes	If any, paid by village collective	No
	Urban-hukou-based minimum living guarantee	Yes	If any, paid by village collective	No
Housing	1) Limited urban-hukou-based low-rent housing; 2) Limited urban-hukou-based low price housing; 3) Contribution-based housing fund	Yes	If any, paid by village collective	No
Education	Nine years of free compulsory education	Yes	Yes, paid by village collective and state collectively	Yes, but extra temporary schooling fee is needed to be paid
	Right to participate in the university entrance exam in the host city	Yes	Yes	No

The national and urban conditions of bordering 55

Category	Item	Col 1	Col 2	Col 3
Health and medicine	Public health services (i.e. free immunization service for children, free family planning services)	Yes	Yes	Yes (2006)
	Urban medical insurance (Higher reimbursement)	Yes	Rural medical insurance	Rural medical insurance
Politics	Urban-hukou-based political rights (one person one vote, have the right to be voted as a deputy to the National People's Congress)	Yes	Have the same right as non-agricultural holder since 2010 (eight persons one vote before 1996, four persons one vote before 2010)	Without the right to vote and to be voted in the host city
	Membership of official trade union	Yes	Yes	Yes (2003)
	Right of honor (i.e. to be nominated a model worker)	Yes	Yes	Yes (2005)
Accident compensation	Full compensation	Yes	Half or even less than half of the non-agricultural hukou holder	Half or even less than half of the non-agricultural hukou holder
Land use	Collective land	No	Have contracted agricultural land, housing land, rural collective bonuses	Have contracted agricultural land, housing land, rural collective bonuses in their hometown
Reproductive right	Second child right	One child policy** (couples where just one parent was a single child have second child right after 2014)	Yes, provided the first child is a girl and both parents hold a rural hukou.	Yes, provided the first child is a girl and both parents hold a rural hukou.

Note: "Yes" means eligible; "No" means ineligible; *: bracketed date denotes the year eligibility was extend to the group. **: The one child policy has been abandoned since 2016.

Source: Compiled by author based on FAN (2002) and on ZHANG, et al. (2014, p.1444)

5.3 Housing reform and its impacts

5.3.1 A brief review of the process of housing reform

In the pre-reform era, the work-unit-based housing welfare system was implemented after the People's Republic of China was established in 1949. This system is characterized by a socialist ideology, a welfare philosophy, and clan traditions (ZHAO and BOURASSA 2003). Housing policy during Mao's era was full of ideology and politics (ZHANG 1997a). The purpose of this welfare system was to provide low-cost, decent housing to urban dwellers (YU 2006), which was regarded as an essential symbol of "the superiority of socialism over capitalism" (LIM and LEE 1990). As mentioned above in connection with the process whereby private land was transferred to state ownership, most urban private housing entered state ownership in the 1950s under the traditional socialist goals of elimination of exploitation and social injustice. There was no housing market in this period. The national government saw it as its duty to provide housing. The state government organized the production, allocation, and administration of housing. Housing was seen as a welfare subsidy allocated to people for low rents or free of rent, and this has become a serious financial burden on the state. Because the housing industry was deemed unproductive, the state was reluctant to invest in development or improved housing conditions (YU 2006). Housing shortages and substandard housing conditions became serious problems during the pre-reform period. In addition, the exclusively administrative allocation of housing inevitably led to corruption. The quasi-clan system brought housing inequity among different work units (ZHAO and BOURASSA 2003).

Housing reform began in 1978 with the aim of transforming the state welfare housing system into a market-oriented system of providing housing. The original and direct driving force behind housing reform was to solve the above-mentioned severe problems. The main elements of housing reform were rent reform, privatization of public housing, and the setting up of a housing market (CHEN and HAN 2014). In 1998, the state ceased to allocate welfare housing altogether and replaced it with a monetarized housing distribution system. This ushered in the new era of market-dominated urban housing (WANG 2001). Housing privatization, commercialization, and socialization have become the main features of the housing system (ZHAO and BOURASSA 2003).

5.3.2 The social spatial impacts of housing reform

One of the most important socio-spatial impacts of housing reform is that it sorts people into different social groups and places of accommodation (WU 2005). Before the housing reform, the sorting process was based on state redistribution. Urban residents commonly accommodated in municipal housing were sorted into various work-unit compounds through state-run redistribution. After housing reform, an open commodity housing market was set up and the state government gradually retreated from providing housing, which came to be dominated by a market mechanism. Different social groups are sorted by the mechanism of market-based allocation, for instance on the basis of housing affordability.

On one hand, after housing monetarization was implemented in 1998, public housing construction stagnated until 2006, leading to a shortage of public housing in urban areas. Meanwhile, limited public housing was only allocated to residents with urban hukou. With China's rapid urbanization, a large class of rural-to-urban migrants emerged who were excluded from the housing security system because they lacked local urban hukou. Many of them were accommodated in urban village where shelter was in good supply and cheap (SHEN 2002; ZHANG, et al. 2003; WU 2008b). On the other hand, most commodity housing was built in the form of gated communities. Although the price of commodity housing varies, the average price is relatively high. Only those who can afford it can buy in and live inside. The result is that upper and middle-income classes are sorted into this higher quality, newly-built commodity housing. Hence, the gated communities and urban villages have emerged to accommodate the respective socioeconomic groups. For instance, CHEN and SUN (2007) have shown that people have been "sorted" into increasingly varied, layered residential spaces in Shanghai. Social stratification, residential segregation, and housing inequality have actually been exacerbated by housing reform (LEE 2000; LEE and ZHU 2006; YU 2006).

5.4 Socio-spatial transformation and urbanization

5.4.1 Socio-spatial transformation

China's economy has undergone rapid economic development for more than 30 years, accompanied by massive socio-spatial restructuring and transformation. State-run planning economy has been undergoing transformation to a market-oriented economy through decentralization, marketization, and globalization (WEI 2001).

First, with decentralization, much administrative power has shifted to local government. By and large the role of local governments has gone from that of implementing central plans to one of steering local economic and social development on their own initiative. The reform of the fiscal system is one of the most important devolutions. It divides taxation in into three parts: a central tax, a local tax and a share tax. In this the central and local government each has its respective tax revenue as well as part of the shared tax revenue. Devolution in the fiscal system has given local governments greater financial power. The reform provides the basis for "local-state corporatism" (OI 1992). Accompanying the fiscal system reform is investment reform, which has granted local governments more administrative power to attract foreign investment in their city. DULBECCO and RENARD (2003) demonstrate that institutional flexibility has emerged under the economic transformation towards market economy. HARVEY (1989) argued that the role of the state had been changing from urban managerialism to urban entrepreneurialism. WU, et al. (2007) more recently pointed out that local governments have resorted to many development strategies to compete with other domestic and global cities, with the philosophy of governance changing from the Keynesian welfare national state to a Schumpeterian workfare post-national regime. However, while most scholars have emphasized the role of local government, MA (2002) has taken another stance, emphasizing that the party-state, as the ultimate decision-maker and regulator, has continuously played an important role in the multiple-scale urban economic actives despite a decentralization of national administrative and financial power to local states.

Second, some scholars have explained China's transition from the perspective of marketization. WU (2008a) identifies neoliberalization as the huge transformation through which a market society was established in China. China's marketization has proceeded in three stages. The first occurred in the realm of products and prices. After the reform, decisions about production, products and their prices are determined more by market mechanisms rather than by central plan. The second stage is that the allocation and distribution of resources such as land, labor and finance has been turning over to the market. The final stage of marketization is privatization, in that a private sector has been permitted to develop.

Third, the reform and opening up policies have attracted massive foreign investments. Opening up to the outside world, China timely caught the opportunity to develop economically with the tide of a global shift. The outlines of the global shift were delineated by DICKEN (2003): global industrial capital has been moving from developed countries to less developed countries. The foreign investment has provided capital for Chinese economic development, promoted employment and stimulated urbanization and economical growth. Hence, the most important social transformation in China has been that from a centrally planned economy to a market-oriented economy. It has activated different actors, especially non-state actors, to act in the city according to a market mechanism.

5.4.2 Urbanization

WU, et al. (2007, p. 5) have argued that the transition of China's urban conditions can be depicted as moving from state-led, extensive industrialization to urban-based, intensive urbanization. Urbanization has been one of the most significant processes in China over the past three decades. The rapid development of urbanization in China has been unfolding on two different tracks. One is traditional government-driven urbanization. The other is spontaneous urbanization derived from local development and spurred by market forces (ZHU 1999). China's urbanization is characterized by neoliberal urbanism and rapid urban-centered wealth accumulation (HE and WU 2009).

The national and urban conditions of bordering 59

At the end of 2014, China's total population on the mainland was 1,367.82 million with more than half (749.16 million) living in cities. The urbanization rate is 54.8% or about three times higher than the 1978 rate (17.9%) (National Bureau of Statistics of China 2015). The magnitude of rural migration to urban areas caught the world's attention, not only for its rapidity but also for the enormous inequality that emerged as a consequence of urbanization under the hukou household registration system. The hukou institution has resulted in only 36% of China's total population having urban hukou in 2014. The floating population (in Chinese: *liudong renkou*), those migrants to cities who lack local urban hukou (LIANG and MA 2004), numbered about 253 million people in 2014 (National Bureau of Statistics of China 2015). Part of the participants in this rapid migration, through the policy of *nongzhuanfei*, managed to achieve hukou transfer and settle down in the city. Another part who lacked urban hukou are unequally excluded from the urban welfare system and "float" in the city.

5.5 The city of Guangzhou and its southern district Panyu

5.5.1 The research region of Guangzhou and Panyu

The city intensively reflects internal restructuring and transformation. Guangzhou was a southern gateway to China in pre-1949 development, but the role of the city declined in national comparison during the period from 1949 to 1978 (XU and YEH 2003). After the reform period, Guangzhou took advantage of its coastal location and the preferential policies it enjoyed as one of the first fourteen open coastal cities. It has since kept at the forefront of reform and opening-up. During the last eight Five-Year-Plan periods, Guangzhou has maintained a higher-than average economic growth rate nationally (Figure 6)

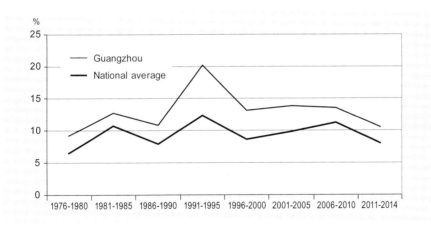

Figure 6: Comparison of the average GDP growth of Guangzhou versus the national average in different periods
Source: *Illustration by author, based on data from Guangzhou Statistical Bureau (2015) and National Bureau of Statistics of China (2015)*

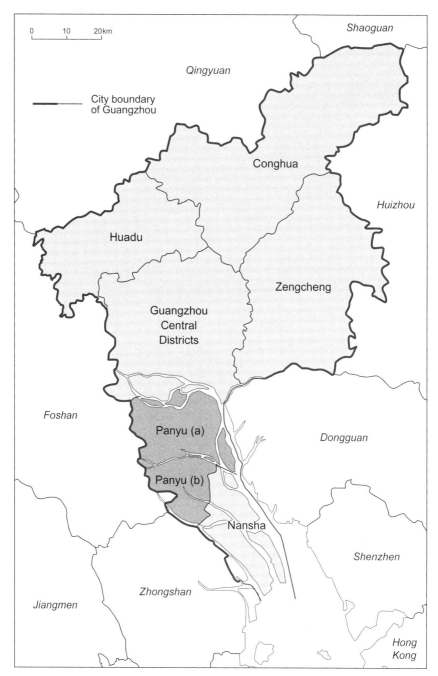

Figure 7: The location of Panyu district
Source: Design by author, cartographic elaboration by Petra Sinuraya

and become the third largest city in China. Nowadays, Guangzhou has a total population of about 13.08 million. However, only 8.42 million (64%) are registered as local (Guangzhou) hukou holders, including 7.66 million urban hukou and 0.76 million rural hukou holders. Its GDP reached 1,670 billion CNY, and its per-capita GDP reached 128,478 CNY, in 2014 (Guangzhou Statistical Bureau 2015).

As Figure 7 shows, Panyu, located in the south of Guangzhou, is separated geographically from the city's central districts by the Pearl River. Panyu has undergone several administrative division adjustments. In 2000, Panyu went from being a "county-level" city to being a district of Guangzhou. Later, in 2005, its southern part was detached to form a new district called Nansha. In 2012, three southern towns (Dongchong, Dagang and Lanhe) in Panyu (the area labeled "Panyu b" on the map) were incorporated into Nansha district. This research treats Panyu as it existed 2005, such that its scope includes both "Panyu a" and "Panyu b". Panyu is home to about 235.9 million people including a floating population of 134.4 million in 2012.

There are several reasons for research on Panyu. First, the Guangzhou region typifies China's economic development and social transformation. The development of Panyu district from a separate county to an integral part of Guangzhou is a dynamic process of a kind that epitomizes Chinese urban development. Second, during the rapid economic development and urbanization in Guangzhou, Panyu has been a key district of residential suburbanization where many gated communities have been built. Third, as will be explored in Chapter 6, residential borderlands are typical phenomena in Panyu district.

5.5.2 Suburbanization as a context of residential borderland development

Suburbanization normally sets in once economic growth and urbanization have progressed to a certain stage. Suburbanization in greater China began in the mid-1980s (ZHOU and MA 2000), but in Guangzhou the process did not set in until the early 1990s. By 2000, it was already remarkable (ZHOU and BIAN 2014). Panyu district, a suburb of Guangzhou, is a center of residential suburbanization. Transportation development and administrative restructuring play important roles in the process of suburbanization affecting Guangzhou and its southern suburb. Essentially, suburbanization between Guangzhou and Panyu can be broadly divided into three stages: a preparation stage (1978-1990), an initial, early stage (1990-2000), and a stage of maturity and rapid development (after 2000) (Table 5).

Table 5: Conditions and features of residential suburbanization in Guangzhou

Time phases and stages	Preparation stage (1978-1990)	Initial and early development stage (1990-2000)	Rapid development and mature stage (after 2000)
Events and conditions in Guangzhou (and Panyu)	• Reform and opening up (1978), • Open coaster cities (1984), • "Front shop, back factory" model of industry development in Pearl River Delta, • Township and village enterprises development in Panyu.	• The improvement of transportation conditions: Luoxi Bridge (1988) and high-speed road, • Property development in Panyu, • Local economic development: Panyu became a county-level city (1992), Panyu as Top 100 most competitive counties in China (Rank, 12,1995).	• Administrative division adjustments: Panyu goes from a county-level city to a district of Guangzhou (2000), • "Southward extension" urban development strategy of Guangzhou (2001), • Public transportation development: Metro lines 3 and 4 (2005), • Nansha district detached from Panyu (2005), • The construction of Guangzhou South Railway Station (2010), • Three less developed southern towns incorporated into Nansha district (2012).
Features	• Rapid urbanization and increasing centripetal force of Guangzhou, • *in situ* urbanization in Panyu.	• Enhanced economic connection between Guangzhou and Panyu, • The main population of suburbanization is upper class and people from Hong Kong.	• Thirty-minute commute to Guangzhou city center, Panyu becomes a part of urban central districts of Guangzhou, • The main population of suburbanization comprises middle class and white collar workers.

Source: Compiled by author

5.5.2.1 Urbanization in two cities (1978-1990)

In this period, although Panyu was governed as part of the sub-provincial city of Guangzhou, it was relatively independent with substantial fiscal and administrative powers of its own. Guangzhou and Panyu were urbanized independently.

Between 1978 and 1990, with its proximity to Hong Kong, economic development in the Pearl River Delta conformed to a model known as "front shop, back factory" that is common to the region's cities: Hong Kong was the front shop and the Pearl River Delta the back factory. The city of Guangzhou experienced rapid urban expansion and development in its eastern and northern precincts (XU and YEH 2003). Under rapid urban expansion, the government of Guangzhou resorted to a fast, far-reaching, low-cost method that bypassed the built-up village area. That expansion strategy led directly to the emergence of the urban village. However, the Pearl River forms a geographic barrier between Guangzhou and Panyu and effectively blocked Guangzhou's expansion toward Panyu. The urban expansion of Guangzhou to the south was limited to its inner suburban area and had not extended as far as the city of Panyu in this period.

Urbanization also took place in Panyu, but according to a different model than Guangzhou. The impetus instead was from below. The pattern was identified by MA and FAN (1994) in their studies of Jiangshu province. In 1984, the national government instituted a policy encouraging rural hukou holders to "leave the land but not the village" to "enter the factory but not the city" (in Chinese: *litu bu lixiang, jinchang bu jincheng*). Under this relaxed hukou policy, together with commercialization of agricultural land, many township and village enterprises arose in Panyu. The extensive and constant emergence of village and township enterprises was captured by the phrase "every village lights up a fire, and every household sets off smoke" (in Chinese: *cuncun dianhuo, huhu maoyan*). The township and village enterprises were central to industrial development. In 1991, the number of village enterprises reached 2,718, and the number of township and county enterprises was 424. The output value of village and township enterprises was 103.2 million and 177.9 million CNY, respectively, which in total accounted for 55.4% of the overall gross industrial output value in Panyu (507.8 million CNY) (Panyu Statistical Bureau 1992). The development of manufacturing, especially of labor intensive industry at the town and village level, attracted many inland migrant workers to the township and village areas of Panyu; and on the other hand it achieved an *in situ* transformation of local villagers in the rural area of Panyu district. A similar transformation pattern has also played out in Fujian province (ZHU 2000).

5.5.2.2 Initial and early stage of suburbanization (1990-2000)

The Luoxi Bridge and Huanan Expressway were built in 1988 and 1998 respectively. This effectively pierced the geographic obstacle posed by the Pearl River and greatly reduced commuting times between Guangzhou and Panyu. The connection between Guangzhou and Panyu strengthened substantially. Due to economic growth and the gradual increase of overall urban robustness in Guangzhou, the urban function spillovers have increasingly strengthened. At the same time economic growth has remained constant in Panyu with the boom of township and village industry and economic overflows from Guangzhou. Due to its rapid economic growth, Panyu was promoted to a "county-level" city governed directly by the Guangzhou government in 1992, and it achieved "Top 100 Counties in China" honors according to which Panyu's economy ranked twelfth among all the counties.

Improvements in transportation stimulated the development of a real estate industry in Panyu. Many large real estate projects such as Luoxi Xincheng, Guangzhou Country Garden, Guangzhou Aoyuan, and Clifford Estate have been constructed in Panyu. A 2001 survey by the Panyu district government found that 116 real estate projects were under construction or completed. The total construction area reached 5,023 ha. Most projects were located in the northwestern part of Panyu close to the city of Guangzhou. Because public transportation lagged, daily commuters between Panyu and Guangzhou city relied mainly on private cars. In this period, suburbanization involved a population from Guangzhou that was mostly upper-class or high-income and chose to live in Panyu as a second home or retreat because the environment in the suburb of Panyu was better than that of the inner city.

5.5.2.3 Rapid development and mature stage (after 2000)

Urban territorialization is one of the major forms of urban transformation. It takes place when a city expands and takes control of a greater area (SHEN 2007, p.309). Urban territorialization was remarkable in Guangzhou. In 2000, the "county-level" cities of Panyu and Huadu were annexed by Guangzhou as city districts. The conceptual plan of Guangzhou in 2001 put forward an adjusted governmental strategy for urban development: it advocated urban construction in Guangzhou to "develop the south, enhance the north, enter the east and integrate the west". The strategy of southward expansion has brought many investments in infrastructure to Panyu district. For instance, new bridges and a new metro system were built, greatly enhancing transit between Guangzhou and Panyu. After the metro system expanded to Panyu, Panyu lay in the thirty-minute commuting circle of Guangzhou. Improved public transportation and lower housing prices than those of Guangzhou's central districts attracted many middle class and white-collar workers from Guangzhou who made Panyu their primary residence. As Figure 8 shows, the local

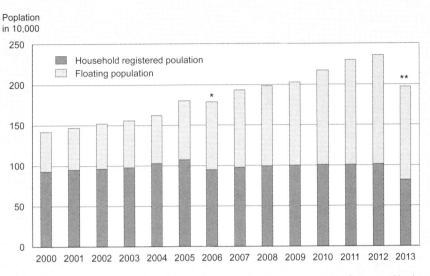

Figure 8: The population development of Panyu district
Source: Illustration by author, based on data from Panyu Branch of Guangzhou Municipal Public Security Bureau, Development and Reform Bureau of Panyu District (2014)

household population remained nearly constant between 2000 to 2012; however, the floating population greatly increased in Panyu. The real estate industry continued to flourish at this stage; according to the Panyu government's survey, the number of real estate projects had risen to 146 in 2009, an increase of 30 projects over 2001.

5.5.3 The policy of "converting villages to communities"

The policy of "converting villages to communities" (in Chinese: *cungaiju*) refers to an effort to transform villagers' agricultural hukou to non-agricultural hukou and to transform the administrative divisions from those of the village to that of a residential community. The policy of converting villages to communities began in the 1980s in the coastal region, especially in the Pearl Rival Delta. Urbanization involved a massive expropriation of agricultural land by the government. Many villages in suburban areas have lost all their land, and the villagers no longer engage in agricultural activities. Hence, the local government launched the policy of "converting villages to communities," which is a concomitant policy to the expropriation of agricultural land.

Converting villages to communities involved two stages. The first lasted from 1984 to 2000. In this phase most urban villages changed their administrative structure from rural villages into communities. The local government led the process without much concern for the will of villagers. After 2000, the state government started to regulate the shift from villages to communities by instituting a policy called "Opinions on Promoting the Construction of Urban Communities" (Ministry of Civil Affairs 2000). The state government encouraged local governments to promote the process of *cungaiju* by defining kinds of villages suited for conversion; but on the other hand the state government regulated local governments' behavior by asking them to offer welfare in the reformed village equivalent to what the urban hukou holders could receive. However, the policy was not carried out fully by local governments. Most of the reformed villages could only enjoy a small fraction of the state welfare. Therefore, *cungaiju* created a new urban hukou with some welfare benefits for villagers, who in exchange permanently lost their land use rights (HONG and CHAN 2005).

The provincial government of Guangdong responded by instituting a detailed policy called the "Opinion to Promote the Construction of Urban Communities" (Guangdong Provincial Bureau of Civil Affairs 2001). This provincial policy requested that all the villages that met the eligibility requirements for administrative conversion should be transformed into urban communities before June, 2002. Because of this policy, a great many villages were converted into urban communities, and the villagers' agricultural hukou was transformed into a new type of urban hukou with some limited welfare benefits. Although the villagers thus have the status of urban hukou holders, they cannot enjoy full welfare as can holders of full urban hukou. According to the policy, financial expenditures on public services in the village, including road maintenance, clean water and sanitation, social security, environmental services, and education, were to be fully publically financed by local government after the administrative conversion. However, only a small part of the expenditure is actually subsidized in practice. Most of these public service expenditures are still charged to village committees (LI 2013). The movement known as "converting villages to communities" has been underway in Panyu district since the early 1990s and has underlain the emergence of the urban villages.

5.6 Summary

Residential borders were cultivated in the social, economic and political settings and came to be represented in the city. The multi-scalar conditions and dynamics of China are the basis of the processes of debordering and rebordering in the city.

The reform of institutions, including the transitions from a strictly restricted to a relaxed hukou system, from a land grant system to a dual land use system, and from public allocation to commercialized housing, have had a strong impact on the creation of borders in residential areas and on sorting people into different residential enclaves. The devolution of the administrative and financial power from the central state to local government has enhanced the role of local government. The social transformations are typified by the southern city of Guangzhou.

Guangzhou has undergone rapid urbanization since 1978, and set up a process of suburbanization after the early 1990s. The urban development strategy of "southward extension" has accelerated the speed of suburbanization towards Panyu district, which has become one of the key regions of real estate development. The development of real estate industry in suburban Guangzhou has led directly to the proliferation of residential borderlands. The next chapter hence is going to explore the phenomenon of residential borderlands in the Panyu district in detail.

6 Residential borderlands in Panyu in Guangzhou

6.1 Residential borderlands in Panyu: spatial distribution

Two residential enclaves, the gated community and its neighboring village, geographically adjacent but physically separated by the walls and fences of gated community: this phenomenon is defined as residential borderland. As explored in Chapter 5, the real estate industry in Panyu district is booming. The land fueling the development is mostly that of local villages. In the course of expropriation, the local government only expropriated the arable and left the village residential land intact. Very common, therefore, is a commercial housing project that has been erected next to a village in suburban area.

The commercial housing projects have mostly taken the form of gated communities in Panyu. There are several practical reasons for the property company to build fences and walls around the communities. Firstly, since the construction land comes from local villages, setting up a fence around the parcel signifies the physical extent of ownership of the land-use rights. Secondly, in the course of Panyu's urban development, economic growth has been led in large part by the township and village industry. A governance vacuum existed in the city of Panyu such that the development of its towns lacked a uniform urban plan at the city level before the mid-1990s. Each town built largely of its own will, leading to a fragmentized construction space in Panyu. Urban infrastructure and public service facilities were mostly concentrated at the city or town center but in suburban areas were in short supply. This lack compelled property companies to construct neighborhood facilities privately in order to attract buyers. For instance, the company Shunde Country Garden built not only neighborhood facilities and amenities such as private schools, supermarkets, and a swimming pool but also independent infrastructure such as a water supply system. Walls and fences around the communities are conducive to managing private facilities for exclusive use. Thirdly, security in rural areas is an important consideration for both housing purchasers and property companies. Most real estate projects in Panyu therefore took the form of a gated community.

Based on a list of real estate projects (146) from the local government as well as on land use data from the Second National Land Survey (SNLS), 134 gated communities were identified in Panyu district. This number derives from an inspection of real estate projects on the Google image map, from an investigation of "gatedness" in property company marketing material, and from visits by the author to projects during the first-stage of fieldwork. This research identifies only gated projects that cover more than 1 ha. Conversely single gated buildings or small-scale gated projects of less than 1 ha area are excluded from the research scope. From the map of spatial distribution of gated communities (Figure 9), residential borderlands have appeared in large number in Panyu, especially in the northwest. As a statistic in ArcGIS derived from land use data, the land area of these gated communities amounts to 3,752 ha in all, including 41 gated projects with a construction area of more than 20 ha.

Based on a buffer analysis in ArcGIS, within a 200-meter buffering zone, 118 gated communities intersect with village residential areas. In a 500-meter buffering zone, 130 gated communities intersect with village residential areas. In a 1,000-meter buffering zone, all the listed gated communities intersect with village residential areas. Apparently, the identified gated communities are all located next to or not far from a local village residential area.

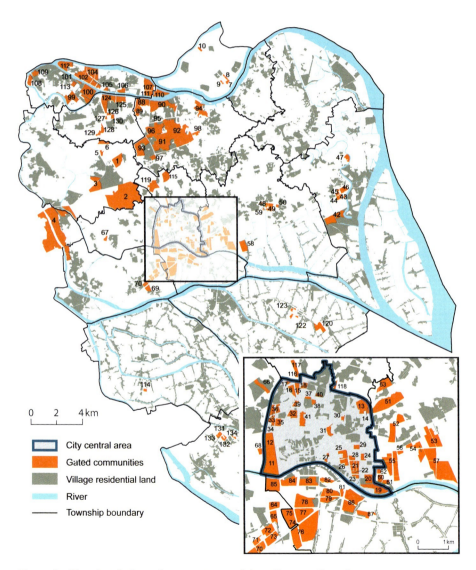

Figure 9: The identified gated communities and the village residential areas
Source: Illustration by author

Residential borderlands in Panyu in Guangzhou 71

Figure 10: The landscape of residential borderland in Panyu
Source: Photographs by author

There are salient differences between the two types of residential enclave. On one side is a modern community with high-rise buildings. On the other side is an old village with a chaotic environment and densely arranged buildings. Figure 10 shows the landscape of residential borderlands in Panyu. Photo (a) shows a typical stark contrast between the high-rises in gated communities and densely-built village (in this example mainly the gated community Xinyue Mingzhu surrounded by villages). Photo (b) shows that the gated community called Shunde Country Garden on the right side juxtaposed with Sangui village on the left. Photo (c) shows razor wire typically installed atop the fences and walls of a gated community in the city. Photo (d) shows self-employed migrants in the village waiting for customers, mostly from the gated community located behind them. In residential borderland, different groups populate the adjacent enclaves. Gated communities accommodate the upper and middle-class people or essentially those with better incomes. The neighboring villages mainly accommodate marginal urban groups: indigenous villagers, rural migrants, and a part of the urban hukou holders.

However, residential borderland is not a phenomenon unique to Panyu district, but rather it has appeared in most capital cities. As one questionnaire survey of urban planners of national scope conducted by author shows[1], 28% of respondents from all over the country agreed that gated communities are located mostly next to local villages in suburban areas in the cities they worked in. However, narrowing in on urban planners from capital cities in the eastern region identified a much higher ratio of agreement. The ratio is 35.2%. One case from Shanghai was also reported where a gated community stood next to a shanty area (IOSSIFOVA 2009). In other words, the residential borderland phenomenon is, to a certain degree, universal in China, especially in coastal cities.

6.2 Three typical residential borderlands

6.2.1 Three types of residential borderlands

Based on the layout (gated or non-gated) and supply model (private or non-private) of neighborhood facilities (e.g., the commercial, educational, and medical facilities) in a gated development project located next to a village, three types of gated communities are identified: a self-sufficient type, an open-oriented type, and a publically supplied type

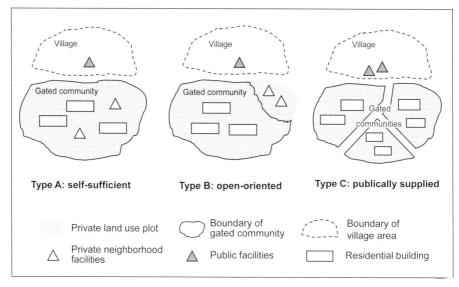

Figure 11: A model of three types of residential borderland
Source: Illustration by author

---

1 In order to explore the general existence of the phenomenon, the question "Is a gated community often adjacent to or neighboring a village in the suburban area in the city where you work?" was put to a massive questionnaire survey assessing urban planning response to gated communities in China. The author conducted it at the Chinese Annual Planning Meeting in Kunming from October 17 to 19, 2012. The question was designed to grasp the prevalence of the phenomenon in China through the eyes of urban planners. The annual planning meeting is attended by over 3,000 urban planners from all over the country. The questionnaire was distributed on tables each day before the meeting and collected after the meeting. 1,000 questionnaires were issued and 871 returned; of these 561 were valid. The respondents come from 28 capital cities, 3 Special Economic Zones (SEZ), and 56 non-capital cities in Mainland China. The results of the survey were presented at the Royal Geographical Society (RGS-IBG) Annual International Conference 2015.

Residential borderlands in Panyu in Guangzhou 73

(Figure 11). The self-sufficient type of gated community entails that most private neighborhood facilities are constructed and enclosed for the purpose of residents' exclusive use (Type A). An open-oriented gated community means that the major private neighborhood facilities are arranged in a common, open area to which outsiders have access (Type B). A publically supplied gated community means that the development project offers few if any private neighborhood facilities. Most neighborhood facilities are supplied instead by urban public financing and located in the surrounding open village area (Type C).

6.2.2 Profile of three corresponding residential borderlands

The hypothesis is that the different models of supply facilities identified above might impact flows of people across the border from a gated community to its neighboring vil-

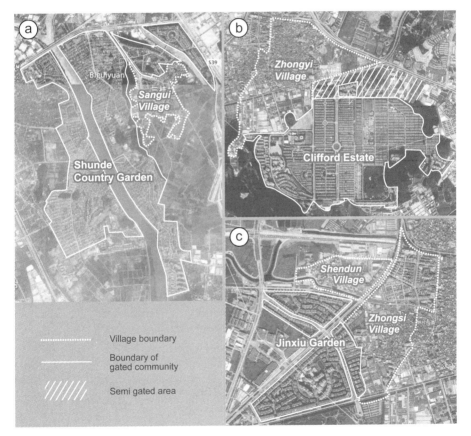

Figure 12: Three residential borderlands: Shunde Country Garden, Clifford Estate, Jinxiu Garden
Source: *Illustration by author, based on image maps from Mapbox & OpenStreetMap, Digital Globe*

Table 6: The profile of three residential borderlands

Name	Communities	Residential area (ha)	Population
Shunde Country Garden borderland	Shunde Country Garden	456	25,000*
	Sangui Village	65	6,600*
Clifford Estate borderland	Clifford Estate	399	32,000 (includes 27,136 mainland residents)
	Zhongyi Village (villages in total)	169	13,871
Jinxiu Garden borderland	Jinxiu Garden	67	14,455
	Shendun and Zhongsi villages	77	15,451

* The population data derives from interviews. Land use data is calculated by the author in ArcGIS based on SNLS data. The other population data sources are local village committees and the SNPC. Population data sourced from SNPC is as of 2010; other sources of population data are as of 2012.

Source: Compiled by author

lage. In order to test the hypothesis, three relevant residential borderlands have been chosen for observation by following. The selected residential borderlands all include a gated community and a neighboring (or non-gated) village. As shown in Figure 12, the selected residential borderlands include the gated community of Shunde Country Garden and neighboring Sangui Village (a), the gated community of Clifford Estate and neighboring Zhongyi Village (b), and the gated community of Jinxiu Garden (or in English: "Beautiful Enjoyment Garden") and neighboring Shendun and Zhongsi Village (c). The locations of these three gated communities are coded respectively as numbers 4, 3, and 2 in Figure 9.

The three selected gated communities were all first built in 1991. Shunde Country Garden is located on the city fringe of Panyu, and most of its area lies in the Shunde district, in the neighboring city of Foshan. Shunde Country Garden is a totally gated community. All its housing and public facilities are enclosed by walls and fences. About 20,000 residents lived inside in 2012 (Table 6). As map (a) in Figure 12 shows, Sangui Village is almost completely encircled by the gated community of Shunde Country Garden with only one road linking it to the outside. Sangui Village has a population of about 6,600.

The second residential borderland is Clifford Estate, located in the northwestern part of Panyu district. It includes Clifford Estate and neighboring Zhongyi Village. The area of

Clifford Estate is 399 ha, on which live about 32,000 residents[2] including 27,136 mainland residents and about 2,700 residents from Hong Kong, Macao, or Taiwan plus about 2,500 foreigners as of 2010 (Zhongcun Subdistrict Office 2014). Clifford Estate is laid out such that all residential buildings and some neighborhood facilities are enclosed, but most private commercial facilities lie in a concentrated, open area. Neighboring Zhongyi Village[3] takes up about 169 ha on which live about 13,871 people. Among them are 4,280 indigenous villagers and 9,591 rural migrants. More detailed socio-demographic characteristics are found at Chapter 7.1.3.

Jinxiu Garden represents the publically supplied gated community model. It lies in northwestern Panyu. All residential buildings there are enclosed in groups. Except for some private education facilities and convenience stores inside the gated area, all commercial facilities lie in the surrounding buildings and are open to the public. Other neighborhood facilities, such as the bank, hospital, food market etc. are supplied in the neighboring area. The neighboring villages are called Shendun and Zhongsi, as is apparent on map (c) in Figure 12. As of 2012, Jinxiu Garden was home to 14,455 residents while the neighboring villages housed 15,451 residents, of whom 3,899 were indigenous villagers and 11,552 rural migrants[4].

6.2.3 Coding gated community residents' activities in neighboring village areas

As mentioned in Chapter 4.2.2, observation by following has been performed across the three case areas. Although the three gated community types differ, they all share the feature of having one or more pedestrian gates. This term refers to less imposing side gates as opposed to the main gated entrances; residents of the gated community use these to pass on foot or bicycle into the respective neighboring village area (Figure 13). The pedestrian gate is a remarkable signal that flows of people exist across the border between two adjacent enclaves and provides an avenue to discover connections between the two enclaves through observation by following of residents who use the pedestrian gates for short trips.

---

2   Data sourced from SNPC. There are different sources of population data for Clifford Estate. Clifford Estate, the company, advertises that more than 100,000 people live there. Actually, the permanent residents in Clifford Estate do not amount to that. A plenary vote was held by residents to decide whether they agreed with an increase in Clifford Estate property management fees in 2014. The company there announced that 33,962 ballots had been issued to all Clifford Estate households resulting in 14,363 votes (8,754 in favor, 5,227 against, 117 abstentions, and 265 invalid). The polling period ran from 6 April to 29 April, 2014. Regardless of participation rate, the result would indicate that about 14,363 households resided in Clifford Estate during that period. Another public announcement by the property management office indicated that about 15,000 cars are maintained in Clifford Estate. Hence, The community-level statistical data from SNPC, which shows 10,652 permanent households and 27,136 mainland residents in Clifford Estate (which number lacks residents from Hong Kong, Macao, Taiwan, and foreigners), is more reliable.
3   Since some interviews took place in residential areas of Zhonger and Zhongsan, a part of Zhonger (19 ha) and Zhongsan (38 ha) villages are included in the research area of Zhongyi Village.
4   The data include Shendun and Zhongsi villages.

Main entrances	Pedestrian gates
Shunde Country Garden (a)	Shunde Country Garden (b)
Clifford Estate (c)	Clifford Estate (d)
Jinxiu Garden (e)	Jinxiu Garden (f)

Figure 13: The main entrances and pedestrian gates of the gated communities
Source: Photographs by author

The pedestrian gates of Shunde Country Garden (picture (b) in Figure 13) and Jinxiu Garden (picture (f) in Figure 13) were chosen as starting points for observation. Because

Clifford Estate is a large-scale community with many subdivisions, a neighborhood shuttle bus operates among them. Clifford Estate is part completely gated area and part commercial and hospital area which is open to the public (Map (b) in Figure 12). The bus connects the two parts. Its use in the open area is restricted to Clifford Estate residents and legal visitors. There is a bus stop named Clifford Hospital Station located nearest Zhongyi Village, and Clifford Estate residents who visit Zhongyi will normally take the shuttle to there and then walk 5 or 10 minutes to reach the village. Therefore, the Clifford Hospital bus stop serves as the departure point for observation by following. Since residents' trips may have multiple purposes, observation by following operated on the principle that only the first destination and purpose were recorded. Observation would then stop rather than shadow the whole journey of each observation object. In all 481 samples from observation by following were collected.

Visits to neighboring villages served diverse purposes generally assignable to nine categories. Coding the collected data involved inductively finding categories for trip purposes by reference to the Chinese Standard of National Industry Classification (CSNIC 2011)[5]. The arrived-at categories are as follows:

1. Retail services: gated community residents visited the neighboring village to buy or sell goods. Included were residents shopping in village commercial facilities such as food markets, grocery stores, pharmacies or lottery shops, or selling things in the village such as second-hand goods or recyclable waste at the recycling shop.
2. Catering services: residents went to eat, e.g., at a restaurant in the village area.
3. Labor services: the resident went to purchase labor, e.g., a household service, sewing, bicycle or electrical appliance repair, get a haircut etc.
4. Intellectual and health services: this category covers visits to service facilities in the neighboring village, such as banks, real estate agencies, telecommunications shops, hospitals etc., to obtain those services.
5. Public transport and postal services: these were visits to the bus station or postal location in the village.
6. Culture, sports and entertainment services: the resident visited a cultural amenity in the village, or an exercise or recreational facility there such as the Ktv, the massage shop, or the tennis or badminton facility.
7. Education services: visiting the village for the purpose of education, including kindergarten, primary school, musical school etc.
8. Working: people are accommodated in gated communities while working in the village area.

---

5   There are many industrial classification standards used in different countries, for instance the International Standard Industrial Classification, the North American Industry Classification System (NAICS), or the Statistical Classification of Economic Activities in the European Community. I chose the Chinese Standard of National Industry Classification (CSNIC) because the research area and economic activities unfolded in China, so a local standard was more suitable to the practical situation. For instance, the lottery industry falls under entertainment in NAICS but under household services in CSNIC.

9. Other: this category covers those observed leaving the gated community and entering village housing. Interviews revealed two kinds of situations for this group. First, some are indigenous villagers who have bought property inside the gated community and split their existence between village and gated community. Second, some are migrant workers or indigenous villagers accommodated in the village but working in the gated community.

6.2.4 The general features of flows of insiders across the border in residential borderland

As empirical data shows, there are strong flows of people across the boundary from a gated community to its neighboring village area regardless of the public service supply model the gated community represents. For instance, although the weather was hot during the empirical study period for observation by following in September in Guangzhou, residents of gated communities frequently and continually visited neighboring villages through the small pedestrian gates.

As the recorded data in Table 7 and evidence from interviews shows, visitors from gated communities have several features in common. First, the female visitors partly outnumbered the males. This is related to the division of family roles in China, where the female in a family normally handles housework. Shopping for food, sending children to school, arranging housekeeping etc. all come into this scope. Second, a portion of the residents are taking care of children during short-distance trips to the neighboring villages. This phenomenon was found at Shunde Country Garden, Clifford Estate, and Jinxiu Garden respectively. Third, retail, catering, and labor services are the three basic, primary aims of residents who went into a village area. Three activities together constituted the majority at Shunde Country Garden and Clifford Estate, while their combined ratio was about one third at Jinxiu Garden. Fourth, the village area is also a destination for other services, such as intellect and health services, public transportation and postal services as well as for culture, sports and entertainment services in all three residential borderlands. Fifth, although each gated community has private education facilities, the educational services, especially kindergarten and primary schools, are insufficient and expensive. Therefore, a certain number of gated community residents send their children to kindergarten or primary school in village areas.

Sixth, according to additional interviews with commercial developers in the village area, some businesses there target the residents of gated communities. For example a night club in Sangui Village, the Zhongfu mall and hotels in Zhongyi Village, and a private musical school in Zhongsi Village are investments or operated by residents from the gated communities. Moreover, operators or employees are increasingly accommodated in the gated community while working in the village. Finally, the results show that there are not only significant economic connections but also social interactions between the two enclaves in each residential borderland.

However, the three residential borderlands displayed some differences. In general, the main purpose of activities in the neighboring villages differed among them. Shunde Country Garden and Clifford Estate were originally positioned as resorts aimed at potential customers from Hong Kong and wealthier segments of Guangzhou or Foshan. Different supply models and layouts of private neighborhood services were chosen: Shunde Country Garden, which is a self-sufficient gated community, opted for exclusive-use

Table 7: Statistical results of the collected data from observation by following

Communities	Shunde Country Garden		Clifford Estate		Jinxiu Garden	
	Count	%	Count	%	Count	%
Total (times)	110		260		111	
Gender (person)	178	100	344	100	186	100
Male	69	38.8	95	27.6	76	40.9
Female	109	61.2	249	72.4	110	59.1
Age (person)						
Young adults	112	62.9	123	35.8	130	69.9
Middle-aged adults	37	20.8	98	28.5	45	24.2
Older adults	29	16.3	123	35.8	11	5.9
With children (times)	20	18.2	26	10	11	9.9
Purposes (times)	110	100	260	100	111	100
(1) Retail services	47	42.7	172	66.2	28	25.2
(2) Catering services	13	11.8	19	7.3	6	5.4
(3) Labor services	16	14.5	31	11.9	8	7.2
(4) Intellectual and health services	5	4.5	13	5	19	17.1
(5) Public transport and postal services	8	7.3	5	1.9	25	22.5
(6) Culture, sport and entertainment	3	2.7	12	4.6	7	6.3
(7) Education services	5	4.5	5	1.9	6	5.4
(8) Working	2	1.8	2	0.8	9	8.1
(9) Other	11	10	1	0.4	3	2.7

Source: Compiled by author

neighborhood facilities; Clifford Estate chose an open-oriented model of public service supply. The main purpose of gated community residents' visits to the neighboring village areas was to obtain low-cost retail, catering, and labor services but only to a limited extent for other types of services. This is because higher-end services are available either inside the gated community or in the city center.

Jinxiu Garden had positioned itself to appeal to local buyers and has attracted many local people as residents. Because most of the neighborhood services are publically financed and the facilities are located in the village area, the structure of activities in the adjacent village is more balanced than that of the other two residential borderlands. Jinxiu Garden and its neighboring village are more functionally connected than the other two residential borderlands.

6.3 Summary

This chapter identified the phenomenon of residential borderland and described the permeability of borders in terms of the flow of residents from a gated community to the vicinity outside. Although a visible, physical border demarcates either enclave, the border is permeable in that vigorous flows of "insiders" cross every day. The constant flow of people across the borders is not determined by the supply model or by the layout of the neighborhood facilities in a gated community. Rather, it is a general phenomenon of insiders pursuing diverse activities in the neighboring villages. The activities can be classified into the above-mentioned nine categories. The gated community is thus neither isolated nor isolating with respect to its surroundings but rather, to a certain extent, is functionally connected to its locality. This chapter provides only a first glimpse of the debordering practices. The next chapter explores the Clifford Estate borderland, which was selected as a single case by which to study debordering and rebordering processes in detail.

7 Urban debordering and rebordering processes

This chapter closely explores a single, typical case to examine the theoretical framework and analyze the processes of urban debordering and rebordering in detail. The residential borderland of Clifford Estate is selected for this purpose for two reasons. First, Clifford Estate is in the Panyu district of Guangzhou, which has undergone rapid economic development and urbanization since 1978. The Panyu district is the center of this suburbanization. The advantage of location and the implementation of a "southward extension" strategy in Guangzhou have made Panyu the key area of development with constant, dynamic changes. Many large-scale gated communities have emerged in Panyu in the past two decades, reflecting this dynamic development. Second, the spatial structure of Panyu is characterized by fragmentation with many residential borderlands. The Clifford Estate borderland represents these as one of the first gated communities constructed in Panyu district. As such, Clifford Estate has attracted much mass media attention.

7.1 The physical border and socio-demographic and economic differences between two contiguous enclaves

7.1.1 The creation of Clifford Estate: historical perspective

Within the suburbanization process in Guangzhou, a large amount of agricultural land has been expropriated since the late 1980s to promote real estate development in Panyu. Clifford Estate was one of the largest such projects. It was developed by the Clifford Group, which was first set up as a joint venture between a private company from Hong Kong and two local government-owned companies. Cooperation with a local government makes it easier for the development company to obtain construction land. Hence a large quantity of construction land has been leased to Clifford Estate, most of it in Zhongyi Village. Except for 15.5 ha of agricultural land set aside, all the agricultural land in Zhongyi Village (more than 267 ha) had been expropriated and transferred to the Clifford Group by 1992.

However, in the 1990s the land was sold through an administrative method which entailed the local government leasing the land by agreement with the private company based on consultations, rather than by auction, at very low prices. The official standard land transfer fee was a low 10 yuan per square meter in Panyu at that time, while villagers were compensated at a much lower rate. After the land was expropriated, indigenous villagers lost the agricultural land they relied on for their living, changing the trajectory of their lives. The loss of land set up potential conflicts between Zhongyi Village and Clifford Estate. As the residents complained:

> "There is nothing to do [after the land was expropriated]; it is very difficult to find a job now. We as the old generation didn't receive much education. All recruitment

prefers the educated workers; they don't want the people without schooling. Many indigenous villagers at my age [above age fifty] didn't have much education then. What can we do? How can we earn money for living?" (No 9, December 05, 2012, indigenous villager)

"We had clean water and beautiful mountains. The pool, the rice field and the dry land were great and enjoyable. The entire village was surrounded by this wonderful natural environment then. Now, all of them are destroyed. It is really frustrating." (No 15, December 05, 2012, indigenous villager)

After the Clifford Estate community was built, a significant line of demarcation between Clifford Estate and Zhongyi Village appeared in the physical environment. As Figure 14 shows, Clifford Estate has modern buildings and a clean, tidy environment with green, open space. On the contrary, as Figure 15 shows, Zhongyi Village has a high density of buildings and a messy, shabby environment with small, limited green space.

Clifford lake   Lakeside recreational space

Horizon unit   Qinyi unit

Figure 14: The architectural environment inside Clifford Estate
Source: Photographs by author

Urban debordering and rebordering processes 83

Handshake buildings

Mixed commercial and recreational space

Bulletin board

Waste collecting store

Figure 15: The living environment in Zhongyi Village
Source: Photographs by author

7.1.2 The constitution of the border

Clifford Estate is a gated community with strict border controls consisting of hard and soft components. The hard components are iron fences, walls, and gates. The soft components are an entry control system that relies on identity cards ("IC") and surveillance staff including guards and shuttle bus drivers. Some guards act as gatekeepers at each door, while others patrol public areas and residential units inside the community. The shuttle bus drivers are also part of the security system, for they check everyone's residential IC who boards the bus outside Clifford Estate. More than 1,000 guards and 40 dogs reportedly patrolled the community during the early development stage of Clifford Estate (SHI 2004). Today there are about 500 guards and 210 bus drivers; meanwhile the use of dogs has been sharply reduced (Interviews No. 14, No. 54).

Entry to the Estate is strictly managed at the gate. Residents must swipe an IC every time they enter. Each visitor's personal information must be registered with the administrative office before it will issue a permit. Normally, guards will call the property owner to check the information given at each visit. Particular attention is paid to young adults but less attention to the elderly or people accompanied by children (Interview No. 54).

7.1.3 Socio-demographic and socio-economic differences between two enclaves

Residents of Clifford Estate (termed "insiders") and residents of the village of Zhongyi (termed "vicinity outsiders") both inhabit the border area. 27,136 permanent mainland residents live in Clifford Estate, and 13,871 residents live in Zhongyi Village (see Appendix 4)[1].

Remarkable socio-demographic and economic differences exist between insiders and vicinity outsiders. One is their age structure. As Figure 16 shows, the residents of either area are mainly between the ages of 19 and 45 (57% and 67% respectively). The proportion of the population above age 61 is 6 percentage points higher in Clifford Estate than in Zhongyi, while the proportion of young residents (ages 19 to 30) in Zhongyi is 11 percentages higher. The difference comes down to the rural migrants living in Zhongyi

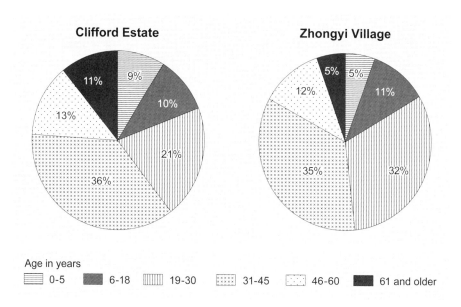

Figure 16: Population age structures for Clifford Estate and Zhongyi Village
Source: Illustration by author, based on data of SNPC, community level (2010, respecting only mainland residents)

---

[1] The SNPC data reflected here is sourced from the raw survey and was not officially adjusted. Official data put the population of indigenous villagers in Zhongyi village at 5,124 in 2010. In addition, a number of Hong Kong, Macao, Taiwanese and foreign residents, about 5200, was not included in the statistical data for Clifford Estate.

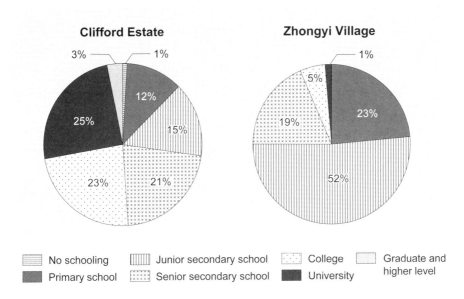

Figure 17: Population education levels for Clifford Estate and Zhongyi Village
Source: Illustration by author, based on data of SNPC, community level (2010, respecting only mainland residents)

who are mainly younger workers. The next striking difference is educational achievement (Figure 17). Mainly, insiders are highly educated while vicinity outsiders are less well educated. Most insiders, or 72.7%, have achievement beyond junior secondary school. Vicinity outsiders have achieved junior secondary school at most, amounting to 75.1%.

Clifford Estate residents are Panyu or Guangzhou citizens, migrants, residents of Hong Kong, Macao, and Taiwan, and foreigners; however, this research focuses on the mainland residents who form the main community population (84%). As Figure 18 shows, based on the hukou structure of mainland residents, 62% of the residents have Guangzhou urban hukou, of whom 32% have local Panyu hukou and 30% Guangzhou hukou. Nevertheless, a major part the Guangzhou or Panyu hukou holders are not indigenous but are permanent migrants who received urban hukou after relocating to Guangzhou (or Panyu). In addition, 38% of residents without Guangzhou hukou are part of the floating population who are able to purchase commercial housing or have relatively advanced education.

Zhongyi is inhabited mainly by indigenous villagers, rural-to-urban migrants, and some urban hukou holders. There are 4,280 indigenous villagers in Zhongyi Village and a small number with Guangzhou hukou. 67% of residents are floating population, including a

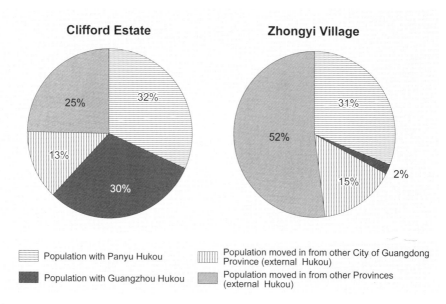

Figure 18: Hukou structure of residents of Clifford Estate and Zhongyi Village
Source: Illustration by author, based on data of SNPC, community level (2010, respecting only mainland residents)

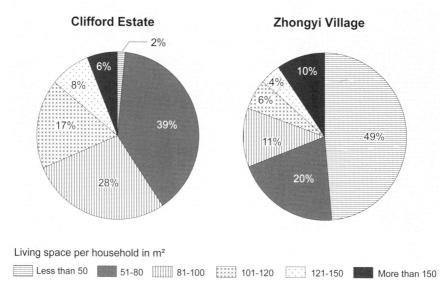

Figure 19: Housing conditions in Clifford Estate and Zhongyi Village
Source: Illustration by author, based on data of SNPC, community level (2010, respecting only mainland residents)

Urban debordering and rebordering processes 87

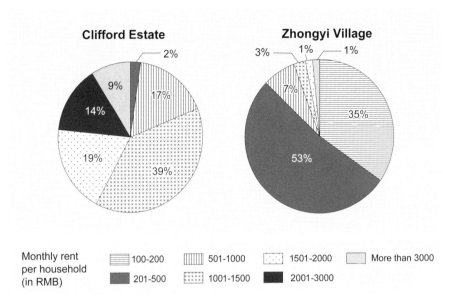

Figure 20: Rental level in Clifford Estate and Zhongyi Village
Source: Illustration by author, based on data of SNPC, community level (2010, respecting only mainland residents)

large group (52%) of migrants from other provinces and another group (15%) of migrants from other cities within the local province.

There is a social and economic gap between the two enclaves. Clifford Estate is inhabited mainly by urban professionals representing middle- or high-income classes, while the residents of Zhongyi Village are mainly lower income. Most of the migrants in Zhongyi Village are manual laborers who work either at nearby factories or as self-employed workers in the low-end services industry.

The two indices demonstrate the economic gap. These are 1) the structure of living space and 2) rental price (Figure 19, Figure 20). The living space per capita in Clifford Estate is 37.8 m² as compared with Zhongyi Village at 18.6 m². 98% of households in Clifford Estate live in a space larger than 50 m², but only 51% of households in Zhongyi inhabit as much or more space. According to the SNPC sampling survey, 86% of housing rentals cost less than 501 yuan in Zhongyi, including 34% costing between 100 and 200 yuan per month. By comparison, no property in Clifford Estate rents for less than 201 yuan per month. 81% of housing there goes for more than 1000 yuan per month.

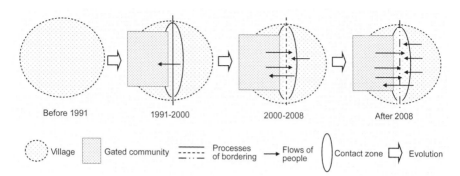

Figure 21: The dynamic processes of bordering between Clifford Estate and Zhongyi Village
Source: Illustration by author

7.2 Functional debordering process and permeability

7.2.1 Functional debordering process

Dynamic processes play out over time between Clifford Estate and Zhongyi, including bordering, debordering and rebordering (Figure 21). The debordering and rebordering processes have different aspects. This section explores functional debordering, which refers to the increasing permeability of the border. Because the Clifford Estate development company bought a large amount of land, the construction of Clifford Estate has been a staggered process. Some land today is still under development by the company. The debordering process breaks down into four phases.

The village of Zhongyi is a sub-village of Zhongcun established during the Song dynasty. However, most of the existing buildings in Zhongyi Village were constructed in the 1950s. Zhongyi village was a contiguous agricultural village before 1991, but since then the construction of Clifford Estate has divided it in two. Most agricultural land of Zhongyi has been expropriated and transferred to the Clifford Estate development company, while the built-up area was kept intact. At the first stage of Clifford Estate development, the developer promoted the project as a resort for potential purchasers in Hong Kong and among Guangzhou's wealthy. Between 1991 and 2000, most of the developed units were villas or low-rise apartments, and the first-generation residents were mainly upper classes who bought into Clifford Estate for a second home. These were, in fact, mostly people from Hong Kong and some of Guangzhou's wealthy, both of which groups spoke mainly Cantonese. For safety and exclusivity, the border between Clifford Estate and Zhongyi was strictly controlled. The insiders' economic consumption took place completely within Clifford Estate or in the city center, and there was almost no flow of residents from the inside to the vicinity outside within the residential borderland. Only building contractors and some service providers who accommodated in Zhongyi Village crossed the border from the vicinity outside.

Urban debordering and rebordering processes 89

Between 2000 and 2008, Clifford Estate underwent a process of localization. With accelerating suburbanization, the Clifford Estate development company shifted its market posture from that of a resort to one of residential real estate in the later stage of the development. They have started to build multi-story and high-rise housing. As the scale of Clifford Estate grew larger with newly built housing, more and more local, middle-income residents moved in. Meanwhile, because the property prices in Clifford Estate increased with improved transportation between Panyu and Guangzhou, some of the Hong Kong investors began to sell their property. Clifford Estate, located in the suburban area between the Guangzhou central districts and the Panyu city center, offered lower housing prices than either. Therefore, many middle-income people from both areas chose to make Clifford Estate their first home.

Thus the new residents are mainly middle-income people who work in Guangzhou central districts or Panyu city center. A great many young residents, especially the floating population, bought property in Clifford Estate through mortgage loans. This group typically works in the central districts of Guangzhou, lives in this suburban area, and commutes daily between the two. Because new residents come from all over the country, the main language spoken in the community shifted from Cantonese to Mandarin.

Under the process of localization, residents' daily needs increased considerably and diversely. Moreover, the price of private commodities and services inside the gated community was much higher than comparable commodities and services offered in the neighbo-

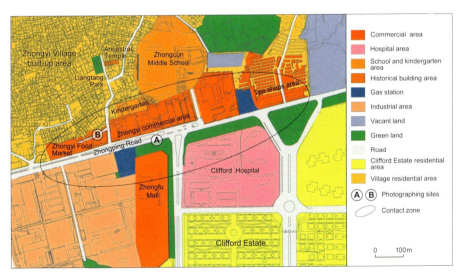

Figure 22: The contact zone between Clifford Estate and Zhongyi Village
Source: Illustration by author, based on the basemap from Guangzhou City Planning Bureau Panyu Branch

Zhongfu Mall   Zhongyi Food Market

Figure 23: The key nodes of flows in the contact zone
Source: Photographs by author

ring village area, so many residents oriented their consumption toward the village vicinity. The economic ties between Clifford Estate and Zhongyi Village were greatly enhanced in this period.

The most important sign of the connection is the emerging "contact zone" (Figure 22). At the bottom right area of the map is Clifford Estate; at the top left is Zhongyi Village. Clifford Estate is separated from Zhongyi's built-up area both physically, by fences and walls, and geographically, by a city road named Zhongping Road. Zhongping Road is a two-lane main city artery used daily by an endless stream of traffic. With the coming of flows of Clifford Estate residents to Zhongyi Village, many shops and service facilities set up on either side of this road, constituting a contact zone where some key nodes of flow have formed. These include Zhongfu mall and Zhongyi food market (Figure 23), which attract many insiders every day. Particularly since the completion of Zhongfu Mall in 2008, the contact zone has become a new commercial center.

7.2.2 Changes to the contact zone over time

"When I first arrived here [Zhongyi village] in 2003, there were a few customers [Clifford residents] visiting here. Most of the stores in this alley had not yet operated. Just two or three fruit stores, two dumpling shops, opened at the entrance to the alley near the street [Zhongping Road]. Not too many residents were coming here until 2005. All these stores were opened between 2005 and 2008. These places were a garment factory before. In addition, the Zhongyi Food Market wasn't like this. All the food and vegetables were sold on the street then. The Zhongyi Food Market was built after I came here, and it was decorated twice afterwards." (No. 27, December 09, 2012, self-employed seamstress)

The interview with a self-employed seamstress who had been working at Zhongyi Village for about ten years shows that the biggest changes in the contact zone occurred in the

Urban debordering and rebordering processes 91

December 2012

October 2013

November 2014

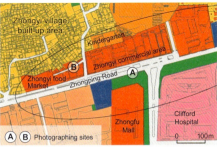
Map extract of Fig. 22

Figure 24: Changes over time to the area around a pedestrian crossing at Zhongping road. It is the main crossing for residents of Clifford Estate going to Zhongyi Village.
Source: Photographs by author (all pictures were taken from site A, see map extract)

December 2012

October 2013

March 2014

Figure 25: Changes over time along a commercial alley in Zhongy Village that leads to the Zhongyi Food Market.
Source: Photographs by author (all pictures were taken from site B, see map extract, Figure 24)

period between 2005 and 2008. During this time the main dynamic was that the contact zone became more commercialized. The dynamic changes were still underway over time in the contact zone. Figure 24 is a set of photographs taken on the same side of a pedestrian crossing of Zhongping Road at different times; it shows the way the facades in the contact zone have developed. From 2012 to 2013, the green trees lining Zhongping Road were cut down, and a sauna shop opened. From 2013 to 2014, the sauna shop was redecorated, and a new sign advertising a private kindergarten and children's park was put up next to it. The picture also shows that the square in front of Zhongfu Mall was being widened during November, 2014. Figure 25 shows the changes to a commercialized alley connecting to the Zhongyi Food Market. The building on the left, which became a hotel, was remodeled and fitted with air conditioning from 2012 to 2014.

The sidewalk parallel to Zhongping Road on the Zhongyi Village side is the only foot path available to the residents of Clifford Estate walking to Zhongyi Food Market. Since such a large member of residents use the sidewalk every day (Figure 26), it has become an informal commercial space. Interviews demonstrate that once upon a time many street peddlers would sell food and vegetables on this sidewalk until a regulation forbid the use of this sidewalk by street peddlers (Interview No. 34). After 2012, the sidewalk was widened as trees along it were cut down. Many informal, self-employed migrants providing moving services, motorcycle taxi, and recycling services would gather on this sidewalk.

Fig. 26: Daily flows of residents returning home on the sidewalk after visiting the Zhongyi Food Market
Source: Photograph by author

It has become the main site of social encounters and a space for the poor and the affluent to mingle and co-exist.

7.2.3 Flows of gated community residents to the neighboring village

"There are so many people shopping in Zhongyi Village every day in the morning that it looks like during the new-year festival." (No. 04, November 17, 2012, Clifford resident)

"I always buy meat and vegetables at Zhongyi Food Market. The other things like daily necessities and snacks I buy at the Clifford market." (No. 18, December 08, 2012, Clifford resident)

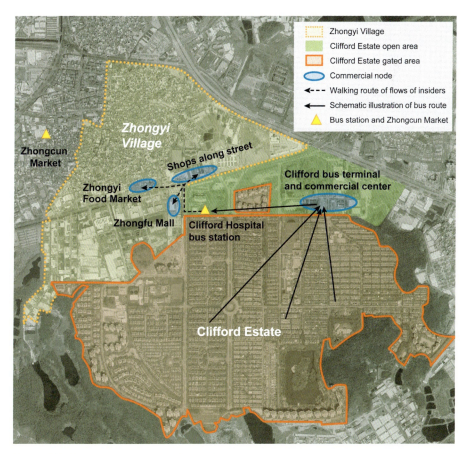

Figure 27: Flows of gated community residents to the neighboring area
Source: Illustration by author based on image maps sourced from Panyu Land District Development Center

Such interviewee statements show that a vigorous flow of residents from Clifford Estate to Zhongyi Village transpires every day. As Figure 27 shows, the Clifford commercial center, Zhongfu Mall, the Zhongyi Food Market and the shops along the street in Zhongyi's built-up area have become the key nodes of the daily flow of the insiders into the vicinity area. The Clifford commercial center in front of the Clifford gated area is linked to each unit of Clifford Estate by a shuttle bus service. Clifford residents can reach the commercial center easily and conveniently. The daily flow of insiders out into Zhongyi follows a particular route. First, they ride the shuttle bus to the Clifford bus terminal, which is adjacent to the Clifford commercial center, and then transfer to another shuttle bus by which they reach the Clifford Hospital station. From here they walk a few minutes either to Zhongfu Mall or to the Zhongyi Food Market area. Some residents ride the public bus further to the Zhongcun Market, a comprehensive farmers' market whose prices are lowest as compared to any above-mentioned market. As analyzed (see Chapter 6.2.3), the observational data reveal that gated community residents visit neighboring villages to pursue one of eight types of activities. These include obtaining retail, catering, and labor services; intellectual and health services; public transportation and postal services; culture, sports and entertainment services; educational services; and employment.

Although most daily needs can be satisfied at the Clifford commercial center, many residents nonetheless choose to make purchases in Zhongyi Village. The main reasons that insiders visit the neighboring village are to obtain particular goods and services cheaply. The Clifford Estate residents constitute a massive daily demand, and although many commercial and public service facilities operate in the Clifford Estate area, they are insufficient. Moreover, the price of goods and services in Clifford Estate is generally higher than those in Zhongyi Village. Hence, many complementary or competitive facilities have been set up in the Zhongyi village area: bank branches, real estate agencies, a shopping mall, and educational facilities. Zhongyi's commercial development reduces the cost of living for Clifford Estate residents. The contact zone has become a functional complement of Clifford Estate. One five-year resident who had gone daily to the Zhongyi Food Market for shopping explained:

> "Before commerce developed in Zhongyi Village, I did grocery shopping in Clifford Estate; it was very expensive. However, after the commerce developed in Zhongyi Village, it has reduced the cost of living for us. It is very convenient for me to go there, and the price of food and goods is cheaper." (No. 8, December 01, 2012, Clifford resident)

Another resident commented:

> "I would sometimes go to Zhongyi Food Market, for I either can't get some services or I feel the price is too expensive in Clifford Estate. The prices at the Zhongyi

Food Market are more affordable. Moreover, there is an old man who offers a sewing service there. I can't find this kind of service in Clifford Estate." (No. 12, December 04, 2012, Clifford resident).

7.2.4 Flows of vicinity outsiders across the border of the gated community

People also flow from the outside to the inside. Residents of Zhongyi Village including the local villagers and migrants who offer commodity or household services can cross the border easily. As one shopkeeper of a grain store in Zhongyi Village said:

> "I have many regular [Clifford] customers who often visit my store. They either give me a call or come to my store to make an order, and then I deliver the grain to their home." (No. 24, December 09, 2012, migrant in Zhongyi Village).

The gated community residents welcome the counter-flow based on beneficial business services. As one resident claimed:

> "There are some pharmacies in Zhongyi Village with good service. Usually after I bought traditional Chinese medicine there, they would decoct it for me and deliver it to my home when it was ready." (No. 8, December 01, 2012, Clifford resident).

The counter-flow serves other purposes besides commerce. One particular hill was a traditional recreational place for indigenous villagers seeking shade during the hot summers. The area was sold to Clifford Estate and exclusively reserved as a leisure place for insiders. However, some indigenous villagers still manage to visit the hill by entering through the strictly controlled borders. Their avenue is knowing other villagers who bought property inside or who work at Clifford Estate as guards or housekeepers. As one indigenous villager said:

> "The frequency with which we go to Clifford Estate varies in different seasons. We often go to the hill inside [Clifford Estate] for shade on summer evenings." (No. 15, December 05, 2012, indigenous villager).

7.3 Functional rebordering

7.3.1 Enhanced barrier effect

The vigorous flow of people from Clifford Estate to Zhongyi Village has not erased the barrier effect of its fences and walls but rather created new private space and a superimposed invisible border. First, the insiders' daily routes around Zhongyi make apparent that they mostly limit their activities to the contact zone. Despite frequent visits to the area, they normally do not venture beyond its commercial facilities and seldom go further

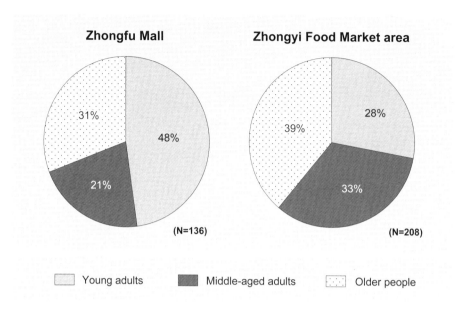

Figure 28: Age structure of gated community residents who visit the neighboring vicinity
Source: Illustration by author based on the data derived from observation by following

into the inner part of Zhongyi. For instance, Zhongyi Liantang park is a main place of recreation for local villagers and rural migrants. Although many of the insiders interviewed said they visit Zhongyi Food Market frequently, only a few of them knew the park, which is located not far from Zhongyi Food Market.

Second, when Zhongfu Mall was built on the same side of the traffic artery as Clifford Estate, it intercepted the flow of residents to the Zhongyi Food Market area. Residents going to Zhongyi Food Market must cross Zhongping Road. The endless stream of traffic on this road makes it another physical barrier between Clifford Estate and Zhongyi. The barrier effect remarkably affects the behavior of young adults. The Zhongyi Food Market is more difficult to reach on foot than Zhongfu Mall, and, most importantly, there is a parking area in front of the mall. Young adults would rather visit Zhongfu Mall than Zhongyi Food Market. As shown in Figure 28, the age structure of insiders who visit Zhongfu Mall reveals that 48% of visitors are young adults while only 28% of young adults visit Zhongyi Food Market area. Visitors to Zhongyi Food Market are mainly middle-aged and elderly, together accounting for 72%. Zhongfu Mall has thus impacted business development in Zhongyi Village. According to some interviews:

"In my family, my mother normally goes to Zhongyi Food Market every two days. As far as I know, working young people like me go to Zhongyi Village only once or twice a week. However, we normally don't go as far as Zhongyi Food Market; we just go to Zhongfu Mall. Only the aged people or the retired elderly who have more spare time would like to go to Zhongyi Food Market area." (No. 21, December 08, 2012, Clifford resident).

"From 2005 to 2008, business was prosperous here [Zhongyi Food Market], people were crowded in the alley [leading to Zhongyi Food Market]. After 2008, there were fewer people due to the development of Zhongfu Mall." (No. 27, December 09, 2012, self-employed seamstress).

Third, the flow of residents going to Zhongyi Village has created new gated private space. For instance, a private gated kindergarten named Oriental Pearl Kindergarten (in Chinese: *Dong mingzhu*) opened in Zhongyi's built-up section and meant to appeal to Clifford residents. Tuition is lower than what the kindergarten in Clifford Estate charges but higher than that of other kindergartens in Zhongyi Village. As one interview shows, the kindergarten is well known in Zhongyi Village, but the high tuition is unaffordable to residents there, who send their children to other kindergartens. This means a new exclusive space has arisen in Zhongyi Village area through the price mechanism:

A: "My grandson is two-and-a-half-year-old, and he is in kindergarten now. The kindergarten is in Zhongsi Village [a neighboring village of Zhongyi]. His father works outside; I pick up my grandson every day, and it only takes less than fifteen minutes."
Q: "Why don't you choose the nearest kindergarten, Oriental Pearl Kindergarten?"
A: "Many residents of Clifford Estate put their children in the Oriental Pearl kindergarten. The tuition fee is higher there, about 7,500 yuan per semester, while it is only 5600 yuan per semester in Zhongsi Village Kindergarten." (No. 42, October 11, 2013, local migrant).

7.3.2 Differentiation of places of consumption

The border effect has, to a certain extent, affected the way vicinity outsiders behave as consumers. When they came, residents of Clifford Estate brought a differentiation of commodity prices in different markets depending how far they lay from Clifford Estate. The further the market from Clifford Estate, the lower its prices. Prices increased substantially in the Zhongyi Food Market area, which pushed many migrants and some indigenous villagers to shop at more distant food markets, *e.g.*, Zhongcun Food Market or Zhongsan village market. Although the flow of insiders into the contact zone increased the likelihood of social encounters between them and the vicinity outsiders who supplied goods and services in Zhongyi Village, the interviews reveal that some low-income residents of Zhongyi Village were priced out of common markets like Zhongfu Mall, Zhongyi Food Market etc. Hence, despite frequent encounters between the insiders and the village-area merchants, differentiation of the consumption places and routes frequented by insiders and poor vicinity outsiders has reduced the likelihood that these groups will encounter one another and interact. These groups' different daily trajectories have created a tunnel-like border:

> "I usually buy food and meat at Zhongcun Food Market, but not in Zhongyi Food Market. There are many Clifford residents shopping in Zhongyi Food Market, and the price is higher than Zhongcun Food Market. If I spent three yuan in Zhongyi Food Market, it would just cost two yuan in Zhongcun Food Market for the same goods." (No. 9, December 03, 2012, indigenous villager).

> "I always buy food and meat in Zhongcun Food Market where the price is much cheaper; however, the price in Xiecun market, a wholesale market, is even lower than Zhongcun Food Market. Although Xiecun market is the farthest one, I prefer to go there whenever I have time." (No. 10, December 03, 2012, migrant in Zhongyi Village).

7.4 Symbolic debordering

7.4.1 The collective identity in Clifford Estate

Because property in Clifford Estate is not cheap, behind the gate lives a socio-economically mainly homogenous group of people who have the economic ability to buy the property. Most of the residents are well-educated urban professionals. There is a collective identity among the residents such that the residents are "superior quality" (in Chinese: *gao suzhi*). As one resident put it:

> "It does not matter where you come from, as long as you live inside. We are at the same [high] level [in Chinese: *dangci*]. The people at this level have many similar hobbies, such as sports and communication. For example, I like playing tennis; there are many residents at this level who have this hobby." (No. 43, October 11, 2013, Clifford resident).

However, the collective identity of Clifford Estate has been undergoing a change from being a homogenous group of wealthy residents to being a mixed-income group of residents. As the scale of the community has become larger and larger, residents with different backgrounds and income levels have come in. The original collective identity of the wealthy has been diluting and shifting to a hybrid identity. The increasing proportion of middle-income people includes many migrants born in rural areas who migrated to Guangzhou. They normally have stable jobs in the city because of their good education. However, following cultural tradition in China, when migrants settle down in the city, they tend to have their parents come from their hometown to live together. Generally, the rural elderly generation is poorly educated and only dimly aware of urban civilization due to lack of exposure and opportunity. The arrival of this older rural generation into the gated community disturbed the original public order of the community with respect to such behaviors as queuing up for the community shuttle bus or avoiding litter. Residents became dissatisfied with the population structure in the community. As one interviewee said:

> "I can't flatter the composition of residents. The restriction on housing purchases is less strict than before; everyone can migrate to everywhere to earn money and make a living now. They [migrants] can buy a flat here just with their identity card [without any restriction] after they earn money. When they feel well and settle down, they get their parents [from rural area] living with them. These people come from all over the country, and have a lot of [uncertain] information. Some are superior quality [in Chinese: *gao suzhi*], and some are inferior quality [in Chinese: *di suzhi*]." (No. 34, December 13, 2012, Clifford resident).

Another resident who had been living in Clifford Estate for more than ten years also complained:

> "Generally speaking, the quality of residents is lower than before. More and more white-collar migrant workers move in and bring their parents from a rural area to live with them. Their parents' generation does not pay too much attention to hygiene and usually litters randomly in public areas. Moreover, after this group of residents comes, they start to get on the bus without queuing. I think that this is related to their accustomed rural living environment. When they come in, they never consider improving their quality! I think Clifford Estate is a high quality and elegant community, but now it is becoming a normal community." (No. 61, November 20, 2014, Clifford resident).

In response to this perceived degradation of community quality, many wealthy residents have left the community, which has diluted the original homogenous structure, essentially, of a wealthy group. It was reported that 80% of the first generation residents – the wealthy ones – had left the gated community of Clifford Estate by 2003 (CHEN and ZHU 2003). With the original order destroyed, the rich set about creating new borders in other places.

7.4.2 Symbolic debordering: a sense of belonging

Frequent visits by insiders to the vicinity area, especially to the contact zone, raised a sense of belonging and attachment to place among those insiders. As residents said:

"I sometimes tell people that I live in Zhongcun ['cun' in Chinese means 'village'. The area of Zhongcun contains both Clifford Estate and Zhongyi Village], rather than tell them exactly that I live in Clifford Estate; because sometimes I don't want the people know my residence in detail." (No. 18, December 08, 2012, Clifford resident).

"We usually said we were going to Zhongcun but actually were going to Zhongyi village. In the native consciousness, we call Zhongyi Village 'small Zhongcun'." (No. 01, September 02, 2012, Clifford resident).

Location information

Administrative Region	Panyu-Clifford
Property Location	Intersection of Canton Road and Jinshan Avenue, Panyu District
Transportation Information	Bus: No1, No 13, No 15, No 301, No 305, No 307, No 288

Featured Information

Advantage	No information
Disadvantage	No information

Building Information

Developer	Clifford Estate Company
Construction Year	2002-01-01
Buildings Category	Houses
Greening Rate	75%

Supporting Information

Property Management Company	Clifford Property Management Ltd.
Property Fee	2.70 RMB/m²/month
Supporting Facility	Kindergarten: Clifford Elite Kindergarten, Clifford Kindergarten, Zhongsan Kindergarten Primary and Middle school: Clifford Estates School, Zhongcun Middle School, Clifford School, Zhongcun Yuying Primary School, Clifford Public School University: Guangdong University of Technology Hospital: Zhongcun Hospital, Clifford Hospital Market: Clifford Market, Zhongfu Mall, Zhongyi Food Market, Din Tai Tea shops area, Changhua commercial street Post Office: Clifford Post Station Bank: Bank of China, ICBC, Agricultural Bank of China, China Construction Bank, China Merchants Bank, Bank of East Asia Other: Clifford Food Court, Clifford Club, Clifford Hotel, Clifford Commercial Street, Zhongfu Mall Cinema, Clifford Hotel and Resort Center. Neighborhood Inner Facility: Basketball courts, Badminton courts, Tennis courts, Squash courts, Water golf, Bowling Alley, Football field, Archery field, Skating rink, Electronic Amusement Park, Swimming pool, Indoor heated swimming pool, Water Park, Diving Hall, Climbing gym

Figure 29: Screenshot of a website promoting a property in Clifford Estate. (The emphasized facilities are all in the village enclave).
Source: Centaline Property Agency Limited (2014); the original version is in Chinese, translated by author

Because the geographical concept of *Zhongcun* encompasses Clifford Estate as well as Zhongyi Village, residents representing that they live in Zhongcun convey that they live either in Clifford Estate or in Zhongyi Village. That insiders do not intentionally distinguish themselves from the poor village means that the territorial stigma towards the poor village has weakened or been eliminated, and that the gated community residents to some extent have embraced the poor, neighboring village. After living in this area for a long time, a local consciousness has formed such that Zhongyi Village has become a metonym for the village of Zhongcun.

As shows in Figure 29, there is another example attesting that the insiders have come to consider the neighboring village as integral: many second-hand housing units in Clifford Estate have come up for sale or rent on the housing market. These properties are introduced, either on websites or in real estate agencies' promotional materials, in such a way that some Zhongyi Village amenities – the Zhongyi Food Market, the Zhongsan primary school, the Zhongcun middle school etc. – are introduced as neighborhood facilities directly attendant to the Clifford Estate properties. Hence, there is a symbolic debordering process of insiders starting to consider some places in the neighborhood village as part of their own rather than regarding the two enclaves as completely isolated places.

7.5 Symbolic rebordering

The weakening of the insiders' geographical stigma is by no means equivalent to full acceptance of the vicinity outsiders. Symbolic debordering is accompanied by symbolic rebordering processes. Spatial strategies of seeking a sense of security and of ordering and othering strengthen the barrier effect at the same time. The border symbolizes security for insiders against vicinity outsiders whom they perceive as a potential source of crime and disorder. The stigma toward vicinity outsiders persists in the minds of the residents of gated community.

7.5.1 Seeking a sense of security

For the residents of gated communities, the physical border is antecedent: the developer erected it before their arrival. Then, having taken up residence on one side of the physical border, they resist opening the border. For them, the fences and walls of gated communities symbolize a sense of security.

Borders as symbol of security
The physical borders in terms of fences and walls create a sense of security. Many interviewees mentioned that the management of entry at the gates benefits security inside (Interviews No. 12, 13, 39, and 47). For instance:

"With enclosed property management, the thieves are fewer, and it is more difficult for them to steal. Even if they come, there is nothing to be stolen. We normally don't keep money at home but deposit it with the bank. If they want to take the furniture, it is hard to do that, for they need a car to carry it. However, outside cars can't enter. The enclosed property management is indeed good for security." (No. 39, October 06, 2013, Clifford resident).

"After so many years of practice, the enclosed property management system is mature now. The outsiders generally are restricted from entering, for the community is closed. I feel safe in our community." (No. 47, October 13, 2013, Clifford resident).

In fact, "enclosed property management" has enhanced the sense of security among residents, for whom a situation without gates and fences is unimaginable. As one resident who bought a villa in Clifford Estate as a second home claimed:

"If there were no fences and walls, I would not feel good about the safety of my property when I am not here." (No. 34, December 13, 2012, Clifford resident).

Another resident compared Clifford Estate with Zhongyi Village, which lacks fences and walls:

"The sense of safety here is better. I don't very much like to go to Zhongyi Village, where it is certainly less safe than here. Although it is not so unsafe, I don't dare to go there in the evening." (No. 21, December 08, 2012, Clifford resident).

The gates and fences are so pervasive that some residents do not consider that gatedness is an abnormal social phenomenon. As one interviewee said:

"You can enter only with the IC card. If anybody can come in without IC card, security becomes a question. In fact, all the not-so-old communities are like us [closed]." (No. 32. December 13, 2012, Clifford resident).

Borders as purchased private service
Security is viewed as a kind of private "public service" provided by the property management company. Residents frequently mentioned that the need for fences and walls follows from their purchasing the service in the first place. It is a duty of the property management company, they argue, to maintain safety inside based on the fact that they charge a management fee:

"Q: Which do you prefer? Loose enclosed property management or strict enclosed property management?

A: I prefer strict enclosed property management.
Q: Why?
A: Basically, it conveys that the management of community is active. If there were not enclosure, why would we need the property management company? Moreover, the property management fees would make no sense.
Q: What do you think the property management fees are used for?
A: The use of the charge is manifold, including community cleaning and greening, security inside, the shuttle bus service…
Q: How much do you need to pay in management fees each month?
A: The charge is actually very high in Clifford Estate. The average is 2.2 yuan per square meter; however, the charge starts at 180 yuan no matter how small your flat is." (No. 18, December 08, 2012, Clifford resident)

Asked why the community needs many guards patrolling inside, aside from managing the enclosure, one resident claimed:

"It is a lack of a secure social environment for us. We are charged so much in management fees; the company should offer the security service for us. If there were not guards patrolling in the community, we would not have to pay so much in management fees." (No. 47, October 13, 2013, Clifford resident).

However, although it reduces the likelihood of crime to have enclosure management and patrols, it does not prevent crime. Not only did interviewees frequently cite burglaries; some even reported murders. One interviewee reported that a burglary took place despite two barriers protecting the neighborhood:

"There is a main door in the Clifford community and a sub-division door in my daughter's residential unit. Most importantly, there were guards patrolling. It was about 9 o'clock in the evening, and it was raining that night. My daughter was in Guangzhou visiting a friend of hers, and my son-in-law stayed at home during that time. In order to avoid the thunder, my son-in-law shut off all the lights and the television. He lay down on a chair to relax and left the door open for the sake of cold, fresh air in the hot summer. In that moment, a thief entered our home. When the thief found somebody at home, the thief ran away immediately. If there had been nobody at home, the burglary would have succeeded. What is the use of enclosure? It is nothing!" (No. 19, December 08, 2012, Clifford resident).

Crime does occur in the community. Four murders have been reported in the last thirteen years (HUANG and XU 2012), and about 100 burglaries took place between April and September, 2014 in Clifford Estate (NETEASE BBS 2014). The most recent murder case involved a hidden corpse in a villa in Clifford Estate and gave rise to a protest by residents directed at the property management company. The residents requested that the property management company secure the community and install CCTV surveillance systems inside.

Therefore with perceptions of external threats real and unreal, security is packaged as a private "public" service by the developers and sold as such to buyers. According to this logic, the border composed of fences and walls represents security. Although the border does not completely prevent crime, it provides or enhances the gated community residents' sense of safety.

Stigma: vicinity outsiders as a potential source of crime
Insider residents distrust and even discriminate against vicinity outsiders and entertain a stereotype about them as the potential source of crime. Most interviewees believed that vicinity outsiders entering the community would bring the crime:

> "I think that enclosed property management is necessary. Because if we opened the door, there would be a lot of security problems from the outsiders coming in. When the outsiders come in, burglary happens easily; maybe even murder would happen as well. Anything is possible." (No. 47, October 13, 2013, Clifford resident).

> "Speaking from morality, I think letting the vicinity outsiders coming in is okay. But speaking personally, it would be better if the outsiders did not come. If they just came in to have a look, or only for a rest, no problem. However, if eighty percent of them may have these purposes, but twenty percent of them might have other purposes, they may be up to deviant things. Eighty percent of them might be good people, but it is difficult to tell about the other twenty percent." (No. 46, October 11, 2013, Clifford resident).

Some residents declare that "enclosed property management" poses a target for nominal groups of outsiders such as salespeople, thieves, and burglars. However, this is actually an example of how residents go about othering the local villagers:

> "I don't want the villagers to enter the Community freely. On the one hand, there are too many residents accommodated inside the community now. On the other hand, if the villagers want to enter our community, there must be some [improper] purposes. If the villagers just want entertainment, they can go to the city park or the lawn outside." (No. 21, December 08, 2012, Clifford resident).

Trust is lacking among people in the society, especially in this megalopolis area to which rapid urbanization has brought so many different people to live together so quickly. The distrust not only pervades between insiders and outsiders but also among the insiders. One resident explained:

> "If I paid for my breakfast with a 100-yuan note in the morning here, the seller has to rub the cash against the wall to check its authenticity. If I paid with a 100-yuan note in my hometown to buy breakfast, the seller never checks it." (No. 43, October 11, 2013, Clifford resident).

And despite enclosed property management, burglaries still happen inside. The residents have started to suspect that the thieves might be gated community residents. Take for example the interviewee reported above who related a burglary during a summer storm. When asked why that had happened despite the community providing "enclosed property management", she replied:

> "This is a mega-scale community; the thieves might have companions living inside. The thieves might come either from outsiders or from insiders." (No. 19, December 08, 2012, Clifford resident).

Frequently, other residents would mention that the source of crime might be inside. One interviewee said:

> "There are lot of thieves now; it is hard to tell who they are. They might be the property owners or the outsiders. Both are possible!" (No. 61, November 20, 2014, Clifford resident).

It was surprising to find that the residents even distrust the neighborhood guards, who they also think might become a source of crime. Employment as a neighborhood guard represents temporary, low-paid work. The property management company often hires inexperienced rural migrants as guards. This is why some residents believe that the guards on patrol on represent superficial security:

> "The guards normally patrol only for the sake of appearances. But the guards sometimes might also be out of line [do something bad]. We can see the people; but it is hard to see their heart." (No. 51, October 13, 2013, Clifford resident).

7.5.2 Ordering and othering

The process of rebordering involves both ordering and othering (VAN HOUTUM and VAN NAERSSEN 2002). As O'DOWD (2002, p.14) argues, "borders are integral to human behavior – they are a product of the need for order, control and protection in human life and they reflect our contending desires for sameness and difference, for a marker between 'us' and 'them'". The residential border orders different groups of people and constructs the order of "inside" versus "outside" in order that a homogenous group of people are sorted. In pursuit of a purified living place, the concomitant process of othering involves the border creating (or excluding) "others". In other words, borders create order and "other" some people as outsiders. Processes of ordering and othering are embedded in the process of symbolic rebordering.

The order of the inside and the outside

For the residents, the border is important to maintain the order of inside and outside. There is a lake inside the gated community that serves as a recreational site for all residents (Figure 30). Residents have voluntarily organized a variety of group activities such as dance, chess, singing etc. Living with one's similar socio-economic group, people conceive of the inside as a safe, orderly space. The ordered space gives residents a tendency to be more willing to communicate with each other. As one resident said:

> "To talk with people, the feeling is totally different between people who are insiders and people who are outsiders. I feel a sense of security inside. On the one hand, everyone knows each other's accommodation status here. Whether we own a flat or just live here, the economic status would not be poor. On the other hand, if the economic status is not poor, then the quality [in Chinese: *suzhi*] of a resident will be better. We can talk casually as we did now, for we inside are as neighbours. If I were

Figure 30: Living space inside the gated community
Source: Photograph by author

outside, generally, I would not talk, and would not have contact with anybody!" (No. 13, December 04, 2012, Clifford resident).

The residents look to borders as a matter of social status, dividing people into different social groups. The better-off groups live inside, while the low-income groups live outside. Residents even believe that social stratification can drive low-income people to work hard and toil for a good life:

"In my opinion, we should have our own circle. The situation of various kinds of people intermingled gives me a sense of disorder. Only under a good order can the people who are not rich have the goal of fighting to live inside." (No. 13, December 04, 2012, Clifford resident).

Creating the others
Bordering is also a process of othering. In order to maintain the purity of place and a "good order", a process of othering the vicinity outsiders unfolds. Residents subconsciously discriminate against vicinity outsiders. Clifford Estate residents need Zhongyi village simply as a matter of economic benefit. The gated community residents attach a stigma to migrants, whom they perceive as dirty. Some depict the relationship between the insiders and the outsiders as a cat-and-mouse relationship:

"It is like in the capital Beijing during the rural Chinese New Year festival. The city is empty, for most of the migrants have left the city. The nannies (in Chinese: *A Yi*) left and the shops closed; there is not even a place to have breakfast. The relationship between us [Clifford Estate] and the residents in Zhongyi Village is like the cat and mouse relationship. We don't want to see them, but we also can't leave them. When we see them, they look dirty and disrupt our living environment. However, when they go away, all the shops are closed and you can't get anything anywhere." (No. 34, December 13, 2012, Clifford resident).

Meanwhile, the vicinity outsiders also express a feeling of segregation and view the insiders as a distant group:

"The relationship between Clifford Estate and Zhongyi Village is like the relationship between the emperor and civilians in ancient times. The emperor lives in the luxurious palace, while the civilians live in surrounding rural area. It is like the Beijing Imperial Palace and the surrounding area in ancient times." (No. 33, December 13, 2012, migrant in Zhongyi Village).

The affluent insiders need the vicinity outsiders economically but exclude them socially. On one hand, when vicinity outsiders who can provide cheap labor services are in short supply, the insiders feel inconvenienced by daily life. But on the other hand when the insiders see the vicinity outsiders, it raises the potential conflict in that the insiders regard the vicinity outsiders as poor and dirty and as a source of disorder. Hence, the insiders do not wish to see them or let them enter their living place. Fences and walls thus construct an order that separates the affluent insiders from poor vicinity outsiders. This order means that the outsiders are excluded socially; but at the same time the border does not destroy the possibility of exchanging economic resources.

7.5.3 Border for whom? The invisible border in Zhongyi Village

The visible physical border in the gated community of Clifford Estate is loaded with multiple meanings. However, its neighboring village, Zhongyi, unrestricted with respect to public entry, exhibits the same processes of seeking a sense of security, of ordering and othering.

7.5.3.1 Security in Zhongyi Village

The rural-urban dual system in China assigns ownership of the land in rural areas to the village collective. Villages have a high degree of autonomy. Financial revenue and expenditures are in the hands of village committees in rural areas. As shown in Table 8, except for some government subsidies, most of financial revenue comes from the autonomous operation of collective lands and businesses. The lease of agricultural lands, markets, stores, and industrial plants are the main sources of revenue in Zhongyi Village, accounting for up to 75%. Expenditures are divided among operations, management, and welfare. Surplus revenue is distributed as a dividend to indigenous village shareholders.

Security has become a public service in the village and represents a collective welfare expenditure. Frequent crimes have made the security expenditure a main component of rural public finances. The cost of maintaining security was 1.3 million yuan in 2011, which accounted for 17% of the total welfare expenditure. The Zhongyi Village committee set up a "self-protection team" using its own financial revenue. The self-protection team hired 43 guards whom it split into three groups. Each group patrols the village in shifts every day. In addition to the guards patrolling the village, there is 24-hour surveillance video installed on every main street. Because it is impossible to close the village, the village committee also encourages every unit to install an access control system.

Despite the guards and the CCTV surveillance system, crime frequents Zhongyi Village. As the Village Committee reported, it occurs almost every month. The most frequent crimes are motorcycle theft and burglary. Five crimes were reported in one month in September in 2014, of which three were cases of motorcycle theft and two were burglaries (Interview No.62).

Table 8: Financial revenue and expenditures of Zhongyi Village (2011)

	Collective income		Collective expenditure	
	Items	Cumulative (10,000 CNY)	Items	Cumulative (10,000 CNY)
Business income	1. Operating revenue	129.76	1. Operating expenditure	170.05
	2. Contract income	1,278.20	Routine maintenance of operating fixed assets	170.05
	Agricultural land lease	64.9	2. Management expenditure	130.26
	Markets, stores, and plants leases	1,213.30	Wages and allowances	31.34
	3. Other income (i.e. bank interest)	46.09	Other (i.e., conferences, elections, transportation, telecommunications, etc.)	98.92
Government subsidies	4. Welfare subsidy	247.3	3. Welfare expenditure	789.86
	Family planning (birth control)	5.15	Family planning (birth control)	14.16
	Compulsory education	148.54	Compulsory education	35.37
	Kindergarten	0	Kindergarten	0.44
	Five Guarantees* for poor households	0	Five Guarantees* for poor households	7.07
	New rural cooperative medical subsidy	5.54	New rural cooperative medical expenses	187.56
	Streetlight, greening and garbage collection	44.57	Streetlight, greening and garbage collection expenses	124.98
	Elderly subsidy	28.38	Elderly subsidy expenses	93
	Public security	0.07	Public security expenses	134.44
	Funeral fee subsidy	0	Funeral expenses	3.4
	Other welfare subsidy	11.16	Other welfare expenses**	189.45
	Balance of last year	3.9	4. Other expenditure***	51.63
	Total	1,701.36	Total	1,141.80

* Poor households in rural area enjoy five specific guarantees including food, clothing, medical care and funeral expenses.
** Other welfare expenses include cultural actives, rural infrastructure maintenance, etc.
*** "Other expenditure" includes insurance, conscription, etc.

Source: Information from Zhongyi Village Committee in 2014

Crime, both perceived and experienced, heightened the defensive posture in villagers' minds and deeds. Some indigenous villagers kept watchdogs to look after their homes. For instance, one indigenous villager related that her gold was stolen during her daughter's wedding, so she now was raising three watchdogs to patrol the house: two in front of the main door and one on the roof (Interview No.42). With modern and traditional technology of keeping watch in village, the "open" village has become a fortress.

7.5.3.2 The ordering process in Zhongyi Village

A process of ordering the space is underway in a rising collective identity for the "Zhongyi Villager". The hukou system has consolidated the collective identity through its attached, collectively offered welfare and the corresponding entitlements. As mentioned in Chapter 5.5.3, a policy has implemented "converting villages to communities". Zhongyi Village was nominally converted into a community in 1992. This does not significantly change residents' entitlement to state-provided welfare. Specifically, a new non-agricultural hukou was created that conferred some eligibility to state benefits but also retained some eligibility for rural rights such as ownership of housing land, to share in collective economic revenue.

Although all the local agricultural hukou was transformed into non-agricultural hukou, the villagers cannot receive as much state welfare as urban hukou holders can. As the Table 8 in the left column shows, after the reform of Zhongyi Village, the village obtained a certain amount of welfare subsidies from the government consisting of items of family planning, education, medical care, street lights, greening, and garbage collection. The government subsidies totaled 2.5 million yuan in 2011. However, some original rural subsidy items have been canceled. One of these is the agricultural subsidy; another is the "Five Guarantees" welfare subsidy for poor households. As the expenditures of Zhongyi Village (right column in Table 8) show, the welfare items are all only partly subsidized. There was a 7.9 million yuan welfare expenditure in 2011, the major part of which, about 5.4 million or 68%, was covered by Zhongyi Village Collective itself. Because the state subsidy is insufficient and the rural preferential policies no longer apply to the reformed village (i.e., which is now a "community"), the villagers complain that under this new type of hukou they "don't have full eligibility to receive the state-provided welfare and are losing their original rural right at the same time". (Interview No. 62).

The process known as "converting villages to communities" is connected with another policy implemented in 2005 called "fixing the share-right to collective economic revenue" (in Chinese: *gufen guhua*). This policy provides that all collective economic revenue be divided into a certain number of shares of stock depending on the number of Zhongyi hukou holders. All the villagers who have Zhongyi hukou and were born before January 1, 2006 can obtain a certain amount of stock. The stock is distributed in fixed proportion to

Urban debordering and rebordering processes　　　　　　　　　　　　　　　　　111

Zhongyi Liantang Park

Ancestral Temple

Figure 31: Recreational space for Zhongyi residents
Source:　　Photographs by author

each villager under a rule of "not reduced after death, not increased for a newborn child". From that point on, the villagers could only collect economic bonuses from the collective based on their respective stock holdings. Children born after 2006 have the right to inherit stock or receive it as a legacy from their family; but no new stock will issue from the village collective. The villagers are faced with choosing for their new born child between non-agricultural hukou with all benefits or Zhongyi agriculture hukou. However, because most of the land has been sold and the retained land and collective economic revenue fixed into stock, "there are not any advantages for a new born baby to choose an agricultural hukou", as one indigenous villager claimed (Interview No. 52).

Hukou has become a strong border demarcating the homogenous group of indigenous villagers. Because the size of anyone's share of village-provided welfare and the village's collective economic bonus are based on Zhongyi hukou, the collective identity of Zhongyi Villagers is enhanced and fixed by the hukou system.

Except for the sorting of the homogenous group of villagers under the hukou system, local villagers feel attached to the village. The influx of Clifford Estate residents has consolidated the local consciousness of Zhongyi Village area. There is a park (*Liangtang* park) and an ancestral temple in the inner space of village where indigenous villagers and migrants normally spend their leisure time (Figure 31). The indigenous villagers regard these places as their own and tend to communicate more easily here:

> "Only in here [in Zhongyi Liantang Park], would I talk to you; if we were outside [outside the village], I would never talk to you. If we were outside, you would go your way, I go mine and never talk; who knows if you are a good person or not." (No. 26, December 9, 2012, indigenous villager).

7.5.3.3 The othering process in Zhongyi Village

For indigenous villagers, the line between Clifford Estate and Zhongyi Village is a subsequent border, even a superimposed border. Different groups of people have settled around the border, including: (a) indigenous villagers who have Zhongyi rural hukou; (b) urban hukou holders, a part whom are employees of the public institutions such as Zhongyi primary school teachers, doctors at the Zhongyi neighborhood health station, and other, laid-off workers, mostly local villagers who worked at street-run state-owned enterprises ("SOEs") or collective-owned enterprises ("COEs") that went bankrupt or were privatized; (c) rural migrants; and (d) the subsequent residents of Clifford Estate. As the indigenous people, the villagers are "othering" the other residents: residents of Clifford Estate, migrants, and local laid-off villagers who hold urban hukou.

Othering the company and the residents of Clifford Estate
The construction of Clifford Estate has brought many advantages for Zhongyi Village. Commercial and service industries in Zhongyi Village have boomed, creating many job opportunities and attracting a large member of migrants to seek accommodation in Zhongyi Village. The market for leased housing in Zhongyi Village has prospered. However, the loss of so much agricultural land has limited local villagers' appreciation of Clifford Estate. As one indigenous villager complained:

> "If the Clifford Estate company had not bought our land, we would have kept it until now and got a better price today ... The development of our village is far behind that of other nearby villages who still have most of their land." (No. 9, December 03, 2012, indigenous villager).

The indigenous villagers also shun the private services supplied by Clifford Estate. An interview with a teacher at Zhongyi middle school shows that some local villagers do not wish to be educated in the private environment of Clifford Estate:

> "There was a period when Clifford Estate International [private high] school would invite excellent local students to study there for free, and provide food and accommodation. The invited local students normally rejected studying there, apart from only one year, when a student accepted the invitation. The villagers did not get used to the private environment and preferred to study in traditional, famous public schools." (No. 15, December 05, 2012, indigenous villager).

The coming of Clifford Estate also brought the disadvantages of modernity. Some residents of Clifford Estate would seek the hotels in Zhongyi Village for vice activities such as drug use and gambling. As one migrant worker who used to work at a hotel in Zhongyi Village said:

"Some residents of Clifford Estate would take drugs in the hotel in Zhongyi Village regularly. I found that when I worked at the hotel as an attendant. Because of the vice activities in the hotel, I resigned my job." (No. 33, December 13, 2012, migrant worker in Zhongyi Village).

Zhongyi Village excludes residents of Clifford Estate through the hukou system as well. The right to access the public primary school is based on the hukou designation, under which only residents with local Zhongyi hukou can access Zhongyi primary school. The supply of private educational facilities in Clifford Estate has become short with more new residents moving in. As chapter 7.4.2 showed, some educational facilities in Zhongyi Village are being promoted among the neighborhood facilities of Clifford Estate. In fact, residents of Clifford Estate are excluded from this state-supported public system because their urban hukou is not designated as Zhongyi village. If Clifford Estate residents want to attend public primary school in Zhongyi Village, they must purchase the service just as the rural migrants.

Othering the migrants
As another segment of the residents of Zhongyi Village, the migrants either work at the village factories or are accommodated at the village. Housing rentals to the migrant workers are one of the main income sources in Zhongyi Village. However, the villagers other the migrants in several ways.

First, migrants are considered a source of disorder in the village. Zhongyi Liantang Park and ancestral temple are two of the main public spaces in Zhongyi Village. Formerly they would remain open all day long, but after some undesirable behaviors arose including overnighting and littering, the village committee hired staff exclusively to look after these places during the day and began to lock the park and ancestral temple during the evening.

Second, migrants are subject to employment discrimination. Zhongyi Village established the security team but would only allow indigenous villagers to do the work. Employment discrimination exists not only between indigenous villagers and rural migrants within the village but also between Clifford Estate residents and rural migrants. The residents of Clifford Estate prefer to hire the local villagers as housekeepers, for instance, for the local villagers have fixed accommodations and village roots.

Third, although the population of rural migrants in Zhongyi Village is greater than that of indigenous villagers and a great many of the rural migrants have lived in Zhongyi Village for a long time, their hukou status bars them from receiving the same public services and welfare as the indigenous villagers. Children's education is the major issue arising from this. Since state-provided public education is exclusively for citizens who have local hukou, the rural migrants without it must either pay additional fees for their children or send them to school in their respective home towns. It is true that the hukou system has become more flexible and migrant workers can obtain urban hukou through a point system; however, even if a migrant's children have the right to attend the local school, they remain isolated within the school. Investigation has revealed that there are two first-grade classes at the Zhongyi primary school and that all indigenous students are in one class while the migrant students are in other classes. Moreover, the government assigns a quota index to the village school every year and requests that the village school recruit more of the migrant workers' children; but in reality the local village sentiment runs against the additional quota index (Interview No. 62).

Othering local villagers who lack Zhongyi hukou

Indigenous villagers do not even stop at othering local, laid-off villagers. One group of local villagers, born and raised in Zhongyi but today with Panyu city hukou registrations, have relinquished their rural hukou, having transferred it to urban hukou at a time when they worked at SOEs or COEs. They subsequently became urban laid-off workers in the course of bankruptcy or privatization of those employers.

One interviewee (No. 48), an indigenous villager with urban hukou, formerly worked at the Zhongcun textile plant, a street-owned COE. During the SOEs/COEs reform period in the 1990s, the Zhongcun textile plant was privatized, and he and many other employees were laid off. This interviewee complained that the villagers no longer accept them:

> "Because we do not have local rural hukou, the village welfare system does not cover us any longer, and they don't even allow us to park our cars in the village parking area. Only the indigenous villagers who have rural hukou can park there. The village collective said we do not belong to Zhongyi Village anymore." (No. 48, October 13, 2013, laid-off worker).

Hence, the hukou system itself has become a stubborn border dividing the people into different groups in Zhongyi Village.

7.6 Social networks in residential borderland

7.6.1 Different types of social relationships between insiders and outsiders

7.6.1.1 Economic connections improved weak social ties

There are strong flows of residents from Clifford Estate to the Zhongyi Village area. But economic connections have not created strong social ties between the insiders and vicinity outsiders. Although many Clifford residents like to shop in Zhongyi Village daily, their contacts are mostly limited to buying and selling. Visits to the village area are only to purchase services and goods, rather than for social contact. As the residents of Clifford Estate describe it:

> "Although I know them by sight, and they know me by sight, it has no meaning. We still don't know each other's name. We are busy shopping; it is not time to talk." (No. 19, December 08, 2012, Clifford resident).

> "We don't have much to talk about when we meet; we just greet each other. Only because we see each other a lot, have we then become familiar." (No. 18, December 08, 2012, Clifford resident).

> "I know the stallholders by sight, for I often buy stuff there; and some hairdressers I know well; but the relationship does not reach the level of friendship. However, I have a regular nanny for house cleaning; I will contact her when I need cleaning service, but I have not learned much about her." (No. 12, December 04, 2012, Clifford resident).

The interview cited below shows how a self-employed seamstress knows many insiders because they frequently visit her store. As the author conducted the interview, some such customers whom she knew arrived, and she would introduce them. Although the relationship between her and the customers did not rise to the level of intimacy, she conversed liberally with the customers while they waited and she readied the clothing:

> "Q: What kinds of people normally come here to have clothes sewn?
> A: Many of them are elderly woman from Clifford Estate.
> Q: Are you on familiar terms with the customers?
> A: Some are familiar, some are not. The customers who come here frequently are familiar.
> Q: Do you know who they are?
> A: To be honest, I can't tell exactly what their names are, but I know a lot about what they do, such as accountants, businessmen." (No. 27, December 09, 2012, self-employed seamstress).

Although insiders and outsiders do not develop friendships, the flow of insiders to the nearby village has important social meaning. First, the residents' visits to the neighboring village area increase the chance of social encounters between the economically privileged groups and the low-income groups, which alleviates the degree of residential segregation. Second, the economic connections have created weak social ties between the gated community residents and some segments of vicinity outsiders; these relationships involve greeting one another or having brief conversations upon meeting. For instance, gated community residents often shop daily in the same store in Zhongyi Village and thereby become familiar with storeowners, who as a group are mainly rural migrants. Moreover, the migrants who work at Clifford Estate providing housekeeping services also create weak social ties with the insiders. The weak social connection is beneficial in terms of increasing mutual understanding.

7.6.1.2 Strong social ties across the border

Besides the proportion of weak social ties across the borders, some kinds of strong social ties also permeate the borders between inside and the vicinity outside. The first kind is clan networks of the villagers. The urbanization process in Panyu district led some of the younger-generation indigenous villagers to purchase housing in Clifford Estate. After they had moved into the gated community, they keep very strong, intimate social ties with their family members and relatives who still live in Zhongyi:

> "My daughter bought a flat inside four years ago; My wife and I live in the village; we always visit my daughter for meals." (No. 38, October 06, 2013, indigenous villager).

> "A nephew on my mother's side and a nephew on my father's side both live inside. I just need a call to enter [Clifford Estate]. Moreover, today there is a wedding celebration [a villager's] being held in the Clifford Estate hotel; I am going to attend and many local villagers will join in as well." (No. 26, December 9, 2012, indigenous villager).

The data collected during observation by following also provide evidence that some indigenous villagers own property inside Clifford Estate (see Chapter 6.2.4). Through the village clan networks, they keep firm social contact with villagers still living outside.

The second kind of strong social tie permeating the border is that of migrants, some of whom have relocated their original kin or clan networks into the area. As explored earlier, the influx of Clifford Estate residents has facilitated commercial development in Zhongyi Village and created many job opportunities. Some well-educated, economically well-situated migrants have bought property in Clifford Estate. Finding job opportunities in Zhongyi, they have encouraged relatives or fellow-townsmen from their places of origin to migrate to Zhongyi Village. Take for instance the case of Interviewee No. 33, a young girl: she and her mother migrated to Zhongyi Village because of her uncle lives inside Clifford Estate and induced them to come.

The third kind of strong tie that permeates the border arises from employment. Some urban hukou holders who work in Zhongyi Village have bought a residence inside and live in the gated community but work for outsiders in the vicinity. For instance, a retired teacher from Zhongcun high school said that many high school teachers in his school had bought housing inside Clifford Estate (Interview No.15). They live in the gated community but work in the village area teaching students from the village.

7.6.1.3 Different social circles

Although many migrant workers, as shop operators and services staff in Zhongyi Village, have built focused economic contacts with insiders and created weak social ties with them, most migrants' lives transpire within their own circles, which seldom intersect with those of insiders. Migrants' circles consist mostly of their original fellow townsmen or *laoxiang* in Chinese, and exclude much social contact with other groups. One migrant depicted the situation as follows:

> "I don't know any person who lives in Clifford Estates; however, I have many fellow townsmen in Zhongyi Village. We are here doing labor work. How can we buy housing inside? We don't have any fellow townsmen living inside." (No. 10, December 03, 2012, Migrant worker in Zhongyi Village).

Figure 32 shows two migrants processing accessories in Zhongsan village park on a self-employed, temporary basis. Both the pictured women are from Hunan province and have

Figure 32: Two migrants processing acessories in a village park
Source: Photograph by author

lived in Zhongsan village for five years. They migrated to Zhongsan Village to join their adult children, and got to know each other as they both recreated in the park. One introduced the other to accessories processing. Mainly they care for their grandchildren and only fill their spare time with such temporary work. A typical day for either of them follows the same trajectory: they see their grandchildren off to kindergarten in the morning and then come to the park in Zhongsan village to this accessories processing. Around noon they both go home to cook for their adult children who also work in the village. After lunch, they return to their accessories processing in the park until four in the afternoon, when they pick their grandchildren from kindergarten and return home. They each typically can process eighty accessories over the course of such a day, at a rate of 0.25 yuan per item; so they can earn about 10 yuan per day per person at it. Typical of the daily life of a rural migrant is that it unfolds together with those of a circle of fellow townsmen and seldom intersects with those of the insiders.

Migrants have formed different "fellow-townsmen groups" based on their regional origins: groups from Hunan or the Jiangxi, for example, which are also referred to as such. As interviewed, one migrant from Ganzhou, Jiangxi province, said:

> "We are a group of decoration workers from Ganzhou. We worked in the city of Xiamen before. Later, some of us migrated here and found a lot of opportunity, and then a large gang of us followed and came here. The number of our fellow townsman is smaller now—about 200 still remain here [many moved on owing to the financial crisis in 2008]—but at the peak it was more than 500." (No. 28, December 9, 2012, migrant worker in Zhongyi Village).

The rural migrants live in Zhongyi Village without any fences or walls separating them. But these groups, indigenous villagers and rural migrants, nonetheless carry on in separate circles. As the interview cited below shows, although the migrants have lived in the city area for a long time, they still have not formed intimate social connections with local villagers or Clifford Estate residents. The most common kind of social tie between migrants and local villagers is an economic one: the landlord-tenant relationship. Rural migrants have few contacts with local people and little attachment to the city or the village even when they have lived there for a long time:

> "Q: How long have you been here?
> A: I have been here for more than twenty years.
> Q: What do you do here?
> A: I am a laborer; I do everything, but mostly work as a builder.
> Q: Does your family stay with you?
> A: Yes, we rent an accommodation here; if my family were not here, I would not stay here for long. However, during my son's schooling, he was in our home town.

It is very expensive to study here. Now he is working at a factory nearby.
Q: Have you ever been to Clifford Estate before?
A: No, I seldom to visit other places; I usually need to work. There is no time to go to other places. After work, I just have a limited rest here [in the village park].
Q: Do you know any local people here?
A: I don't know anybody; I seldom contact others, and seldom talk to others." (No. 2, September 02, 2012, migrant worker in Zhongyi Village).

There are several reasons for resident rural migrants' detachment from the village. First, the migrants' hukou as well as their roots remain in their respective home town, and the city provides little social welfare that would enable them to uproot and settle down. Second, rural migrants have high mobility in the city. Most of them are self-employed, engaging in temporary, informal jobs. They change jobs frequently. The high mobility of rural migrants restricts the formation of stable social relationships with the local villagers. Third, there is a language barrier to migrants' integrating into the local village. Most rural migrants do not speak Cantonese, the main language of the local villagers; and some cannot even speak Mandarin well. The language barrier restricts rural migrants' communication with the local villagers.

7.6.1.4 The decline in social contacts

Although the weak and strong social ties permeating the border demonstrate the process of debordering of social networks, the fences and walls have reconstructed a border that cleaves two social networks out of adjacent enclaves. After some outsiders moved into the gated community, the social connections between them and the vicinity outsiders went into retreat. As outsiders have reported, after a friend moves into the gated community of Clifford Estate, social contact between them declined or even vanished, the friends becoming alienated:

"A friend of mine bought a flat in Clifford Estate. I visited his flat once a time a long time ago, and he had given me his telephone number then. The telephone member was written down on a piece of newspaper, and I put it in my pocket but forgot to take it out when the clothes were being washed. Since the telephone number vanished, we haven't had any more contact." (No. 9, December 03, 2012, indigenous villager).

"I visited a friend of mine in Clifford Estate twice, but that was in the early 2000s. After that, we didn't contact one another anymore. I don't know whether he has moved away or not, or even died. [Q: How do you know each other?] He is a fellow townsman of mine; there was a time when he would come to visit me, but he didn't do that again afterwards." (No. 16, December 05, 2012, migrant in Zhongyi Village).

One indigenous villager who usually enters Clifford Estate for shade during the summer used to interact with many Clifford residents inside. (He was introduced in Chapter 7.2.4). However, according to his statements, this did not lead to significant social ties:

> "Q: As you usually go to Clifford Estate for shade, do you know any residents there?
> A: There are a few, even if I know one or two of them, just because we meet a lot on the hill when I take shade there. However, they are not local [Guangzhou] people who can speak Cantonese; they come from different places, such as Hunan, Jiangxi, and Sichuan.
> Q: Do you keep contact with them?
> A: No, we only have a talk during the recreation inside [in Clifford Estate], just a chat together, nothing more." (No. 15, December 05, 2012, indigenous villager).

7.6.2 Neighborhood relationships among insiders

In fact there is a lag of social interactions within the gated community. The interactions and communications between neighbors are weak in Clifford Estate. Interviewees frequently mentioned that people are busy working, and there was little opportunity for them to see each other and no time to communicate even with neighbors:

> "We normally don't see each other; we go to work in the morning and come back in the evening. After we back home, the door is always closed. It is rare to communicate." (No. 47, October 13, 2013, Clifford resident).

> "Everyone's life-circle is not so large. Our circle is limited to colleagues or a small group of friends. It is very difficult to create a new circle or enter other circles [after moving in]. As you know, everybody faces huge pressure at work; there are only one or two days off in a week." (No. 43, October 11, 2013, Clifford resident).

An elderly resident bought a residence in Clifford Estate as place live in retirement. He normally stays at home and expresses a lonely emotion due to the scant connections with neighbors:

> "I don't know the next-door neighbors, for they always have the door and windows closed. It is hard to see them. I normally watch TV at home. When it is time to cook, I go out to buy food and meat, and then come back home. Sometimes I just go to Clifford Lake to have a break." (No. 7, December 01, 2012, Clifford resident).

Public space, such as the lake and the community club at Clifford Estate, is a collective recreation space for the residents. Daily communication and contact mostly happen here. However, the daily contact does not form intimate relationships. As one resident said:

> "We are familiar with each other; however, we don't visit each other. We just sit together and have a talk here [in the public area]. The topic is daily family life. For example: how many children do you have? What do they do? Do you live with your son or your daughter? We are not close contacts." (No. 19, December 08, 2012, Clifford resident).

Due to the rapid development of the economy and urbanization, a large population has migrated from rural to urban areas, or from less developed inland cities to the developed coastal cities. Different people have come together in a very short period of time, and the old neighborhood relationships were disrupted in the wake of the migration while new neighborhood relationships are still forming. The city residents come from everywhere but lack roots in the new places. Residents inhabit the same community, but everyone is a stranger to each other. As one resident who missed the intimate neighborhood relationship in his home town said:

> "When my parents lived in the home town, the neighborhood relationship was totally different from here. Our family kept very good relationships with the neighbors next-door, upstairs and downstairs. If one family did something, it attracted the other neighbors to do something together. For example, if one family sent their children to take lessons, the neighbors would follow suit and do the same. Moreover, we would often make a plan to travel together. The neighborhood relationship is very harmonious." (No. 43, October 11, 2013, Clifford resident).

7.6.3 The transformation of social networks in residential borderland

The social network dimension of the border indicates a separation of the social ties permeating the border between the gated community and the urban village. As Figure 33 shows, a transformation of social relationships among the residents has taken place in the residential borderland. The transformation has involved simultaneous processes of debordering and rebordering in the social networks dimension. Different levels of social contacts, i.e., economic connections, weak social connections, normal social connections, and strong social connections (for discussion of the definitions, see Chapter 3.2.4), have transgressed the borders.

7.6.3.1 Types of social networks in the 1980s

In the pre-reform period, Zhongyi villagers were a homogeneous group. Strong social connections and intimate social ties existed among them, and collectively were called the "village clan network". When in the 1980s some factories sprang up Zhongyi Village, rural migrants came to live, and they changed the population structure and broke up the homogeneity. In this period, most of the migrants were first-generation migrants who stood in landlord-tenant relationships with indigenous villagers. Within this group of migrants, there were two types of social ties. The first type was the original kinship or the "fellow-townsmen" relationship of people from the same village migrating together to the same city. Their social activities continue to follow these fellow-townsmen circles, which are characterized by very strong mutual social ties. The second type of social ties among migrants was the new collegial relationships among migrants working in the same factory. These were weaker social ties.

7.6.3.2 Types of social networks in the 1990s

The village area has been divided into two parts by the construction of Clifford Estate since the 1991. In the 1990s, most of the residents in Clifford Estate were either people from Hong Kong or wealthy people from Guangzhou who had second homes in Clifford Estate. Within Clifford Estate was thus a highly homogenous, wealthy group of people. Three types of social connections were prevalent among gated community residents. First were original social circles formed before the residents moved to the gated community, in situations where several owners who already knew one another purchased properties at the same time. Second were newly-formed social connections, e.g., neighborhood or club relationships among residents who met through participation in specific common interest community clubs. Third were the weak social connections formed as a matter of daily living in the same place, such as from talking with or greeting one another at recreation in a public area.

Social connections between the insiders of Clifford Estate and the vicinity outsiders of Zhongyi Village were rare. Only a few economic connections existed where some local villagers were employed, say, as housekeepers. Because the indigenous villagers could speak Cantonese and had permanent housing in Zhongyi Village, the insiders preferred to hire the local villagers rather than the rural migrants, who were typically excluded from such housekeeping services at first.

7.6.3.3 Types of social networks after 2000

Since 2000, the process of suburbanization has accelerated. Many middle-class residents have moved into Clifford Estate, and the economic connection between Clifford Estate and Zhongyi Village has substantially increased. Accordingly, the mainly economic contacts as well as some types of social contacts permeating the border between the enclaves have been transformed. In this stage, various types of social relationships have emerged across the border, as discussed in Chapter 7.6.1.

Within the gated community, there are weak, fragile social connections among the residents (see Chapter 7.6.2) that have remained essentially the same since the 1990s. Most

Urban debordering and rebordering processes 123

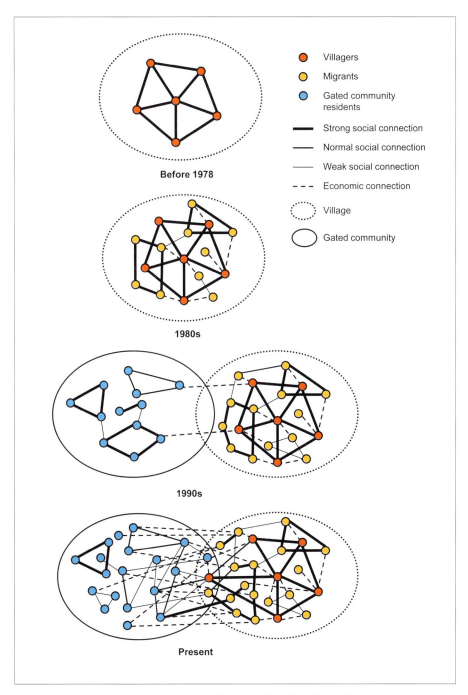

Figure 33: Transformation of social networks in residential borderlands
Source: Illustration by author

residents keep to the basic unit of single family and do not form stable, intimate social ties with their neighbors. However, the scale of the social circles involving "fellow townsmen" of rural migrants in the village increased from the 1990s into the 2000s. Second-generation migrations have come in a process known as chain migration. The original circles of fellow-townsmen have expanded and constituted different "groups" of migrants (see Chapter 7.6.1.3). Although the migrants have been living in the city area for a long time, the relationship between them and the local villagers has remained mostly one of the economic connections embodied in the landlord-tenant relationship. The relationship between the migrants and the residents of the gated community also consisted mainly of economic contacts.

7.7 Actions of the developer and government

7.7.1 Actions of the developer

The development company plays an important role in shaping the bordering process, not only between the gated community and the neighboring village, but also between the gated community and the city. Clifford Estate is a project developed by an entity known as Clifford Group, while the management of the property is controlled by a subsidiary, the Clifford Property Management Limited Company ("CPMLC"). The developer is directly responsible for the management and perpetuation of the border. The developer built the fences and walls that divided the village territory into two parts and constructed the splintered urban infrastructure. Clifford Estate was built with its own infrastructure unconnected to the system in Zhongyi Village. The developer left Zhongyi Village wholly out of consideration during construction. As one interview shows:

> "After Clifford Estate was built, the land surface was rigidified. Before, rain was absorbed by the land and ponds, and it was hard to flood our village. But now after a heavy rain, the water rushes to a flood and the roads are engulfed. Several years ago, a heavy rain led to a flood. The beds in some dwellings situated in the low places were flooded." (No. 15, December 05, 2012, indigenous villager).

The debordering processes meant that, with the increasing flows of people into the neighboring area, the gated community had less ability to shutter itself off. First, the ability of developers to counter these flows is weakened. The strong flows of gated community residents into the neighboring village area created conditions for commercial development in Zhongyi Village. The commercial and service industries in Zhongyi Village have developed in competition with and as a challenge to commercial operations in Clifford Estate. The developer once even wanted to impede residents from going out. One interviewee described how in the early period after Zhongfu Mall had been built, many residents drove to Zhongfu Mall to shop there. The property management company at that point arranged for some guards to strictly monitor the Clifford private streets connecting to

Zhongfu Mall and would not allow the residents to park their cars on the street near the mall in order to deter residents from going there (Interview No. 61).

Second, the ability of residents themselves to shutter themselves off has also decreased. Residents want the management company to strictly control public entry. However, the entry restrictions in Clifford Estate are loosening contrary to the wishes of the residents. Observations during the first two stages of fieldwork in 2012 and 2013 indicated that every time a visitor entered Clifford estate, a guard would examine his or her IC. But during the third stage of fieldwork in 2014, the company had loosened its "enclosed property management". It started to employ middle-aged, female guards. The visiting procedure has been simplified such that visitors could enter by registering their information but without being checked.

The loosening of "enclosed property management" is a reaction of the property management company to the rising cost of its undertaking. Once the system was in place, the company had to confront the cost of maintenance under inflation. In order to guarantee the high quality of its "enclosed property management" service, the management has had to raise its fees frequently. At the latest increase, many residents expressed dissatisfaction and refused to pay[2]. Some residents do have the economic ability to pay the higher management fee, but with more and more price-conscious residents moving into the community, higher management fees became unpopular. Thus it has been hard to maintain the high quality of such a gated private service, and the company has started to hire female guards and simplified the complex, strict entry procedure as a cost-saving measure.

The loosened "enclosed property management" is a processes of debordering which is also accompanied by rebordering processes. The regressive management of the borders makes for further dissatisfaction on the part of residents toward the developer. For example, when one interviewee realized the company had loosened its management of the gate, she felt disappointed and declared that she wanted to move to another gated community (Interview No. 21).

7.7.2 Actions of local government

The governance of gated community
The main strategies of local government toward gated communities are on one hand to integrate it into the city – for instance, by asking the development company to build more neighborhood facilities and shoulder more social responsibility – but on the other hand to encourage "enclosed property management" in order to maintain neighborhood security and social stability.

---

2   The management fee hike was a result of a plenary vote in 2014 which was mentioned in Chapter 6.2.2. However, due to lack of transparency of the vote, many residents reject the result.

Clifford Estate, a large-scale community, has constructed comparatively comprehensive neighborhood facilities and amenities such as middle schools, a hospital, supermarkets, restaurants and so on. For a long time, the gated community of Clifford Estate has been likened to an independent kingdom. Its operated mostly in isolation from local government. As one resident put it, Clifford Estate was a good place to escape from the "one child" birth control policy several years ago because it has a private hospital which the government could not easily inspect. When government officials did come, they would be denied entry or misled by the guards (Interview No. 45).

The administrative blank space has been filling in since 2008. Due to a sharp increase in the cost and need for social affairs management as the number of residents grew, the Clifford Estate company chose to cooperate with local government. In 2008, the Clifford community committee was set up inside Clifford Estate as a subdivision of the government of Panyu. In order to solve the problem of a shortage of primary education in Clifford Estate, the property company of Clifford Estate decided to cooperate with local government to build a public primary school inside. The structure of the cooperation was such that Clifford Estate provided private land while local government provided financial and administrative support.

From the perspective of security, the government is a stakeholder in the production of gated communities. Maintaining social stability is a foremost political concern of the government, because gatedness is a direct, effective means of keeping neighborhood security, which in turn is directly conductive to social stability (MIAO 2003). In order to create "safe and harmonious communities", sealed management of residential areas is a basic policy in China. As one interviewee said:

> "The enclosed property management is sometimes strict, and sometimes loosened. For instance, if there has been a serious crime, the local government would come to inspect the work of enclosed property management. In these periods, the enclosure is very strict." (No. 18, December 08, 2012, Clifford resident).

Hence, the need for gatedness only serves the economic interests of the developers. Providing security is considered as a promotional strategy for the development company. The security service decays when the security costs rise and cannot be offset by the management fee. The residents and the authorities are the ones who really need "enclosed property management" in a community. The residents need borders for security and for ordering and othering; the authorities need the borders to achieve their political goal of social stability.

The "splintering urbanism" of local government

GRAHAM and MARVIN (2001) introduced the notion of "splintering urbanism". The phenomenon of residential borderland is actually a reflection of splintering urbanism in the

Urban debordering and rebordering processes 127

actions of local authorities. In spite of the engagement of local government in the social affairs of Clifford Estate, there has been no will to integrate Clifford Estate and Zhongyi Village. The government considers Clifford Estate and Zhongyi Village as two different developmental entities and is not motivated to seek integration of the two contiguous enclaves. There is no cooperation with respect to cultural activities, either by Clifford Estate or the local government, or between Clifford Estate and Zhongyi Village.

The urban planners and the government share the same urbanism about the residential borderlands. They understand the two contiguous enclaves as two separate parts rather than as a whole. One local urban planner questioned any need to integrate Clifford Estate and Zhongyi Village, on the basis that they represent two totally different developmental units (Interview No. 56). A Clifford resident complained:

> "If the government wants to integrate us, they should build a bridge across Zhongping Road, where a great many residents walk through to Zhongyi Village every day. However, they won't do it even though several car accidents have happened due to the busy traffic." (No. 12, December 04, 2012, Resident of Clifford Estate).

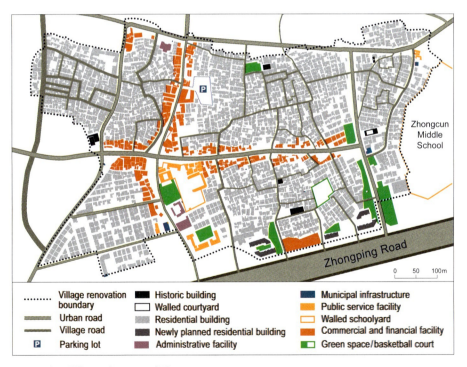

Figure 34: Village planning of Zhongyi
Source: *The general planning layout of village renovation 2008 (Guangzhou City Planning Bureau Panyu Branch); translated and partly redrawn by author*

As Figure 34 shows, the urban planning of Zhongyi Village, implemented in 2008, reflects the planners' splintering urbanism. The plan provides for most of the commercial facilities to be arrayed around the middle of the village rather than at the outer part of the village. Clifford Estate, however, is located adjacent to the village, to the southeast. Despite its huge impact on the development of Zhongyi Village, Clifford Estate was not labeled on the map. Most importantly, the contact zone close to Clifford Estate is planned for residential use in spite of the fact that, as mentioned in Chapter 7.2.1, most of the buildings in this contact zone have actually changed to a commercial use (Figure 22).

7.8 Summary

In summary, the debordering and rebordering processes in residential borderland can be depicted in terms of three respective dimensions: the functional dimension, the symbolic dimension, and the social network dimension (Table 9).

The vigorous flows of people across the border every day indicate a debordering process with respect to the physical borders of fences and walls. The flows of people from the gated community to village area are characterized as functional exchange of money, goods, and services. Insiders who frequent the neighboring village area, especially the contact zone, are changing their minds with respect to these places, having found a sense of belonging and a regard for some of the adjacent area in the neighboring enclave as a part of their daily life. Meanwhile, economic interactions between the insiders and the vicinity outsiders have created significant social meanings. Buyers and sellers have become familiar with each other and maintain weak social ties; they greet and carry on brief

Table 9: Debordering and rebordering processes in residential borderland

Processes in different dimensions	Functional	Symbolic	Social networks
Debordering	Flows of people (goods, services), Commercialization of the contact zone	A sense of belonging	Different levels of social connections across the border e.g., clan networks, kinship
Rebordering	Enhanced barrier effect, Differentiation of places of consumption	Seeking a sense of security, Ordering and othering	Differentiation of social circles, Diminished social contact

Source: Compiled by author

conversations with one another. Although they do not amount to friendship or intimacy, the weak social ties are conductive to increasing social understanding among each group as between the affluent and the poor. But due in particular to the accelerated process of suburbanization, a localization process has come about in Clifford Estate out of which some strong social ties have emerged across the border. For instance, the younger generation of villagers who owns housing inside keeps strong social contacts with their family members or relatives in the village. Moreover, some insiders are working in the vicinity enclave. Hence, the debordering process to some extent alleviates the degree of segregation between two enclaves.

However, the debordering process is accompanied by a rebordering process. The economic need of affluent residents in the village area has created a new, private, bounded space. The rise of consumer prices in the contact zone, for example at Zhongyi Food Market, has led poorer vicinity outsiders to change their original places of consumption. This differentiation in places of consumption has created a new tunnel-like border. Nor has the insiders' rising sense of belonging to places in the vicinity brought complete acceptance of the residents. In order to maintain the homogeneity of community and exclusive use of the private residential space, the insiders are othering the vicinity outsiders. The stigma or stereotypes associated with vicinity outsiders as potential sources of crime and disorder persist in the minds of insiders. The insiders begrudge the outsiders any entry into their living space. The affluent group and the poor group are actually living in different social circles although they have settled down next to each other. The insiders need the poor vicinity outsiders only economically but exclude them socially.

Therefore, the residential borderland is a transitional space between inclusion and exclusion. It exhibits a mixture of processes of debordering and rebordering.

8 Synthesis: understanding debordering and rebordering processes in residential borderland

"Our understanding of bordering processes, and policies, is critical to our understanding of what borders are; We need to focus on the agency of borders that is the activities of social, economic and political individuals and the processes of production and re-production of borders – the bordering and de-bordering praxis – which at a given time in history and within a giving space – are economically, politically and culturally embedded." (BRUNET-JAILLY 2011, p. 3)

8.1 Debordering and rebordering processes in residential borderland

Bordering processes consist of bordering, debordering and rebordering. In this study, the main focus lies on the processes of debordering and rebordering, which in general take place after a border has been created. Debordering and rebordering together denote a cyclical process, either aspect of which occurs simultaneously with the other, but not such that it leads to contradiction. As Figure 35 shows, the processes of debordering and rebordering are outcomes of the interaction of agency and structure. That is, the practices of debordering and rebordering in functional, symbolic, and social network dimensions, as actions which are enabled and constrained by different actors, are embedded in structural and contextual dynamics at different spatial scales. In the residential borderland, the border is constructed and reconstructed through the practices of debordering and rebordering in their functional, symbolic, and social network dimensions.

With regard to the functional dimension, flows of people, goods, and services are making the physical border more permeable and increasing the economic connections and social encounters between the affluent groups and low-income groups. Indeed, the process of functional debordering was initiated when the border was set up. For instance, the construction workers who built Clifford Estate and were accommodated in the vicinity village crossed the border into the gated community every day after the border was set up. The border therefore regulates flows rather than prevents them. Since 2000, the residential border has become more and more permeable for increasing flows of people, goods and services across it (see Chapter 7.2). Residents of the gated community cross the border to the vicinity village for the purpose of obtaining differentiated goods and services. The remarkable outcome of functional debordering is the emergence of a commercialized contact zone.

However, functional rebordering is creating new, private spaces by means of enhancing the barrier effects and even producing new, tunnel-like borders. The construction of Zhongfu Mall intercepted the flow of insiders to Zhongyi Food Market. The new private kindergarten and commercial shops in the Zhongyi Village area are creating new, exclu-

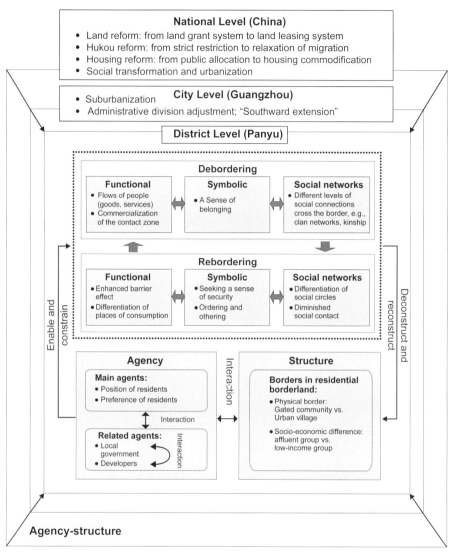

Figure 35: The performance of debordering and rebordering and their agential and structural factors
Source: Illustration by author

sively private space as well. The arrival of gated community residents has raised prices for goods and services in the contact zone substantially. For instance, Zhongyi Food Market was originally a place for local villagers and migrants to shop; but since prices have gone up, the poor villagers and rural migrants have started to source their daily necessities farther afield at cheaper markets. The shift in the location of consumption for local, poor residents and differentiation in the trajectories of daily activities have reduced the likelihood of regular encounters between the gated community residents and the poor, vicinity outsiders. All together it is creating a tunnel-like border.

Symbolic debordering generates a sense of belonging to various places in the village. The insiders' frequent visits to certain village locations generate an attachment to place. The Clifford residents have started to regard the neighboring village as a part of the space in which their lives unfold. Property agencies promoting housing in Clifford Estate have begun to bundle facilities in the neighboring village as though they were community amenities.

Symbolic rebordering of the gated community is a matter of adopting the spatial strategies that go along with seeking a sense of security and ordering and othering. Such strategies strive toward a purification of space. Although "gated property management" does not put an end to crime in the community, the fences and walls reduce the likelihood of crime and increase residents' sense of security. Ordering and othering are simultaneous processes. The residential border of the gated community divides the people into insiders and outsiders and constructs an order consisting of "inside" and "outside" and of "us" and "them". Within the homogeneous community residents are more willing to communicate with other people, increasing the sense of community; but order and security concerns in the community lead residents to other the outsiders. First, the residents stigmatize the outsiders whom they regard as potentially threatening and as a source of disorder. Second, the border serves as a symbol of social status including the affluent while excluding the "others", for whom housing within is unaffordable. When the original order and quality of the community went into decline as the community grew to include less highly educated residents, residents became dissatisfied with the composition of the community. Many rich residents moved out. Third, the most common relationship between the residents of the gated community and the vicinity outsiders from the urban village is depicted as a "cat and mouse" relationship (see Chapter 7.5.2).

Social ties do permeate the physical border. But the border is strengthened by a rebordering current in social networks. In the case study area, social networks across the border between the gated community of Clifford Estate and the urban village of Zhongyi have shifted from being almost non-existent to presenting an array of different types. Since 2000, the gated community of Clifford Estate has undergone localization. The entry of price-sensitive residents has strengthened the economic connection between the gated community and the urban village (see Chapter 7.6.1). The economic connection has improved weak social ties, for instance; and village kinship and clan network connections have also spread across the border. However, the insiders and the vicinity outsiders nonetheless move in two different social circles. First, strong economic connections obtain between them but these do not give rise to deeper-level relationships such as friendship. Second, the border dilutes pre-existing friendships. Third, the indigenous village clan networks are not unaffected by the fences and walls: the younger generation of indigenous villagers that has moved into the gated community has kept strong connections to its family members and relatives through the kinship network, but social contacts with the other villagers is reduced due to the barrier of fences and walls reducing likelihood of encounter among them.

8.2 The role of structures: contextual and institutional factors

8.2.1 The role of social transformation

In the wake of economic reform and accompanying rapid economic development in China, society has undergone massive transformations (see Chapter 5.4). Social transformation is reflected in the dimensions of globalization, devolution and marketization. Globalization has brought great foreign direct investment ("FDI") in China. FDI has driven industrial as well as real estate development and become the main source of urban development. Particularly in the Pearl River Delta, FDI in part from Hong Kong has accelerated urban sprawl and the suburbanization of Guangzhou and stimulated town and village industrial development in the suburbs. This has led both upper and middle classes to seek new commercial housing in the suburbs and migrants to work at factories set up at the villages. The devolution of power to the urban government has unleashed local government actors, who have more power to set policy and promote urban development. The study of the conditions of processes of debordering and rebordering should therefore focus on the city level. Marketization of China's land use and housing provision has promoted commercial housing development and provided the residents with more residential choices.

The 1979 strategy to allow some people to "get rich first" has contributed to the emergence of a new middle class and a spatial division between rich and poor and between urban and rural. Social stratification in the city is reflected in the residential borderland area at the micro-scale, with one part gated community (belonging to urban system) and another part urban village (belonging to rural system). The dual Chinese system of urban and rural areas has created differences and asymmetries on either side of a residential borderland. The same differences and asymmetries meanwhile drive flows of people across the border. The vicinity outsiders, who are mainly rural migrants, are a less expensive work force than the residents of the gated community, and this difference is rooted in the massive income gap between the country's urban and the rural areas. Hence, the most important difference lies in the price of goods and services between the gated community and the urban village, which is the direct impetus driving the residents of the gated community to shop in the village area.

Social inequality has caused an increase in crime rates in China. Liu (2006) reported that while the annual average rate of real GDP growth was 9.05 % between 1990 and 2002, with GDP reaching $1.23 trillion in 2002, China has become the world's sixth largest economy. At the same time its total official crime rate increased from 55.91 incidents per 100,000 people in 1978 to 337.5 incidents per 100,000 people in 2002. Granted, the official crime rate was low as compared to Western counties. But the unofficial crime rate may be higher when one considers the bribery and corruption that have been widely observed in China (Zhang 2013). Crime in the city is frequent, and residents generally feel unsafe. For instance, in the urban village of Zhongyi, burglary and motor cycle theft are the most frequent crimes (see Chapter 7.5.3.1). In response to this, the village has been implementing many crime prevention measures including security patrols, video surveillance, and access control systems to buildings. Crime prevention has become one of the main village public service expenditures. The social discourse of crime has motivated residents to seek a sense of security in the city.

8.2.2 The role of institution

At the national level, a set of institutional reforms characterize a post-Mao era. These include the land reform (see Chapter 5.1), the hukou system reform (see Chapter 5. 2), and the housing reform (see Chapter 5.3). The main goal of China's reforms is to change the socialist-planned economy to a market-oriented economy. The reform of institutions has a strong impact on the creation and perpetuation of the border in the residential area.

First, land reform has underlain the formation of residential borderland. The land-use system has been transforming from a land grant system into a land leasing system since the late 1980s. One of the outcomes has been the establishment of a land market. However, due to the government monopoly on the supply of urban land, the land market excludes rural villagers. In the process of land expropriation, the local governments expropriated the agricultural land in villages, while bypassing built-up areas in villages in order to reduce the cost of compensating the villages for the expropriation. The requisitioned land was changed into urban land while built-up village areas kept their character during the process of urbanization. Where the requisitioned land became the site of a new gated community next to a village, there emerged the phenomenon of residential borderland.

Second, the hukou system has divided the people into different groups and pushed rural migrants to aggregate in urban villages. Post-Mao era relaxation of internal movement restrictions significantly underlies the process of urbanization. However, the hukou-based state welfare system is still under-reformed. Without urban hukou, the rural migrants are excluded from the urban welfare system. In particular, they are excluded from the public housing system in cities and are unable to obtain the expensive housing available through the market. Urban villages, as urban low-rent areas, have become a habitat for the rural migrants.

An invisible border exists in the urban village which has been consolidated by the institution of the hukou system. The assignment of hukou, which determines who in the village shall receive village welfare and other corresponding entitlements, consolidated a collective group identity of "Zhongyi villagers". The hukou system divides the residents of Zhongyi Village into three groups: indigenous villagers, rural migrants, and other indigenous villagers who hold urban hukou. The economic status of the group of indigenous villagers is superior to that of the other two groups, for they are eligible to benefit from the village collective's welfare and economic interests. The rural migrants and the local laid-off villagers who hold urban hukou are excluded from this welfare system. In the inferior position, the rural migrants and the other group of indigenous villagers comprising laid-off employees of SOEs/COEs constitute the main group of urban poor.

The hukou institution has also played the important role in excluding subsequent residents: those of Clifford Estate. Hukou employs categories of rural and urban as well as a location attribution (see Chapter 5.3). The entitlement to state-provided or village collective-provided welfare is not only based on urban or rural hukou but also on the distinction of local (in Chinese: *bendi*) hukou and non-local or external (in Chinese: *wailai*) hukou. All Zhongyi Village collective welfare and other resources are allocated to villagers based on their local (Zhongyi) hukou status. Therefore the location attribute of hukou excludes subsequent residents of Clifford Estate from the public welfare provided at Zhongyi village, including from such public goods as education.

Third, the housing reform has been sorting the population in a such way that favors affluent segments moving into commodity housing. The housing reform has brought a transformation from public allocation to commodification. The state government has retreated from providing commodity housing, which is now mainly supplied through the market and offers superior conditions as compared to other types of housing in the same parts of a given city for a higher price. Hence, affordability has become the main market mechanism sorting people into different residential areas. Sorting by affordability means that the gated communities are mostly inhabited by the higher income groups while urban villages mostly are home to low-income groups.

In addition, an important outcome of institutional reforms has been the activation of non-state actors who are less restricted in shaping the practices of debordering and rebordering. With respect to creating a concrete border (bordering), different local actors, i.e., the local Panyu government, the villagers of Zhongyi, and most importantly the developers have erected the walls and fences of Clifford Estate. The power elites, among them the Panyu government and village cadres (with the political power) and the developer (with the financial power) are cooperatively creating the border in residential borderland. In the practice of debordering and rebordering, the residents of the gated community, the residents of the village, the developers and the local government are different actors with different motivations pursuing their own goals.

8.2.3 The role of urbanization and suburbanization

After launching reforms and the open-door policy, China has undergone rapid economic development accompanied by rapid urbanization (see Chapter 5.5.2). The impact of urbanization is national because migration happens not only within a city from the rural area to urban area but also massively among cities from less developed regions to more developed regions. A huge rural population has migrated to the cities, especially to the megacities, in a short time, which has led to a fragmentation of social networks in the residential borderland. The population migration has brought the old, original social networks to collapse, but new social networks have not yet emerged. The residents of gated communities come from all around the country. Although among the insider community different types of social ties are developing (see Chapter 7.6.1), relationships in the neighborhood are generally fragmented and characterized by indifference. The residents within Clifford Estate are far from forming intimate social ties among themselves let alone intimate social ties between themselves and the outsiders.

However, rapid urbanization has been followed by a suburbanization which has promoted the process of debordering by changing the population structure in the suburban area. Guangzhou, China's third largest city, exemplifies the trend. Since the administrative reform that integrated the previously independent city of Panyu into Guangzhou as one of its districts, Guangzhou has adjusted its urban development strategy to favor a "develop the south" approach. Panyu has thus become the main suburbanization area of Guangzhou. Many middle-class citizens have chosen to live in suburban Guangzhou. Against the backdrop of these processes, the gated community of Clifford Estate has undergone the transformation known as localization, whereby the population structure of the community has changed from mainly consisting of Hong Kong residents and Guangzhou's rich to being mainly middle class. This transformation in Clifford Estate has reshaped the relationship between the gated community and its neighboring village.

8.3 The role of actors: position, preference and motivation

8.3.1 The role of residents' positions

The role of position has been prominently advanced as a key to understanding how people come to live in different residential areas (see, e.g., WU and LI 2005; LI and HUANG 2006; CHEN and SUN 2007). Different people are individually positioned in society in terms of their resources such as income and property. Socio-economic status plays an important role in driving the processes of debordering and rebordering.

As mentioned in Chapter 7.6.3, economic and social connections strengthened dramatically during the transformation of residential borderland from the 1990s to the 2000s. In this the residents' position played an important role. In the 1990s, the residents were mainly upper class with the economic capacity to afford the expensive private services inside gated community. Most of the residents' consumption took place within it. Therefore, there was almost no directly economic connection between the gated community residents and the residents of neighboring village. But since 2000 with suburbanization, the homogenous group of wealthy residents in the gated community has transformed into a mixed-income group. The middle-income residents purchased housing with the help of mortgages and elderly residents moved from rural areas to Clifford Estate solely for the purpose of joining their adult children. These are price-sensitive groups and have become the main driving force behind flows of people from the inside to the outside vicinity. The position change of the social group living in Clifford Estate has led to the debordering process. Meanwhile, changes in some villagers' and rural migrants' positions are also driving them to purchase houses inside the gated community.

The position difference between the residents inside and outside the gated community has also caused differentiation in places of consumption. Residents of the gated community visit the vicinity village area in order to purchase daily necessities, of course; however, their purchasing power is stronger than that of the vicinity outsiders. For this reason the shopping locales such as the Zhongyi Food Market and the Zhongfu Mall in the contact zone are mainly occupied by insiders. Many vicinity outsiders by the same token were priced out of these markets. Therefore, the functional rebordering process as a whole is a consequence of a socio-economic status difference.

8.3.2 The role of residents' preference

As O'Dowd (2002, p. 25) observed, "some actors have a vested interest in maintaining borders as barriers; others wish to develop their bridging role; others still use borders as a positive economic resource in ways which seek to benefit from their bridging and barrier functions simultaneously". The debordering and rebordering processes are largely a consequence of individual preference. The insiders have the ability and capacity to make decisions about whether to maintain contacts to the vicinity outsiders and vice versa.

In the social networks dimension of debordering and rebordering, the individual's preference is a strong driving force. Some insiders express a preference for purchasing food at a particular stall in the village market just because they feel an individual stallholder is good or the products or services are better. After constantly visiting the same stall, they get to know the stallholder. Some people would enjoy talking to and are willing to befriend the vicinity outsiders. Strong social ties come about between insiders and outsiders this way, even if this applies only to a limited group of community residents. But at the same time many residents avoid talking to and stigmatize vicinity outsiders as a potential source of crime and disorder. Thus security concerns affect the residents' preference with regard to communicating with the vicinity outsiders.

In addition, the individual's linguistic dialect is also a factor determining residents' preferences. As interviews have shown, speaking the same dialect can bridge the distance between the insiders and outsiders. Most of the insider interviewees said they had gotten to know somebody while shopping in the vicinity village because an outsider spoke their dialect. The residents of Clifford Estate originate from all over the country and their dialects differ accordingly. Encountering an outsider who speaks the same dialect makes an insider more open to an exchange. In terms of the preference of the residents, the local dialect is important in constructing social ties between the two enclaves.

8.3.3 The role of local government and developers

MADRAZO and KEMPEN (2012) point out that discussion of the role of players in China's divided cities should not focus only on individuals but also on entities such as state or local government or the developers. These figures, as related actors, are motivated by different concerns and are very important drivers of the processes of debordering and rebordering.

The local (Panyu) government encouraged middle-income classes from Guangzhou central districts to reside in Panyu but failed to provide enough corresponding public facilities. One local policy was that migrants could obtain local urban hukou after purchasing property in Panyu. This local policy, implemented between 1998 and 2003, attracted many urban professionals and has accelerated the process of residential suburbanization. In addition, the state government implemented a national housing mixing policy in 2006. It mandated that housing units with a floor area less than 90 m^2 must account for 70 % of the total floor area of all new development projects. This policy has to a certain extent forced the developer of Clifford Estate to consider building more small-sized apartments in subsequent real estate development. However, as local government has been retreating from the supply of public facilities, the supply of neighborhood public services is mainly left to unwilling developers. The result has been a shortage of public services in the suburban area, even in the gated community, and this has pushed residents there to seek complementary services in vicinity village area.

Although there are strong flows of residents across the border in residential borderland, the local government does not promote the integration of residential borderland. The splintering urbanism of the urban planning system regards the gated community as an urban section but the urban villages as a rural section. The local government, adopting a "divide-and-conquer" strategy of urban development, does not see the residential borderland as a whole but rather as two, separate parts (see Chapter 7.7.2). For instance, although a city road impedes the flow of insiders to Zhongyi's built-up village area, the local government does not recognize the problem and as a practical matter has refused to erect a pedestrian bridge across the busy road.

In the urban village, the local government tries to eliminate the identity difference between indigenous villagers and urban citizens through its policy of converting rural villages into urban communities (see Chapter 7.5.3.2). However, because of the complex interests attached to the hukou designation, the rural hukou of indigenous villagers was transferred to urban hukou in name only. The policy as it stands has not eliminated the difference between the rural and the urban. In fact, the collective identity of Zhongyi indigenous villagers was actually consolidated by the policy of "fixing the share-right to collective economic revenue" which realigned the share allocation scheme.

For the state government actor, the neighborhood is a basic unit of public administration. Social stability is one of the most important central goals of the central government. Security at the neighborhood level is an effective method to ensure social stability (see Chapter 7.7.2). The political goal of social stability has led the local government to encourage developers to erect and maintain fences and walls in residential neighborhoods. The developers are also driving the processes of debordering and rebordering. The developer of Clifford Estate has adjusted its property development strategy at different stages. At first the developer sought to position the property as a resort and marketed it mainly in Hong Kong. After suburbanization got underway in Guangzhou, the more recent development projects have been positioned as residential properties and advertised in local markets. The change in the housing supply structure in Clifford Estate has changed the demographic structure of community. However, as the scale of the community has become larger and larger, the neighborhood facilities in the gated community have come to be in short supply. Therefore, village facilities in the vicinity have become complementary facilities for those in the gated community. In addition, the private developers who have renovated and turned the village's buildings to commercial use in the contact zone and built new, private commercial locales there are clearly promoting functional debordering and rebordering processes.

9 Final conclusion

The reforms in China have brought enormous economic, social and political transformation to the city of Guangzhou. With suburbanization around the city numerous urban borders have emerged along the lines of gated communities and urban villages. A typical spatial phenomenon is the juxtaposition of gated communities and urban villages in the suburban area as a consequence of urban transformation. The dynamics of bordering processes have been examined substantially at national borders in political geography; however, not much attention has been paid to the border at the scale of the neighborhood. How processes of debordering and rebordering are performed at neighborhood borders is not fully clear, nor is it clear what drives those processes. Urban borders are at least as important to people's daily life practice as national borders in most cases. Neighborhood borders exhibit many similarities to national borders. Empirical study of neighborhood borders is useful for improving our understanding of the processes of debordering and rebordering.

Three empirical questions were addressed in this study. The first question concerns how processes of debordering and rebordering are performed at the neighborhood borders; the last two concern the structural and agency factors which shape theses processes. This study has developed a theoretical framework by combining the theoretical conceptions of bordering and structuration theory to interpret the dynamics of neighborhood borders in suburban Guangzhou. By adopting new theoretical perspectives on national borders in political geography into the study of urban borders in suburban Guangzhou, this study not only contributes to our understanding of urban conditions, borderland urbanism, and social segregation in China and beyond, but also helps to enrich the debate of social theory.

9.1 Empirical findings

As to the first research question, the empirical findings demonstrate that the processes of debordering and rebordering unfold simultaneously along functional, symbolic, and social network dimensions in suburban Guangzhou.

There are vigorous flows of people from the gated communities to the neighboring villages regardless whether the gated community is self-sufficient with regard to neighborhood facilities and services. The daily activities of the gated community residents who visit the village area in suburban Guangzhou are diversified. The flows of people from a gated community into the adjacent village serve functional exchange purposes, namely the exchange of money, goods, and services. Most importantly, the gated community insiders frequenting the adjacent village area have created a contact zone that is the site of most economic interaction and social encounters. The insiders' frequent visits to the contact zone have led them to feel they belong to these places. It has become a place of co-existence and a platform for social interaction. Hence, two contiguous enclaves — the gated community and the urban village— are not isolated units but to a certain extent are functionally connected to each other.

SABATINI and SALCEDO (2007) have already described the functional and symbolic aspects of debordering processes at the neighborhood border. However, the novelty of the present empirical finding is that some kinds of social networks debordering persist at the neighborhood border in suburban Guangzhou as the contiguity of a gated community and an urban village has given rise to the formation of some kinds of social networks. A transformation of the social ties linking the gated community to its vicinity urban village has taken place such that, whereas there were no social ties across the border at first, now some kinds of social ties permeate the border. For instance, economic contact has improved social connections across the border, and some villagers' clan networks have crossed the border as well. The residential borderland is becoming a unit for constituting social networks even if there is a border separating the enclaves. This has escaped the dominant view of social networks as something that form within the neighborhood or workplace.

Moreover, this study shows that the process of debordering is in fact accompanied by a process of rebordering. Differentiation of the places at which each group—gated community residents and neighboring village residents—satisfies its consumer needs leads to the emergence of a tunnel-like border such that each group's daily activities follow different trajectories. The study explains the processes of rebordering in the gated community as spatial strategies of place-making. The strategies include seeking a sense of security and ordering and othering. As the empirical evidence shows, although crime is not eliminated inside, gated management has increased residents' sense of security. The ordering and othering processes strongly pursue a bounded space that enables homogenous groups to be sorted and separated from the others. The border constructs the order of "inside" and "outside" as well as the homogenous groups of "us" and "them".

The results illustrate that urban borders are becoming more permeable and flexible in the course of debordering process while the urban space is still divided and fragmented by rebordering processes of seeking a sense of security, and of ordering and othering. Residential borderland is a transitional space in a state between inclusion and exclusion.

As to the second and third research questions, the research has explored structure and agency factors. The dynamics of bordering processes are an outcome of the interaction of the two. Non-state actors are playing a more important role than before. The affluent, the indigenous villagers, the migrants, and the urban poor have become the main actors in bordering practices. Each has its motivation to create, maintain, reconstruct and deconstruct the border. For individual residents, income has determined their position.

When price-sensitive residents moved into Clifford Estate, flows of people from the gated community to the neighboring village greatly increased. Moreover, with the reduction of spatial distance between the affluent and the poor, the individual's preference has become an important factor, something which has received little attention in the Chinese context.

The dynamics of bordering processes epitomize social transition. The processes of debordering and rebordering are activated as the various actors follow their own motives. But they are also embedded in multi-scalar structural conditions and contextual dynamics. The national institutional reforms, i.e. the hukou system, the land use system, and the housing system, together with social transformation and urbanization have all underlain these processes. It ought to be highlighted what institutional factors are paramount among these structural factors. Especially the hukou system is a permanent force that maintains urban borders.

9.2 Theoretical contributions and future perspectives

Inspired by structuration theory which emphasizes the duality of agency and structure and informed by theoretical conceptions of national borders, this research has developed a theoretical framework for analyzing borders at the neighborhood scale. The theoretical conception of "borders as processes" including debordering and rebordering processes in functional, symbolic and social network dimensions is extended in this study through immersion in structuration theory. Structuration theory constitutes a bridge between national border theory and the micro-scale of borders and contributes to the ontological understanding of the driving forces of bordering processes. That is, the processes of debordering and rebordering are an outcome of the interaction of agency and structure.

Some aspects of the empirical study make theoretical contributions. First, the empirical findings highlight the dimension of social networks bordering. Existing research into debordering and rebordering around national borders only distinguishes borders into territorial, functional, and symbolic dimensions (see, e.g., O'DOWD 2002; STETTER 2005; FERRER-GALLARDO 2008; SENDHARDT 2013). Social networks are assigned to the functional dimension without further distinction or discussion. The present empirical findings have found that social networks are important to these processes, for social contact is integral to everyday urban practice. Therefore, the social networks dimension is distinguished from the functional dimension at the micro-scale of borders and should draw more research attention in urban border studies.

Second, the empirical findings of this study extend theoretical concepts of functional, symbolic and social networks borders. Combining the empirical findings, a matrix was formed of different types of borders (functional, symbolic and social-networks) and processes (debordering and rebordering) (see Chapter 7.8). The empirical findings concluded in the matrix between types of borders and dimensions of process have extended the concepts of bordering as set out in Chapter 3.2.

Third, the present study organically synthesizes the contents of security, institution, identity, othering and ordering into a systematical framework. These are among the concepts from border theory which are innovatively applied to urban borderlands. Particularly the theoretical concepts of othering and ordering have been merged into the theoretical framework. These extend our understanding of symbolic rebordering. Not only is there a highly visible border constituted by the fences and walls of the gated community; there is also an invisible border in the urban village. The insiders are permanently othering the outsiders by various means at the neighborhood border. The affluent residents of the gated community need the vicinity outsiders economically as a source of cheap labor, services, and goods but exclude them socially, reject them freely entering their living space, and stereotypically view them as a source of crime and disorder. The invisible border in the urban village reflects the othering (or exclusion) of institution. Based on the household registration (hukou) system in China, only villagers who have Zhongyi Village hukou status are eligible to benefit from the village collective's welfare and economic interests. The indigenous villagers are institutionally othering their own set of others, in this case the rural migrants and a particular segment of urban hukou holders among the indigenous villagers. Access to the state-provided public education services in Zhongyi Village is also controlled by hukou status. This excludes the residents of the gated community.

The approach to multidimensional processes of debordering and rebordering avoids a linear perspective and contributes to a more holistic understanding of urban dynamics and conditions in China. The theoretical framework thus also incorporates flexibility, which is useful for analyzing residential borderlands in other cities in China and beyond.

This study has raised several related topics for future research. First, flows of people across the residential border are not limited to the residential borderland. Flows from inside the gated community to the vicinity outside or vice versa is not an exclusive domain. There are also strong flows of people beyond this limitation of place. Within the context of suburbanization and the international background of Clifford Estate residents, flows of people across the Clifford Estate border also include flows between the local community and the urban centers of Panyu or Guangzhou as well as between the local community and Hong Kong or other international cities. The commuting and long-distance travel behaviors, as cross-border practices, can be topics for research in the future.

Second, residential borderlands consist of a gated community and an (urban) village. There are three types of residential borderlands. This study focuses on one type of residential borderland in a suburban area. Many other residential borderlands exist in the city center. What is the nature of the relationship between the gated community and the urban village in a city center where mature public facilities are found? Comparative research among different locations such as between the suburbs and city center, between a local city and other cities, and among different types of residential borderlands will certainly consolidate the empirical findings of this study. Such extended research will also accumulate more valuable results.

Third, in the social networks dimension of debordering and rebordering, a massive survey employing the questionnaire method would provide greater detail about the features of the social networks between two enclaves. In addition, information technology enables social contact across borders. The impact of the internet and social networking software on the construction of social networks between two enclaves also would be a new direction in the future research.

10 References

ACKLESON, J. (2003): Directions in border security research. In: The Social Science Journal 40 (4), pp. 573-581.

ACKLESON, J.M. (1999): Discourses of identity and territoriality on the US-Mexico border. In: Geopolitics 4 (2), pp. 155-179.

AGNEW, J. (1994): The territorial trap: The geographical assumptions of international relations theory. In: Review of International Political Economy 1 (1), pp. 53-80.

AGNEW, J. (1996): Book Review on A. Paasi: Territories, Boundaries and Consciousness. In: Geografiska Annaler B 78, pp. 181-182.

ALBERT, M. and L. BROCK (1996): Debordering the world of states: New spaces in international relations. In: New Political Science 18 (1), pp. 69-106.

ALBERT, M., Y. LAPID and D. JACOBSON (Eds.), (2001): Identities, Borders, Orders: Rethinking International Relations Theory. Minneapolis: University of Minnesota Press.

ALDOUS, T. (1992): Urban Villages: A Concept for Creating Mixed-Use Urban Developments on a Sustainable Scale Urban Villages Group, London.

ALVAREZ, R.R. (1995): The Mexican-Us Border: The Making of an Anthropology of Borderlands. In: Annual Review of Anthropology 24, pp. 447-470.

ANDERSON, J. (2001): Theorizing State Borders: 'Politics/Economics' and Democracy in Capitalism. In: CIBR/WP01-1. Belfast: CIBR Working Papers in Border Studies.

ANDERSON, J. and L. O'DOWD (1999): Borders, Border Regions and Territoriality: Contradictory Meanings, Changing Significance. In: Regional Studies 33 (7), pp. 593-604.

ANDERSON, J., L. O'DOWD and T.M. WILSON (2003): New Borders for a Changing Europe: Cross-Border Cooperation and Governance. Frank Cass, London.

ANDERSON, M. (1996): Frontiers: Territory and State Formation in the Modern World. Polity Oxford.

ATKINSON, R. and S. BLANDY (2005): Introduction: International perspectives on the new enclavism and the rise of gated communities. In: Housing Studies 20 (2), pp. 177-186.

ATKINSON, R. and J. FLINT (2004): Fortress Uk? Gated Communities, the Spatial Revolt of the Elites and Time-Space Trajectories of Segregation. In: Housing Studies 19 (6), pp. 875-892.

BALIBAR, E., (1998): The borders of Europe, In: Cosmopolitics: Thinking and Feeling Beyond the Nation, CHEAH, P. and B. ROBBINS (eds.), University of Minnesota Press, Minneapolis, pp. 216-229.

BANERJEE, P. and X. CHEN (2013): Living in in-between spaces: A structure-agency analysis of the India–China and India–Bangladesh borderlands. In: Cities 34, pp. 18–29.

BAUDER, H. (2011): Toward a Critical Geography of the Border: Engaging the Dialectic of Practice and Meaning. In: Annals of the Association of American Geographers 101 (5), pp. 1126-1139.

BECK, U. (2000): What Is Globalization? Polity Press, Cambridge.

BLAKELY, E.J. and M.G. SNYDER, (1997a): Divided We Fall: Gated and Walled Communities in the United States, In: Architecture of Fear, ELLIN, N. (ed.), Princeton Architectural Press, New York.

BLAKELY, E.J. and M.G. SNYDER (1997b): Fortress America: Gated Communities in the United States. Bookings Institution Press, Washington DC.

BOGGS, W. (1940): International Boundaries, a Study of Boundary Functions and Problems Columbia University Press, New York.

BONACKER, T., (2006): Krieg Und Die Theorie Der Weltgesellschaft. Auf Dem Weg Zu Einer Konflikttheorie Der Weltgesellschaft, In: Den Krieg berdenken.Kriegsbegriffe Und Kriegstheorien in Der Kontroverse, GEIS, A. (ed.), Nomos, Baden-Baden, pp. 75-94.

BONACKER, T., (2007): Debordering by human rights: The challenge of postterritorial conflicts in world society, In: Territorial Conflicts in World Society.Modern Systems Theory, International Relations and Conflict Studies, STETTER, S. (ed.), Routledge, London, pp. 19-32.

BREITUNG, W. (2011): Borders and the city—intra-urban boundaries in Guangzhou (China). In: Quaestiones Geographicae 30 (4), pp. 55-61.

BREITUNG, W. (2012): Enclave Urbanism in China: Attitudes Towards Gated Communities in Guangzhou. In: Urban Geography 33 (2), pp. 278-294.

BRUNET-JAILLY, E. (2005): Theorizing borders: an interdisciplinary perspective. In: Geopolitics 10 (4), pp. 633-649.

BRUNET-JAILLY, E. (2011): Special Section: Borders, Borderlands and Theory: An Introduction. In: Geopolitics 16 (1), pp. 1-6.

CALDEIRA, T.P.R. (1996): Fortified enclaves: The new urban segregation. In: Public Culture 8 (2), pp. 303-328.

CALDEIRA, T.P.R. (2000): City of walls: crime, segregation, and citizenship in São Paulo. Univeristy of California Press, Berkeley.

CANEY, S. (2005): Justice Beyond Borders: A Global Political Theory. Oxford University Press, Oxford.

CASTELLS, M. (1996): The rise of the network society. Blackwell, Oxford.

Centaline Property Agency Limited (2014): 小区信息: 祈福新村蝶舞轩 Enghlish: The Introduction of Residential Neighborhood: A Unit of Cifford Estate Named Diewu Xuan. In: The official website of Centaline Property Agency Limited, URL: http://gz.centanet.com/xiaoqu/qifuxincundiewuxu/info/ (Accessed: 22.07.2015).

CHAN, K.W. (2009): The Chinese Hukou System at 50. In: Eurasian Geography and Economics 50 (2), pp. 197–221.

CHAN, K.W. and W. BUCKINGHAM (2008): Is China Abolishing the Hukou System? In: The China Quarterly (195), pp. 582-606.

CHEN, J. and X. HAN (2014): The Evolution of the Housing Market and its Socio-Economic Impacts in the Post-Reform People's Republic of China: A Survey of the Literature. In: Journal of Economic Surveys 28 (4), pp. 652-670.

CHEN, P. and Z. ZHU (2003): 富户为何撤离"中国第一村"祈福. English: Why Rich Residents Left : "China's First Village" Clifford Estate. In: Asia-Pacific Economic Times, Published Date: 15.07.2003, URL: http://www.southcn.com/estate/news/gzls/200307150626.htm (Accessed: 22.05.2015).

CHEN, X. and J. SUN (2007): Untangling a global – local nexus: sorting out residential sorting in Shanghai. In: Environment and Planning A 39, pp. 2324 - 2345.

CHEN, X.M., (2009): Pacific Rim, In: International Encyclopedia of Human Geography, KITCHIN, R. and N. THRIFT (eds.), Elsevier, Oxford, pp. 66-71.

CHENG, T. and M. SELDEN (1994): The Origins and Social Consequences of China's Hukou System. In: The China Quarterly (139), pp. 644-668.

CHUNG, H. (2010): Building an Image of Villages-in-the-City: A Clarification of China's Distinct Urban Spaces. In: International Journal of Urban and Regional Research 34 (2), pp. 421-437.

CHUNG, H. and S.-H. ZHOU (2011): Planning for Plural Groups? Villages-in-the-City Redevelopment in Guangzhou City, China. In: International Planning Studies 16 (4), pp. 333-353.

COLEMAN, M. (2005): U.S. statecraft and the U.S.–Mexico border as security/economy nexus. In: Political Geography 24 (2), pp. 185-209.

COY, M. (2006): Gated communities and urban fragmentation in Latin America: the Brazilian experience. In: GeoJournal 66 (1-2), pp. 121-132.

CRUZ, S.S. and P. PINHO (2009): Closed Condominiums as Urban Fragments of the Contemporary City. In: European Planning Studies 17 (11), pp. 1685-1710.

CSNIC (2011): The State Administration of Quality Supervision Inspection and Quarantine, National Standardization Management Committee. Gb/T 4754-2011 Industrial Classification for National Economic Activities. Standards Press of China, Beijing, (in Chinese).

DAVIS, M. (1992): City of Quartz: Excavating the Future in Los Angeles. Vintage, London.

Development and Reform Bureau of Panyu district (2014): Panyu District Statistical Yearbook. URL: http://fagai.panyu.gov.cn/Showbook.aspx?iyear=2014&id=1840&upid=8 (Accessed: 23.12.2015).

DICKEN, P. (2003): Global Shift: Reshaping the Global Economic Map in the 21st Century. Sage, London.

DIENER, A.C. and J. HAGEN (2009): Theorizing Borders in a 'Borderless World': Globalization, Territory and Identity. In: Geography Compass 3 (3), pp. 1196-1216.

DONG, X.-Y. (1996): Two-tier land tenure system and sustained economic growth in post-1978 rural China. In: World Development 24 (5), pp. 915-928.

DONNAN, H. and T. M.WILSON (1999): Borders Frontiers of Identity, Nation and State. Oxford, New York.

DOUGLASS, M., B. WISSINK and R.V. KEMPEN (2012): Enclave urbanism in China: Consequences and interpretations. In: Urban Geography 33 (2), pp. 167-182.

DOWNE-WAMBOLDT, B. (1992): Content analysis: Method, applications, and issues. In: Health Care for Women International 13 (3), pp. 313-321.

DULBECCO, P. and M.-F. RENARD (2003): Permanency and Flexibility of Institutions: The Role of Decentralization in Chinese Economic Reforms. In: The Review of Austrian Economics 16 (4), pp. 327-346.

DUNN, K., (2005): Interviewing, In: Qualitative Research Methods in Human Geography, HAY, I. (ed.), Oxford University Press, Melbourne, pp. 79-105.

DYCK, I. and R.A. KEARNS, (2006): Structuration Theory: Agency, Structure and Everyday Life, In: Approaches to Human Geography, AITKEN, S. and G. VALENTINE (eds.), SAGE, London,Thousand Oaks, New Delhi, pp. 86-97.

FAINSTEIN, S.S., I. GORDON and M. HARLOE (1992): Divided Cities: New York & London in the Contemporary World. Blackwell, Oxford.

FAN, C.C. (2002): The Elite, the Natives, and the Outsiders: Migration and Labor Market Segmentation in Urban China. In: Annals of the Association of American Geographers 92 (1), pp. 103-124.

FENG, D., W. BREITUNG and H. ZHU (2014): Creating and defending concepts of home in suburban Guangzhou. In: Eurasian Geography and Economics 55 (4), pp. 381-403.

FERRER-GALLARDO, X. (2008): The Spanish–Moroccan border complex: Processes of geopolitical, functional and symbolic rebordering. In: Political Geography 27 (3), pp. 301-321.

FOLDVARY, F.E., (2006): The economic case for private residential government, In: Private Cities: Global and local perspectives, GLASZE, G., C. WEBSTER and K. FRANTZ (eds.), Routledge, London and New York, pp. 31-44.

FRANKLIN, B. and M. TAIT (2002): Constructing an Image: The Urban Village Concept in the Uk. In: Planning Theory 1 (3), pp. 250-272.

GANS, H. (1962): The Urban Villagers: Group and Class in the Life of Italian Americans. Anchor, New York.

GIDDENS, A. (1979): Central problems in social theory: action, structure and contradictions in social analysis. University of California Press, Cambridge.

GIDDENS, A. (1984): The Constitution of Society: Outline of the Theory of Structuration. Polity Press, Cambridge.

GIDDENS, A. (1985): The nation-state and violence. Polity press, Cambridge.

GIROIR, G., (2006): The Purple Jade Vilas (Beijing): a golden ghetto in red China, In:

Private Cities: Global and local perspectives, GLASZE, G., WEBSTER, C. J. and FRANTZ, K. (ed.), Routledge, London, pp. 142–152.

GLASZE, G. (2005): Some Reflections on the Economic and Political Organisation of Private Neighbourhoods. In: Housing Studies 20 (2), pp. 211-233.

GOIX, R.L. (2005): Gated communities: Sprawl and social segregation in Southern California. In: Housing Studies 20 (2), pp. 323-343.

GOIX, R.L. and E. VESSELINOV (2013): Gated Communities and House Prices: Suburban Change in Southern California, 1980–2008. In: International Journal of Urban and Regional Research 37 (6), pp. 2129-2151.

GOLD, R.L. (1958): Roles in Sociological Field Observations. In: Social Forces 36 (3), pp. 217-223.

GOODMAN, R., K. DOUGLASA and A. BABACANA (2010): Master Planned Estates and Collective Private Assets in Australia: Research into the Attitudes of Planners and Developers. In: International Planning Studies 15 (2), pp. 99-117.

GOTTDIENER, M. and R. HUTCHISON (2010): The new urban sociology. Westview Press, Boulder.

GRAHAM, S. and S. MARVIN (2001): Splintering Urbanism. Routledge, London and New York.

GRANOVETTER, M.S. (1973): The Strength of Weak Ties. In: American Journal of Sociology 78 (6), pp. 1360-1380.

GRANT, J. (2005): Planning Responses to Gated Communities in Canada. In: Housing Studies 20 (2), pp. 273 - 285.

Guangdong Provincial Bureau of Civil Affairs (2001): 关于印发广东省城市基层管理体制改革工作实施方案的通知, English: The Opinion to Promote the Construction of Urban Communities. URL: http://search.gd.gov.cn/detail?record=151&channelid=16317 (Accessed: 20.05.2015).

Guangzhou Statistical Bureau (2015): Guangzhou statistical yearbook. China Statistics Press, Beijing,(in Chinese).

HAO, P., S. GEERTMAN, P. HOOIMEIJER and R. SLIUZAS (2013): Spatial Analyses of the Urban Village Development Process in Shenzhen, China. In: International Journal of Urban and Regional Research 37 (6), pp. 2177-2197.

HARTSHORNE, R. (1936): Suggestions on the terminology of political boundaries. In: Annals of the Association of American Geographers 26 (1), pp. 56-57.

HARTSHORNE, R. (1950): The Functional Approach in Political Geography. In: Annals of the Association of American Geographers 40 (2), pp. 95-130.

HARVEY, D. (1989): From Managerialism to Entrepreneurialism: The Transformation in Urban Governance in Late Capitalism. In: Geografiska Annaler. Series B, Human Geography 71 (1), pp. 3-17.

HAUGAARD, M. (1997): The constitution of power. Manchester University Press, Manchester.

HAZELZET, A. and B. WISSINK (2012): Neighborhoods, Social Networks, and Trust in

Post-Reform China: The Case of Guangzhou In: Urban Geography 33 (2), pp. 204-220.
HE, S. (2013): Evolving enclave urbanism in China and its socio-spatial implications: the case of Guangzhou. In: Social & Cultural Geography 14 (3), pp. 243-275.
HE, S., Y. LIU, F. WU and C. WEBSTER (2010): Social Groups and Housing Differentiation in China's Urban Villages: An Institutional Interpretation. In: Housing Studies 25 (5), pp. 671-691.
HE, S. and F. WU (2009): China's Emerging Neoliberal Urbanism: Perspectives from Urban Redevelopment. In: Antipode 41 (2), pp. 282-304.
HENG, C.K. (1999): Cities of aristocrats and bureaucrats: The development of medieval chinese cityscapes. Singapore University Press, Singapore.
HERBERT, S., (2010): A Taut Rubber Band: Theory and Empirics in Qualitative Geographic Research, In: The Sage Handbook of Qualitative Geography, DELYSER, D., S. HERBERT, S. AITKEN, M. CRANG and L. MCDOWELL (eds.), Sage, London.
HO, P. and M. SPOOR (2006): Whose land? The political economy of land titling in transitional economies. In: Land Use Policy 23 (4), pp. 580-587.
HOLDICH, T.H. (1916): Political Frontiers and Boundary Making. MacMillan, London.
HONG, S. and K.W. CHAN (2005): Tudi zhengyong yu defang zhengfu de xingwei (Land Expropriation and Local Government Behavior). Hong Kong: Hong Kong Baptist University, Centre for China Urban and Regional Studies, Occasional Paper, N0. 58.
HOWITT, R. (1998): Scale as relation: musical metaphors of geographical scale. In: Area 30 (1), pp. 49-58.
HSIEH, H.-F. and S.E. SHANNON (2005): Three Approaches to Qualitative Content Analysis. In: Qualitative Health Research 15 (9), pp. 1277-1288.
HU, X. and D.H. KAPLAN (2001): The emergence of affluence in Beijing: residential social stratification in China's capital city. In: Urban Geography 22 (1), pp. 54-77.
HUANG, B. and C. XU (2012): 藏尸别墅邻居相继搬离. English: Hidden Corpse Found in a Villa; Neighbors Successively Move Away,. In: Yangcheng Evening News, Published Date: 06.07.2012, URL: http://www.ycwb.com/ePaper/ycwb/html/2012-07/06/content_1433373.htm (Accessed: 20.05.2015).
HUANG, Y. (2006): Collectivism, political control, and gating in Chinese cities. In: Urban Geography 27 (6), pp. 507–525.
IOSSIFOVA, D. (2009): Blurring the joint line? Urban life on the edge between old and new in Shanghai. In: Urban Design International 14 (2), pp. 65–83.
IOSSIFOVA, D. (2013): Searching for common ground: Urban borderlands in a world of borders and boundaries. In: Cities 34, pp. 1-5.
IOSSIFOVA, D. (2015): Borderland urbanism: seeing between enclaves. In: Urban Geography 36 (1), pp. 90-108.
JIRÓN, P. (2010): Mobile Borders in Urban Daily Mobility Practices in Santiago De Chile. In: International Political Sociology 4 (1), pp.66-79.

JIRÓN, P., (2011): On Becoming La Sombra/The Shadow, In: Mobile Methods, BUSCHER, M., J. URRY and K. WITCHGER (eds.), Routledge, Oxon, pp. 36-53.

JOHNSON, C., R. JONES, A. PAASI, L. AMOORE, A. MOUNTZ, M. SALTER and C. RUMFORD (2011): Interventions on rethinking 'the border' in border studies. In: Political Geography 30 (2), pp. 61–69.

JOHNSON, R.B. and A.J. ONWUEGBUZIE (2004): Mixed Methods Research: A Research Paradigm Whose Time Has Come. In: Educational Researcher 33 (7), pp. 14-26.

JONES, R. (2009): Categories, borders and boundaries. In: Progress in Human Geography 33 (2), pp. 174-189.

JONES, S.B. (1943): The description of international boundaries. In: Annals of the Association of American Geographers 33, pp. 99-117.

JONES, S.B. (1959): Boundary concepts in setting time and space. In: Annals of the Association of American Geographers 49 (3), pp. 241-255.

JORGENSEN, D.L. (1989): Participant observation: A methodology for human studies. Sage, Newbury Park, CA.

KARAMAN, O. and T. ISLAM (2012): On the dual nature of intra-urban borders: The case of a Romani neighborhood in Istanbul. In: Cities 29 (4), pp. 234–243.

KELIANG, Z. and R. PROSTERMAN (2007): Securing Land Rights for Chinese Farmers: A Leap Forward for Stability and Growth. In: Cato Development Policy Analysis Series 3, pp. 1-17.

KNAPP, R. (2000): China's walled cities. Oxford University Press, Oxford.

KOLOSSOV, V. (2005): Theorizing Borders: Border Studies: Changing Perspectives and Theoretical Approaches. In: Geopolitics 10 (4), pp. 606-632.

KONRAD, V. and H. NICOL (2008): Beyond Walls: Re-Inventing the Canada-United States Borderlands. Ashgate, London.

KRISTOF, L.K.D. (1959): The Nature of Frontiers and Boundaries. In: Annals of the Association of American Geographers 49 (3), pp. 269-282.

KUNG, J.K.S. (2002): Choice of Land Tenure in China: The Case of a County with Quasi Private Property Rights. In: Economic Development and Cultural Change 50 (4), pp. 793-817.

LECHEVALIER, A. and J. WIELGOHS (2013): Borders and Border Regions in Europe. Changes, Challenges and Chances. Transcript Verlag, Bielefeld.

LEE, J. (2000): From Welfare Housing to Home Ownership: The Dilemma of China's Housing Reform. In: Housing Studies 15 (1), pp. 61-76.

LEE, J. and Y.-P. ZHU (2006): Urban governance, neoliberalism and housing reform in China. In: The Pacific Review 19 (1), pp. 39-61.

LEIMGRUBER, W., (1991): Boundary values and identity: the Swiss-Italian transborder region, In: The Geography of Border Landscapes, RUMLEY, D. and J. MINGHI (eds.), Routledge, London, pp. 43–62.

LEMANSKI, C. (2006): Spaces of Exclusivity or Connection? Linkages between a Gated Community and its Poorer Neighbour in a Cape Town Master Plan Development.

In: International Journal of Urban and Regional Research 30 (3), pp. 564–586.

Lɪ, L. (2013): "村改居"10年 相关政策仍未落实到位. Enghlish: After 10 Years of the Policy Issued, the Policy of Cungaiju Was Still under Performed. In: Guangzhou Daily, Published Date: 21.01.2013, URL: http://news.dayoo.com/guangzhou/201301/21/73437_28559785.htm (Accessed: 02.06.2015).

Lɪ, S.-M. and Y. Hᴜᴀɴɢ (2006): Urban Housing in China: Market Transition, Housing Mobility and Neighbourhood Change. In: Housing Studies 21 (5), pp. 613-623.

Lɪ, S.-ᴍ., Y. Zʜᴜ and L. Lɪ (2012): Neighborhood Type, Gatedness, and Residential Experiences in Chinese Cities: A Study of Guangzhou. In: Urban Geography 33 (2), pp. 237-255.

Lɪᴀɴɢ, Z. and Z. Mᴀ (2004): China's Floating Population: New Evidence from the 2000 Census. In: Population and Development Review 30 (3), pp. 467-488.

Lɪᴍ, G.C. and M.H. Lᴇᴇ (1990): Political ideology and housing policy in modern China. In: Environment and Planning C: Government and Policy 8 (4), pp. 477-487.

Lɪɴ, G.C.S. and S.P.S. Hᴏ (2005): The State, Land System, and Land Development Processes in Contemporary China. In: Annals of the Association of American Geographers 95 (2), pp. 411-436.

Lɪɴᴄᴏʟɴ, Y.S. and E.G. Gᴜʙᴀ (1985): Naturalistic Inquiry. SAGE, Beverly Hills,CA.

Lɪᴘᴘᴜɴᴇʀ, R. and B. Wᴇʀʟᴇɴ, (2009): Structuration Theory, In: International Encyclopedia of Human Geography, Kɪᴛᴄʜɪɴ, R. and N. Tʜʀɪꜰᴛ (eds.), Elsevier, Oxford, pp. 39-49.

Lɪᴜ, J. (2006): Modernization and crime patterns in China. In: Journal of Criminal Justice 34 (2), pp. 119-130.

Lɪᴜ, Y., S. Hᴇ, F. Wᴜ and C. Wᴇʙsᴛᴇʀ (2010): Urban villages under China's rapid urbanization: Unregulated assets and transitional neighbourhoods. In: Habitat International 34 (2), pp. 135-144.

Lɪᴜ, Y. and Z.G. Lɪ (2010): A review of studies on gated communities since the 1990s: From international to domestic perspectives. (in Chinese: 20世纪90年代以来封闭社区国内外研究述评,人文地理). In: Human Geography 113, pp. 10-15.

Lɪᴜ, Y. and F. Wᴜ (2006): Urban poverty neighbourhoods: Typology and spatial concentration under China's market transition, a case study of Nanjing. In: Geoforum 37 (4), pp. 610-626.

Lᴏᴡ, S. (2001): The Edge and the Center: Gated Communities and the Discourse of Urban Fear. In: American Anthropologist 103 (1), pp. 45-58.

Lᴏᴡ, S. (2003): Behind the Gates: Life, Security and the Pursuit of Happiness in Fortress America. Routledge, London.

Lᴜɴᴅᴇ́ɴ, T. and D. Zᴀʟᴀᴍᴀɴs (2001): Local co-operation, ethnic diversity and state territoriality – The case of Haparanda and Tornio on the Sweden – Finland border. In: GeoJournal 54 (1), pp. 33-42.

Lʏᴅᴇ, L.W. (1915): Some frontiers of tomorrow: An aspiration for Europe. A. & C. Black., London.

LYNCH, K. (1960): The Image of the City. The M.I.T. Press, Cambidge.
MA, L.J.C. (2002): Urban transformation in China, 1949-2000: a review and research agenda. In: Environment and Planning A 34 (9), pp. 1545-1569.
MA, L.J.C. and M. FAN (1994): Urbanisation from Below: The Growth of Towns in Jiangsu, China. In: Urban Studies 31 (10), pp. 1625-1645.
MADRAZO, B. and R.V. KEMPEN (2012): Explaining divided cities in China. In: Geoforum 43 (1), pp. 158–168.
MANZI, T. and B.S. BOWERS (2005): Gated Communities as Club Goods: Segregation or Social Cohesion? In: Housing Studies 20 (2), pp. 345-359.
MAXWELL, J.A. (2012): Qualitative Research Design: An Interactive Approach. SAGE, Thousand Oaks, CA.
MCKENZIE, E. (1994): Privatopia: Homeowners Associations and the Rise of Residential Private Communities. Yale University Press, New Haven.
MCKENZIE, E. (2005): Constructing the Pomerium in Las Vegas: A Case Study of Emerging Trends in American Gated Communities. In: Housing Studies 20 (2), pp. 187-203.
MEINHOF, U. (2002): Living (with) borders: identity discourses on east-west borders in Europe. UK: Ashgate, Aldershot.
MIAO, P. (2003): Deserted streets in a jammed town: the gated community in Chinese cities and its solution. In: Journal of Urban Design 8 (1), pp. 45 - 66.
MILES, M.B. and A.M. HUBERMAN (1994): Qualitative data analysis: An expanded sourcebook. Sage, Thousand Oaks, CA.
MINGHI, J.V. (1963): Boundary Studies in Political Geography. In: Annals of the Association of American Geographers 53 (3), pp. 407-428.
Ministry of Civil Affairs (2000): 民政部关于在全国推进城市社区建设的意见, English: Opinions on Promoting the Construction of Urban Communities. URL: http://www.njyhmz.gov.cn/s/11131909/t/223/10/6e/info4206.htm (Accessed: 20.05.2015).
MURRAY, C., (2004): Rethinking neighbourhoods: From urban villages to cultural hubs, In: City of quarters: urban villages in the contemporary city, BELL, D. and M. JAYNE (eds.), Aldershot and Burlington, Ashgate.
National Bureau of Statistics of China (2015): China Statistical Yearbook. China Statistics Press, Beijing, (in Chinese).
NetEase BBS (2014): 祈福新村的治安极度恶化, English: Public Security Deteriorates Sharply in Clifford Estate. In: NetEase BBS, Published Date: 26.09.2014. URL: http://bbs.gz.house.163.com/bbs/house_0q5s/456396170.html (Accessed: 20.05.2015).
NEVINS, J. (2002): Operation Gatekeeper and Beyond: The War on" Illegals" and the Remaking of the Us–Mexico Boundary. Routledge, London.
NEWMAN, D., (2003a): Boundaries, In: A Companion to Political Geography, AGNEW, J., K. MITCHELL AND G. TOAL (eds.), Blackwell Publishers, Malden, pp. 123-137.

NEWMAN, D. (2003b): On borders and power: A theoretical framework. In: Journal of Borderlands Studies 18 (1), pp. 13-25.

NEWMAN, D. (2006a): Borders and Bordering: Towards an Interdisciplinary Dialogue. In: European Journal of Social Theory 9 (2), pp. 171-186.

NEWMAN, D. (2006b): The lines that continue to separate us: borders in our 'borderless' world. In: Progress in Human Geography 30 (2), pp. 143-161.

NEWMAN, D. and A. PAASI (1998): Fences and neighbours in the postmodern world: boundary narratives in political geography. In: Progress in Human Geography 22 (2), pp. 186-207.

O'CONNELL, D.C. and S. KOWAL (1999): Transcription and the Issue of Standardization. In: Journal of Psycholinguistic Research 28 (2), pp. 103-120.

O'DOWD, L. (2002): The Changing Significance of European Borders. In: Regional & Federal Studies 12 (4), pp. 13-36.

OHMAE, K. (1990): The borderless world. HarperCollins, New York.

OHMAE, K. (1995): The End of the Nation State. Free Press, London.

OI, J.C. (1992): Fiscal Reform and the Economic Foundations of Local State Corporatism in China. In: World Politics 45 (1), pp. 99-126.

PAASI, A. (1996): Territories, boundaries, and consciousness: The changing geographies of the Finnish-Russian boundary. Wiley, Chichester.

PAASI, A. (1999): Boundaries as Social Practice and Discourse: The Finnish-Russian Border. In: Regional Studies 33 (7), pp. 669-680.

PAASI, A. (2005): Generations and the 'Development' of Border Studies. In: Geopolitics 10 (4), pp. 663-671.

PAASI, A. (2009a): Bounded Spaces in a 'Borderless World': Border Studies, Power and the Anatomy of Territory. In: Journal of Power 2 (2), pp. 213-234.

PAASI, A., (2009b): Political boundaries, In: International Encyclopedia in Human Geography, KITCHIN, R. and N. THRIFT (eds.), Elsevier, London, pp. 217-226.

PAASI, A., (2011): A Border Theory: An unattainable dream or a realistic aim for border scholars?, In: The Ashgate Research Companion to Border Studies, WASTL-WALTER, D. (ed.), Ashgate, London, pp. 11-31.

Panyu Statistical Bureau (1992): Panyu Statistic Yearbook. Panyu Statistical Bureau, Panyu.

PARKER, N., N. VAUGHAN-WILLIAMS, L. BIALASIEWICZ, S. BULMER, B. CARVER and R. DURIE (2009): Lines in the Sand? Towards an Agenda for Critical Border Studies. In: Geopolitics 14 (3), pp. 582-587.

POW, C.-P. (2007a): Constructing a new private order: gated communities and the privatization of urban life in post-reform Shanghai. In: SOCIAL & CULTURAL GEOGRAPHY 8 (6), pp. 813-833.

POW, C.-P. (2007b): Securing the 'civilised' enclaves: Gated communities and the moral geographies of exclusion in (post-) socialist shanghai. In: Urban Studies 44 (8), pp. 1539-1558.

POW, C.P. and L. KONG (2007): Marketing the Chinese Dream Home: Gated Communities and Representations of the Good Life in (Post-) Socialist Shanghai. In: Urban Geography 28 (2), pp. 129-159.

PRESCOTT, J.R.V. (1965): The geography of frontiers and boundaries. Hutchinson University Library, London.

PRESCOTT, J.R.V. (1987): Political Frontiers and Boundaries. Allen and Unwin, London.

QIAN, J. (2014): Deciphering the Prevalence of Neighborhood Enclosure Amidst Post-1949 Chinese Cities: A Critical Synthesis. In: Journal of Planning Literature 29 (1), pp. 3-19.

RAGIN, C.C., (1992): Cases of "What is a case?", In: What Is a Case ?: Exploring the Foundations of Social Inquiry, RAGIN, C. C. and H. S. BECKER (eds.), Cambridge University Press, Cambridge, pp. 1-18.

READ, B.L. (2008): Assessing Variation in Civil Society Organizations: China's Homeowner Associations in Comparative Perspective. In: Comparative Political Studies 41 (9), pp. 1240-1265.

ROITMAN, S. (2005): Who segregates whom? The analysis of a gated community in Mendoza, Argentina. In: Housing Studies 20 (2), pp. 303 - 321.

ROITMAN, S. (2010): Gated communities: definitions, causes and consequences. In: Urban Design and Planning 163 (1), pp. 31-38.

RUMFORD, C. (2006): Theorizing Borders. In: European Journal of Social Theory 9 (2), pp. 155-169.

SABATINI, F. and R. SALCEDO (2007): Gated communities and the poor in Santiago, Chile: Functional and symbolic integration in a context of aggressive capitalist colonization of lower-class areas. In: Housing Policy Debate 18 (3), pp. 577-606.

SALCEDO, R. and A. TORRES (2004): Gated communities in Santiago: wall or frontier? . In: International Journal of Urban and Regional Research 28 (1), pp. 27-44.

SASSEN, S. (2013): When the center no longer holds: Cities as frontier zones. In: Cities 34, pp. 67–70.

SAYER, A. (1992): Method in Social Science: A Realist Approach.

SENDHARDT, B., (2013): Border Types and Bordering Processes:A Theoretical Approach to the Eu/Polish-Ukrainian Border as a Multi-Dimensional Phenomenon, In: Borders and Border Regions in Europe. Changes, Challenges and Chances, LECHEVALIER, A. and J. WIELGOHS (eds.), transcript Verlag, Bielefeld, pp. 21-43.

SHEN, J. (2002): A study of the temporary population in Chinese cities. In: Habitat International 26 (3), pp. 363-377.

SHEN, J. (2007): Scale, state and the city: Urban transformation in post-reform China. In: Habitat International 31 (3–4), pp. 303-316.

SHI, X. (2004): The Pattern of Real Estate. Guangdong Economic Press, Guangzhou (in Chinese).

SOJA, E.W., (2005): Borders unbound: Globalization, regionalism, and the postmetropolitan transition, In: B/ordering space, HOUTUM, H. V., O. KRAMSCH and W. ZIERHOFER (eds.), Ashgate, Burlington, pp. 33–46.

SONG, W. and X. ZHU (2009): China Gated Communities: The Negative Social Effects of Social Differentiation (in Chinese: 中国封闭社区——社会分异的消极空间响应, 规划师). In: Planners 25 (11), pp. 82-86.

SONG, Y., Z. YVES and C. DING (2008): Let's Not Throw the Baby out with the Bath Water: The Role of Urban Villages in Housing Rural Migrants in China. In: Urban Studies 45 (2), pp. 313-330.

SPRADLEY, J.P. (1980): Participant observation. Holt, Rinehart & Winston, New York.

SPYKMAN, N.J. (1942): Frontiers, Security and International Organization. In: Geographical Review 32 (3), pp. 430-445.

STETTER, S. (2005): Theorizing the European Neighbourhood Policy: Debordering and Rebordering in the Mediterranean. In: EUI, Robert Schuman Centre for Advanced Studies Working Paper RSCAS No. 34, Internet web site for the European University Institute, Florence.

STETTER, S. (2008): Territories We Make and Unmake.The Social Construction of Borders and Territory in the Age of Globalization. In: Harvard International Review, September.

TANG, Y. (1989): Urban land use in China: Policy issues and options. In: Land Use Policy 6 (1), pp. 53-63.

TAO, R., (2008): Hukou reform and social security for migrant workers in China, In: Labour Migration and Social Development in Contemporary China, MURPHY, R. (ed.), Routledge, London, pp. 73-95.

TEDDLIE, C. and A. TASHAKKORI (2006): A general typology of research designs featuring mixed methods. In: Research in the Schools 13 (1), pp. 12-28.

THUILLIER, G. (2005): Gated communities in the metropolitan area of Buenos Aires, Argentina: a challenge for town planning. In: Housing Studies 20 (2), pp. 255 - 271.

TIAN, L. (2008): The Chengzhongcun Land Market in China: Boon or Bane? — a Perspective on Property Rights. In: International Journal of Urban and Regional Research 32 (2), pp. 282-304.

VAN HOUTUM, H. (2000): An overview of European geographical research on borders and border regions. In: Journal of Borderlands Studies, 15 (1), pp. 57-83.

VAN HOUTUM, H. (2005): The Geopolitics of Borders and Boundaries. In: Geopolitics 10 (4), pp. 672–679.

VAN HOUTUM, H. and T. VAN NAERSSEN (2002): Bordering, Ordering and Othering. In: Tijdschrift Voor Economische En Sociale Geografie 93 (2), pp. 125–136.

VAN KEMPEN, R. (2007): Divided cities in the 21st century: challenging the importance of globalisation. In: Journal of Housing and the Built Environment 22 (1), pp. 13-31.

VESSELINOV, E. (2008): Members Only: Gated Communities and Residential Segregation in the Metropolitan United States. In: Sociological Forum 23 (3), pp. 536-555.

VESSELINOV, E. (2012): Segregation by Design: Mechanisms of Selection of Latinos and Whites into Gated Communities. In: Urban Affairs Review 48 (3), pp. 417-454.

VILA, P., (2003): The Limits of American Border Theory, In: Ethnography at the Border, VILA, P. (ed.), University of Minnesota Press, Minneapolis, pp. 306-341.

WANG, H., C. ZHAO, M. XIAOKAITI, Y. ZHOU and R. ZHAO (2012): Dual Land Market and Rapid China's Urbanization: Problems and Solutions. In: Chinese Studies 1 (1), pp. 1-4.

WANG, J. and S. LAU (2008): Forming foreign enclaves in Shanghai: state action in globalization. In: Journal of Housing and the Built Environment 23 (2), pp. 103-118.

WANG, Y. and S. SCOTT (2008): Illegal Farmland Conversion in China's Urban Periphery: Local Regime and National Transitions. In: Urban Geography 29 (4), pp. 327-347.

WANG, Y.P. (2001): Urban Housing Reform and Finance in China: A Case Study of Beijing. In: Urban Affairs Review 36 (5), pp. 620-645.

WANG, Y.P., Y. WANG and J. WU, (2010): Private rental housing in 'urban villages' in Shenzhen: problems or solutions? , In: Marginalization in Urban China: Comparative Perspectives, WU, F. and C. WEBSTER (eds.), Palgrave Macmillan, Basingstoke, pp. 153–174.

WEBER, R.P. (1990): Basic content analysis. Sage, Beverly Hills, CA.

WEBSTER, C. (2001): Gated cities of tomorrow. In: Town Planning Review 72 (2), pp. 149-169.

WEBSTER, C. (2002): Property rights and the public realm: gates, green belts, and Gemeinschaft. In: Environment and planning B 29, pp. 397-412.

WEHRHAHN, R. (2003): Gated Communities in Madrid: Zur Funktion von Mauern im europäischen Kontext [Gated Communities in Madrid: On the Function of Walls in the European Context]. In: Geographica Helvetica 58, pp. 302-313.

WEHRHAHN, R. and R. RAPOSO, (2006): The rise of gated residential neighborhoods in Portugal and Spain: Lisbon and Madrid, In: Private Cities: Global and Local Perspectives, GLASZE, G., C. WEBSTER and K. FRANTZ (eds.), Routledge, London, pp. 170–189.

WEI, Y.D. (2001): Decentralization, marketization, and globalization: the triple processes underlying regional development in China. In: Asian Geographer 20 (1-2), pp. 7-23.

WHEATLEY, P. (1971): The pivot of the four quarters: A preliminary enquiry into the origins and character of the ancient Chinese City. Edinburgh University Press, Edinburgh.

WILSON, T.M. and H. DONNAN (1998): Border identities: Nation and state at international frontiers. Cambridge university press, Cambridge.

WISSINK, B., R.V. KEMPEN, Y. FANG and S.-M. LI (2012): Introduction – Living in Chinese Enclave Cities. In: Urban Geography 33 (2), pp. 161-166.

WU, F. (2005): Rediscovering the 'Gate' under Market Transition: From Work-Unit Compounds to Commodity Housing Enclaves. In: Housing Studies 20 (2), pp. 235-254.

WU, F. (2008a): China's great transformation: Neoliberalization as establishing a market society. In: Geoforum 39 (3), pp. 1093-1096.

WU, F. (2010): Gated and packaged suburbia: Packaging and branding Chinese suburban residential development. In: Cities 27 (5), pp. 385-396.

WU, F. and Z. LI (2005): Sociospatial Differentiation: Processes and Spaces in Sub-districts of Shanghai. In: Urban Geography 26 (2), pp. 137-166.

WU, F. and K. WEBBER (2004): The rise of "foreign gated communities" in Beijing:between economic globalization and local institutions. In: Cities 21 (3), pp. 203-213.

WU, F., J. XU and A.G.-O. YEH (2007): Urban development in post-reform China: state, market, and space. Routledge, Abingdon and New York.

WU, F., F. ZHANG and C. WEBSTER (2013): Informality and the Development and Demolition of Urban Villages in the Chinese Peri-Urban Area. In: Urban Studies 50 (10), pp. 1919-1934.

WU, W. (2008b): Migrant Settlement and Spatial Distribution in Metropolitan Shanghai. In: The Professional Geographer 60 (1), pp. 101-120.

XU, J. and A.G.O. YEH (2003): Guangzhou. In: Cities 20 (5), pp. 361-374.

XU, M. and Z. YANG (2008): Theoretical debate on gated communities: genesis,controversies, and the way forward. In: Urban Design International 13, pp. 213–226.

XU, M. and Z. YANG (2009): Design history of China's gated cities and neighbourhoods: Prototype and evolution. In: Urban Design International 14, pp. 99-117.

YANG, X. (1993): Household Registration, Economic Reform and Migration. In: International Migration Review 27 (4), pp. 796-818.

YIP, N.M. (2012): Walled Without Gates: Gated Communities in Shanghai. In: Urban Geography 33 (2), pp. 221-236.

YU, Z. (2006): Heterogeneity and dynamics in China's emerging urban housing market: two sides of a success story from the late 1990s. In: Habitat International 30 (2), pp. 277-304.

ZHANG, J. (2012a): The Hukou System as China's Main Regulatory Framework for Temporary Rural-Urban Migration and Its Recent Changes. In: DIE ERDE 143 (3), pp. 233-247.

ZHANG, L. (2001): Strangers in the City: Reconfiguration of Space, Power, and Social Networks within China's Floating Population. Stanford University Press, Stanford.

ZHANG, L. (2012b): Economic Migration and Urban Citizenship in China: The Role of Points Systems. In: Population and Development Review 38 (3), pp. 503-533.

ZHANG, L., (2013): Crime data and criminological research in contemporary China, In: The Routledge Handbook of Criminology Chinese, CAO, L., I. Y. SUN and B. HEBENTON (eds.), Routledge, London and New York, pp. 171-179.

ZHANG, L., S.X.B. ZHAO and J.P. TIAN (2003): Self-help in housing and chengzhongcun in China's urbanization. In: International Journal of Urban and Regional Research 27 (4), pp. 912-937.

ZHANG, M., C.J. ZHU and C. NYLAND (2014): The Institution of Hukou-Based Social Exclusion: A Unique Institution Reshaping the Characteristics of Contemporary Urban China. In: International Journal of Urban and Regional Research 38 (4), pp. 1437-1457.

ZHANG, X.Q. (1997a): Chinese housing policy 1949-1978: the development of a welfare system. In: Planning Perspectives 12 (4), pp. 433-455.

ZHANG, X.Q. (1997b): Urban land reform in China. In: Land Use Policy 14 (3), pp. 187-199.

ZHAO, Y. and S.C. BOURASSA (2003): China's Urban Housing Reform: Recent Achievements and New Inequities. In: Housing Studies 18 (5), pp. 721-744.

Zhongcun Subdistrict Office (2014): 祈福社区简介,English: The Profile of Clifford Estate. URL: http://www.zhongcun.gov.cn/news/html/?1540.html (Accessed: 13.05.2015).

ZHOU, C. and Y. BIAN (2014): The Growth and Distribution of Population in Guangzhou City in 1982-2000 (in Chinese: 1982~2010年广州市人口增长与空间分布演变研究,地理科学). In: Scientia Geographica Sinica 34 (9), pp. 1085-1092.

ZHOU, Y. and L.J.C. MA (2000): Economic restructuring and suburbanization in China. In: Urban Geography 21 (3), pp. 205-236.

ZHU, J. (1994): Changing Land Policy and Its Impact on Local Growth: The Experience of the Shenzhen Special Economic Zone, China, in the 1980s. In: Urban Studies 31 (10), pp. 1611-1623.

ZHU, Y. (1999): New Paths to Urbanization in China: Seeking More Balanced Patterns. Nova Science Publication, New York.

ZHU, Y. (2000): In Situ Urbanization in Rural China: Case Studies from Fujian Province. In: Development and Change 31 (2), pp. 413-434.

List of Appendices

Appendix 1: List of questions of semi-structured interviews	165
List of questions for residents of Clifford Estate	165
List of questions for residents of Zhongyi Village	166
Appendix 2: Interview list	167
Appendix 3: A List of gated communities in Panyu District	175
Appendix 4: The SNPC statistic data of Clifford Estate and Zhongyi Village	179

List of questions of semi-structured interviews

List of questions for residents of Clifford Estate

1) How long have you lived in Clifford Estate?
2) Have you been to Zhongyi Village before? How often do you go there (How many times a week)? What is the purpose of your trips there?
3) Where do you see the village people most?
4) Do you know anyone who lives in Zhongyi Village? If yes, how did you get to know them?
5) Do you like to talk to the villagers? Have you made friends with any? Do you talk to them when you are shopping in the Zhongyi market? Where have the villagers come from? Are they indigenous villagers or migrant workers?
6) What connection do you have to Zhongyi Village? Do you think Zhongyi Village is a part of your life? Or, how important is Zhongyi Village in your everyday life? What changes have happened in Clifford Estate? I.e., the number and structure of the residents, the estate environment. Do you feel more isolated or integrated than you did before?
7) Do you go to Zhongyi Village more often than before? What is the reason for this change?
8) With respect to security, do you have different feelings between when you are in Clifford Estate and when you are in the Village?
9) Do residents send their children to the village school? Do you know anyone who has sent their children to the village school? Conversely, do you know if any village residents send their children to school in Clifford Estate?
10) What do you think is the function of the gates of Clifford Estate? Why do you need the walls and fences? Would you like to open the gate? Would you like to let the residents of Zhongyi Village come to Clifford Estate?
11) Is the entry restriction in Clifford Estate stricter than before?
12) Does the property management company organize any activities to enhance the connection between the estate and the village? If yes, have you taken part?
13) Are there any cultural activities held that include both Clifford Estate and Zhongyi Village?

List of questions for residents of Zhongyi Village

1) Are you a local villager or a migrant worker? [If migrant worker:] Where do you come from? How long have you been living here?
2) What do you do here? How did you find this job?
3) Have you been inside Clifford Estate before? If yes, how often have you been there? What is the purpose of your visits there? How about the residents living inside Clifford Estate?
4) Have you known anybody living inside Clifford Estate? How do you know them?
5) Have any villagers bought property inside Clifford Estate? How many have done this?
6) Have you had any connection with Clifford Estate?
7) What are the impacts of Clifford Estate on the village? Do any of these impacts affect you?
8) Where have you seen Clifford Estate residents most? Are you interested in talking or making friends with them?
9) What kind of people live inside Clifford Estate?
10) What kind of changes have happened in Zhongyi Village?

Appendix 2

Interview list

Number of interview (No)	Date of Interview	Gender	Estimated age	Job	Interviewee status	Place of Interview	Origin of the interviewee	Duration of interview (min)
1	02.09.2012	F	60s	Retired	Property owner	Bus station of Clifford Estate	Clifford Estate	10
2	02.09.2012	M	50s	Migrant work	Rural migrant	Zhongyi Liantang Park	Zhongyi village	12
3	12.09.2012	M	30s	Property agent	NDA	Clifford residential estate	Zhongyi village	50
4	17.11.2012	M	60s	Retired	Property owner	Clifford shopping area	Clifford Estate	29
5	01.12.2012	F	60s	Retired	Property owner	Bus station of Clifford Estate	Clifford Estate	12
6	01.12.2012	F	60s	Retired	Relatives of property owner	Zhongyi village	Clifford Estate	10
7	01.12.2012	F	60s	Farmer	Relatives of property owner	On the way home to Clifford Estate	Clifford Estate	10
8	01.12.2012	F	30s	NDA	Property owner	On the way home to Clifford Estate	Clifford Estate	5
9	03.12.2012	M	50s	Retired	Indigenous villager	Zhongyi Liantang Park	Zhongyi village	50

Number of interview (No)	Date of Interview	Gender	Estimated age	Job	Interviewee status	Place of Interview	Origin of the interviewee	Duration of interview (min)
11	04.12.2012	M	80s	Retired	Property owner	Clifford Estate, lake side	Clifford Estate	19
12	04.12.2012	F	30s	NDA	Property owner	Clifford Estate, lake side	Clifford Estate	20
13	04.12.2012	M	30s	Gold and foreign exchange	Property owner	Clifford Estate, lake side	Clifford Estate	39
14	05.12.2012	M	50s	Clifford bus driver	Clifford Estate Staff	On Clifford shuttle bus	Clifford Estate staff	23
15	05.12.2012	M	60s	Retired teacher	Indigenous villager	Zhongyi Liantang Park	Zhongyi village	55
16	05.12.2012	M	50s	Retired	Rural migrant	Zhongyi Liantang Park	Zhongyi village	26
17	05.12.2012	M	40s	Self employed Fish wholesale	Indigenous villager (From other village)	Zhongyi Liantang Park	Zhongyi village	45
18	08.12.2012	F	20s	NDA	Property owner	Clifford Estate, lake side	Clifford Estate	33
19	08.12.2012	F	80s	Retired	Property owner	Clifford Estate, lake side	Clifford Estate	78
20	08.12.2012	2M	20s, 30s	Computer Department of Clifford	Clifford Estate Staff	Clifford Estate, lake side	Clifford Estate staff	41

Appendix 2   169

21	08.12.2012	F	30s	Teacher	Property owner	a Restaurant in Clifford Estate commercial area	Clifford Estate	61*
22	09.12.2012	M	30s	Immigrant worker	Rural migrant	Zhongyi Liantang Park	Zhongyi village	25
23	09.12.2012	F	60s	Retired and take care of children	Rural migrant	Zhongyi Liantang Park	Zhongyi village	55
24	09.12.2012	M	20s	Grain stores owner	Rural migrant	Xiangguan Restaurant in Zhongyi village	Zhongyi village	15
25	09.12.2012	M	30s	Immigrant worker	Rural migrant	Zhongyi Liantang Park	Zhongyi village	15
26	09.12.2012	M	60s	Member of Painting Association/retired	Indigenous villager	Zhongyi Liantang Park	Zhongyi village	57
27	09.12.2012	F	40s	a self-employed street seamstress	Rural migrant	Zhongyi Food Market	Zhongyi village	55
28	09.12.2012	M	30s	Logistics and porter	Rural migrant	Zhongyi Food Market	Zhongyi village	25
29	09.12.2012	F	30s	Housewife	Property owner	Zhongyi Food Market	Clifford Estate	15
30	13.12.2012	F	20s	Unemployed	Rural migrant	Zhongyi Liantang Park	Zhongyi village	25
31	13.12.2012	F	50s	Unemployed	Rural migrant	Zhongyi Liantang Park	Zhongyi village	20
32	13.12.2012	F	30s	Renter	Renter	Clifford Estate, lake side	Clifford Estate	8

Number of interview (No)	Date of Interview	Gender	Estimated age	Job	Interviewee status	Place of Interview	Origin of the interviewee	Duration of interview (min)
33	13.12.2012	2F	20s,50s	Bakery staff (A mother and daughter)	Rural migrant	Clifford Estate, lake side	Zhongyi village	30
34	13.12.2012	F	40s	Film Editor	Property owner	Clifford Estate, lake side	Clifford Estate	74
35	05.10.2013	M	30s	Marketing personnel	Property owner	Clifford Estate, lake side	Clifford Estate	98
36	06.10.2013	M	50s	Migrant work	Rural migrant	Zhongyi Liantang Park	Zhongyi village	50
37	06.10.2013	M	80s	Retired	Indigenous villager	Zhongyi Liantang Park	Zhongyi village	60
38	06.10.2013	M	50s	Retired	Indigenous villager	Informant's home	Zhongyi village	20
39	06.10.2013	F	50s	Retired	Property owner	Clifford Estate, lake side	Clifford Estate	53
40	06.10.2013	F	60s	Retired	Relatives of property owner	Clifford Estate, lake side	Clifford Estate	40
41	11.10.2013	F	20s	Housewife	Rural migrant	Zhongyi Liantang Park	Zhongyi village	23
42	11.10.2013	F	50s	NDA	Local migrant	Zhongyi Liantang Park	Zhongyi village	57

Appendix 2   171

43	11.10.2013	M	30s	Sales manager	Property owner	Clifford Estate, lake side	Clifford Estate	36
44	11.10.2013	M	60s	Retired teacher	Property owner	Clifford Estate, lake side	Clifford Estate	65
45	11.10.2013	M	40s	NDA	Property owner	On the shuttle bus to city center	Clifford Estate	51
46	11.10.2013	M	60s	Retired	Property owner	Tianhuju sub district in Clifford Estate	Clifford Estate	70
47	13.10.2013	M	30s	Property industry	Property owner	Clifford Estate, lake side	Clifford Estate	74
48	13.10.2013	M	50s	Laid-off worker	Indigenous villager (with urban hukou)	Zhongsan Park	Zhongsan village	58
49	13.10.2013	F	50s	Migrant work	Rural migrant	Zhongsan Park	Zhongsan village	35
50	13.10.2013	M	20s	Migrant workers	Rural migrant	Zhongsan Park	Zhongsan village	30
51	13.10.2013	M	60s	NDA	Property owner	Clifford Estate, lake side	Clifford Estate	48
52	13.10.2013	M	60s	Retired	Indigenous villager	Zhongyi Liantang Park	Zhongyi village	28
53	13.10.2013	M	30s	Migrant workers	Rural migrant	Zhongyi Liantang Park	Zhongyi village	36
54	13.10.2013	M	30s	Guard	Rural migrant	Bus station of Clifford Estate	Clifford Estate staff	56
55	27.10.2013	F	30s	Urban planners	NDA	NDA	Panyu district	97
56	27.10.2013	M	50s	Urban planners	NDA	NDA	Panyu district	35
57	10.11.2014	M	40s	NDA	Rural migrant	Zhongyi Liantang Park	Zhongyi Village	35

Number of interview (No)	Date of Interview	Gender	Estimated age	Job	Interviewee status	Place of Interview	Origin of the interviewee	Duration of interview (min)
58	10.11.2014	M	50s	Retired	Indigenous villager	Informant's home	Zhongyi village	25
59	10.11.2014	2F	50s,50s	Migrant workers	Rural migrant	Zhongsan Park	Zhongyi village	31
60	10.11.2014	M	60s	Retired teacher	Indigenous villager (with Urban Hukou)	Informant's home	Zhongyi village	57**
61	10.11.2014	F	30s	NDA	Property owner	Clifford Estate, lake side	Clifford Estate	60
62	12.11.2014	6 M, 1 F	NDA	Village cadres	Zhongyi village committees	Meeting room of Zhongyi village	Zhongyi village	150
63	29.08.2012	M	30s	A teacher at Shunde Gountry Garden private school	Accommodated in Shunde Gountry Garden	Shunde Gountry Garden	Shunde Gountry Garden	90
64	10.12.2012	F	60S	Retired	Indigenous villager	Informant's home	Sangui village	60
65	10.12.2012	6 F	50s	Retired	Property owner	Dongyuan of Shunde Gountry Garden	Shunde Gountry Garden	50
66	10.12.2012	2M	30s,40s	cooks of a village restaurant	renters in village	Sangui village park	Sangui village	50
67	15.12.2012	M	30s	migrant worker	floating people	Sangui village park	Sangui village	30

Appendix 2

| 68 | 26.08.2012 | M | 30s | a civil servant of Zhongcun village | Indigenous villager and property owner of Jinxiu Garden | On the bus to Zhongcun village | Jinxiu Garden and Zhongcun village | 30 |
| 69 | 23.12.2012 | M | 30s | self employment venture | property owner of Jinxiu Garden | Bus station | Jinxiu Garden | 20 |

*Long term contact, three interviews in different fieldwork phases, **No 15 is the first interview with this interviewee

List of gated communities in Payu district

No	Town/ Subdistrict	Gated communities	Area (ha)
1	Zhongcun	Nanguo Aoyuan	52.8
2	Zhongcun	Clifford Estate	399.9
3	Zhongcun	Jinxiu Garden	67.8
4	Zhongcun	Shunde Country Garden	456.4
5	Zhongcun	Xiangjiang Estate	8.3
6	Zhongcun	Xiangjiang Estate	18.8
7	Xiaoguwei	Daxue Shiguan	5.9
8	Xiaoguwei	Xinghui Wenhua	5.3
9	Xiaoguwei	Xinghui Wenyu	3.6
10	Xiaoguwei	Xinghui Wenhan	5.4
11	Shiqiao	Overseas Chinese Town	30.0
12	Shiqiao	Xicheng Garden	21.0
13	Shiqiao	Huasheng Estate	6.8
14	Shiqiao	Qiaofu Garden	6.8
15	Shiqiao	Hongxi Garden	4.5
16	Shiqiao	Junlin Skyscraper	4.8
17	Shiqiao	Qiaoji Garden	1.6
18	Shiqiao	Yongyalang	3.0
19	Shiqiao	Huangsha Villa	16.1
20	Shiqiao	Boli Garden	7.6
21	Shiqiao	Easten Garden	7.8
22	Shiqiao	Xinye Garden	1.9
23	Shiqiao	Dong Xingyuan	1.8
24	Shiqiao	Shentai Garden	2.4
25	Shiqiao	Dong Huiyuan	5.3
26	Shiqiao	Dongsha Villa	4.3
27	Shiqiao	Ruiheyuan	1.6
28	Shiqiao	Dexin Estate	2.3
29	Shiqiao	Dongxiuyuan	2.5
30	Shiqiao	Huaying Mingyuan	1.3
31	Shiqiao	Yipin Haojing	4.3
32	Shiqiao	Kangleyuan	6.5
33	Shiqiao	Kangyuyuan	2.5

No	Town/ Subdistrict	Gated communities	Area (ha)
34	Shiqiao	Jiaoyu Huating	1.1
35	Shiqiao	Kangyuyuan	4.4
36	Shiqiao	Kangyuyuan	9.3
37	Shiqiao	Laifuyuan	1.4
38	Shiqiao	Kangfu Garden	2.0
39	Shiqiao	lvying Garden	2.2
40	Shiqiao	Baiyun Garden	1.5
41	Shiqiao	Beiliyuan	7.3
42	Shilou	Asian Games Town	70.7
43	Shilou	Kangleyuan Estate	7.9
44	Shilou	Lvyi Estate	6.6
45	Shilou	Baileyuan	8.5
46	Shilou	Zhuangshi Estate	20.0
47	Shilou	Mingren Villa	15.2
48	Shiji	Huting Garden	8.8
49	Shiji	Longji Garden	21.4
50	Shiji	Jiahu Garden	4.4
51	Shiji	Dongfangbaiyun	32.2
52	Shiji	Donghua Garden	18.2
53	Shiji	City Garden	23.3
54	Shiji	Cuiyong Huating	13.7
55	Shiji	Dongyi Xinqu	28.0
56	Shiji	Donghanyuan	1.9
57	Shiji	Jinhaian Garden	53.6
58	Shiji	Donghuzhou Garden	36.7
59	Shiji	Lvting Garden	1.6
60	Shiji	Dongsheng Mingzhu	3.9
61	Shiji	Dongyuhuating	3.8
62	Shiji	Dongsheng Garden	1.5
63	Shiji	Cuizhuyuan	11.6
64	Shawan	Shidaihaoting	7.7
65	Shawan	Agile Jinguancheng	8.0
66	Shatou	Hutu Garden	7.1

No	Town/ Subdistrict	Gated communities	Area (ha)
67	Shatou	Yongjing Villa	7.3
68	Shatou	Baocuiyuan	2.3
69	Qiaonan	Jinshalishui	15.9
70	Qiaonan	Hejin Garden	22.5
71	Qiaonan	Huayuan Estate	4.2
72	Qiaonan	Jinshawan Garden	10.3
73	Qiaonan	Clifford watertown	10.6
74	Qiaonan	Haolong Garden	7.9
75	Qiaonan	Huilong Garden	13.4
76	Qiaonan	Panyu Olympic Garden	56.9
77	Qiaonan	Langtaoju	17.7
78	Qiaonan	Newcentury Garden	21.5
79	Qiaonan	Lvtingyayuan	7.3
80	Qiaonan	Huijing Garden	11.6
81	Qiaonan	Lvtingyayuan	2.4
82	Qiaonan	Huahui	5.4
83	Qiaonan	Huijing Newtown	14.9
84	Qiaonan	Huijing Newtown	13.1
85	Qiaonan	Huayangnianhua	18.6
86	Qiaonan	Debao Garden	29.6
87	Qiaonan	Kangchengshuijun	7.3
88	Nancun	Star River	55.9
89	Nancun	Guangdi Garden	31.0
90	Nancun	Huanan Newtown	103.2
91	Nancun	Hunan country Garden	210.4
92	Nancun	Agile Garden	201.5
93	Nancun	Jinxiuxiangjiang	89.2
94	Nancun	Agile Jianqiao Garden	62.3
95	Nancun	Pearl River Estate	85.9
96	Nancun	Xiangxin	29.9
97	Nancun	Dexun Estate	65.6
98	Nancun	Zizai City	12.1
99	Nancun	Qinghuafang	11.6
100	Luopu	Guangzhou Country Garden	70.0

Appendix 3

No	Town/ Subdistrict	Gated communities	Area (ha)
101	Luopu	Lijiang Garden	94.6
102	Luopu	Luoxi Xincheng	99.1
103	Luopu	Guangao Garden	19.3
104	Luopu	Guangzhou Olympic Garden	36.7
105	Luopu	Donghai Garden	7.5
106	Luopu	Lvdai Garden	16.5
107	Luopu	Shanhuwanpan	54.1
108	Luopu	Bilihua	22.7
109	Luopu	Bilihua	16.3
110	Luopu	Laiyinghuayuan	5.1
111	Luopu	Xinghaiwan	39.5
112	Luopu	Zhujiang Garden	27.5
113	Luopu	Nantian Mingyuan	53.5
114	Lanhe	Changjiangshuma	5.1
115	Donghuan	Wanbo Garden	34.1
116	Donghuan	Diecui Liting	1.7
117	Donghuan	Mingcuiyuan	4.9
118	Donghuan	Panyi Garden	3.2
119	Donghuan	Huhao Garden	45.0
120	Dongchong	Mingyuan Villa	36.9
121	Dongchong	Dongfayuan	1.6
122	Dongchong	Wanxin Garden	2.3
123	Dongchong	Jinxiu Newtown	8.8
124	Dashi	Huli Estate	100.7
125	Dashi	Bingjianglvyuan	4.8
126	Dashi	Lijingyuan	5.3
127	Dashi	Jirilishe	5.7
128	Dashi	Jincheng Garden	14.0
129	Dashi	Tianlong Garden	7.8
130	Dashi	Xinyue Mingzhu	8.2
131	Dagang	Huicui Haoyuan	8.4
132	Dagang	Haogan Garden	9.2
133	Dagang	Lvtingyayuan	3.6
134	Dagang	Yinpin Garden	3.5

The SNPC Statistic data of Clifford Estate and Zhongyi Village (2010)

Item	Clifford Estate		Zhongyi Village	
	Count	%	Count	%
Total Population (person)	27136	100	13871	100
Total Households (household)	10736	100	3290	100
Age (person)	27136	100	13871	100
0-5	2372	8.7	761	5.5
6-18	2793	10.3	1506	10.9
19-30	5563	20.5	4416	31.8
31-45	9890	36.4	4829	34.8
46-60	3576	13.2	1619	11.7
61 and older	2942	10.8	740	5.3
Education (person)	24764	100	13110	100
No schooling	224	0.9	40	0.3
Primary school	2862	11.6	3053	23.3
Junior secondary school	3685	14.9	6754	51.5
Senior secondary school	5335	21.5	2416	18.4
College	5783	23.4	678	5.2
University	6089	24.6	165	1.3
Graduate and higher level	786	3.2	4	0.0
Hukou structure of residents	27136	100	13871	100
Population with Panyu hukou	8588	31.6	4280	30.9
Population with Guangzhou hukou	8257	30.4	271	2.0
Population moved in from other city of Guangdong Province (external hukou)	3575	13.2	2092	15.1
Population moved in from other provinces (external hukou)	6716	24.7	7228	52.1
Housing conditions (household)	10736	100	3290	100
Less than 50 m^2	169	1.6	1597	48.5
51-80 m^2	4188	39.0	675	20.5
81-100 m^2	3012	28.1	373	11.3
101-120 m^2	1850	17.2	194	5.9
121-150 m^2	861	8.0	135	4.1
More than 150 m^2	656	6.1	316	9.6
Average floor space of building (m^2/person)	37.8	100	18.6	100

Item	Clifford Estate		Zhongyi Village	
	Count	%	Count	%
Sample survey of rental level (household)	90	100	197	100
100~200 Yuan per month	0	0	68	34.5
200~500 Yuan per month	2	2.2	103	52.3
500~1000 Yuan per month	15	16.7	14	7.1
1000~1500 Yuan per month	35	38.9	5	2.5
1500~2000 Yuan per month	17	18.9	3	1.5
2000~3000 Yuan per month	13	14.4	1	0.5
More than 3000 Yuan per month	8	8.9	3	1.5

Ältere Bände der
Schriften des Geographischen Instituts der Universität Kiel
(Band I, 1932 - Band 43, 1975)
sowie der
Kieler Geographischen Schriften
(Band 44, 1976 - Band 83, 1991)
sind teilweise noch auf Anfrage im Geographischen Institut der CAU erhältlich.
Das vollständige Verzeichnis finden Sie auf der Homepage des Instituts.

Band 84
Neumeyer, Michael: Heimat. Zu Geschichte und Begriff eines Phänomens. 1992. V, 150 S. ISBN 3-923887-26-4. 9.00 €

Band 85
Kuhnt, Gerald und Zölitz-Möller, Reinhard (Hrsg): Beiträge zur Geoökologie aus Forschung, Praxis und Lehre. Otto Fränzle zum 60. Geburtstag. 1992. VIII, 376 S., 34 Tab. und 88 Abb. ISBN 3-923887-27-2. 19,00 €

Band 86
Reimers, Thomas: Bewirtschaftungsintensität und Extensivierung in der Landwirtschaft. Eine Untersuchung zum raum-, agrar- und betriebsstrukturellen Umfeld am Beispiel Schleswig-Holsteins. 1993. XII, 232 S., 44 Tab., 46 Abb. und 12 Klappkarten im Anhang. ISBN 3-923887-28-0. 12,20 €

Band 87
Stewig, Reinhard (Hrsg.): Stadtteiluntersuchungen in Kiel, Baugeschichte, Sozialstruktur, Lebensqualität, Heimatgefühl. 1993. VIII, 337 S., 159 Tab., 10 Abb., 33 Karten und 77 Graphiken. ISBN 923887-29-9. 12.30 €

Band 88
Wichmann, Peter: Jungquartäre randtropische Verwitterung. Ein bodengeographischer Beitrag zur Landschaftsentwicklung von Südwest-Nepal. 1993. X, 125 S., 18 Tab. und 17 Abb. ISBN 3-923887-30-2. 10,10 €

Band 89
Wehrhahn, Rainer: Konflikte zwischen Naturschutz und Entwicklung im Bereich des Atlantischen Regenwaldes im Bundesstaat São Paulo, Brasilien. Untersuchungen zur Wahrnehmung von Umweltproblemen und zur Umsetzung von Schutzkonzepten. 1994. XIV, 293 S., 72 Tab., 41 Abb. und 20 Fotos. ISBN 3-923887-31-0. 17,50 €

Band 90
Stewig, Reinhard (Hrsg.): Entstehung und Entwicklung der Industriegesellschaft auf den Britischen Inseln. 1995. XII, 367 S., 20 Tab., 54 Abb. und 5 Graphiken. ISBN 3-923887-32-9. 16,60 €

Band 91
Bock, Steffen: Ein Ansatz zur polygonbasierten Klassifikation von Luft- und Satellitenbildern mittels künstlicher neuronaler Netze. 1995. XI, 152 S., 4 Tab. und 48 Abb. ISBN 3-923887-33-7. 8,60 €

Band 92
Matuschewski, Anke: Stadtentwicklung durch Public-Private-Partnership in Schweden. Kooperationsansätze der achtziger und neunziger Jahre im Vergleich. 1996. XI, 246 S., 16 Tab., 34 Abb., und 20 Fotos.
ISBN 3-923887-34-5. 12,20 €

Band 93
Ulrich, Johannes und Kortum, Gerhard.: Otto Krümmel (1854-1912): Geograph und Wegbereiter der modernen Ozeanographie. 1997. VIII, 340 S. ISBN 3-923887-35-3. 24,00 €

Band 94
Schenck, Freya S.: Strukturveränderungen spanisch-amerikanischer Mittelstädte untersucht am Beispiel der Stadt Cuenca, Ecuador. 1997. XVIII, 270 S. ISBN 3-923887-36-1. 13,20 €

Band 95
Pez, Peter: Verkehrsmittelwahl im Stadtbereich und ihre Beeinflussbarkeit. Eine verkehrsgeographische Analyse am Beispiel Kiel und Lüneburg. 1998. XVII, 396 S., 52 Tab. und 86 Abb. ISBN 3-923887-37-X. 17,30 €

Band 96
Stewig, Reinhard: Entstehung der Industriegesellschaft in der Türkei. Teil 1: Entwicklung bis 1950, 1998. XV, 349 S., 35 Abb., 4 Graph., 5 Tab. und 4 Listen.
ISBN 3-923887-38-8. 15,40 €

Band 97
Higelke, Bodo (Hrsg.): Beiträge zur Küsten- und Meeresgeographie. Heinz Klug zum 65. Geburtstag gewidmet von Schülern, Freunden und Kollegen. 1998. XXII, 338 S., 29 Tab., 3 Fotos und 2 Klappkarten. ISBN 3-923887-39-6. 18,40 €

Band 98
Jürgens, Ulrich: Einzelhandel in den Neuen Bundesländern - die Konkurrenzsituation zwischen Innenstadt und "Grüner Wiese", dargestellt anhand der Entwicklungen in Leipzig, Rostock und Cottbus. 1998. XVI. 395 S., 83 Tab. und 52 Abb.
ISBN 3-923887-40-X. 16,30 €

Band 99
Stewig, Reinhard: Entstehung der Industriegesellschaft in der Türkei. Teil 2: Entwicklung 1950-1980. 1999. XI, 289 S., 36 Abb., 8 Graph., 12 Tab. und 2 Listen.
ISBN 3-923887-41-8. 13,80 €

Band 100
Eglitis, Andri: Grundversorgung mit Gütern und Dienstleistungen in ländlichen Räumen der neuen Bundesländer. Persistenz und Wandel der dezentralen Versorgungsstrukturen seit der deutschen Einheit. 1999. XXI, 422 S., 90 Tab. und 35 Abb.
ISBN 3-923887-42-6. 20,60 €

Band 101
Dünckmann, Florian: Naturschutz und kleinbäuerliche Landnutzung im Rahmen Nachhaltiger Entwicklung. Untersuchungen zu regionalen und lokalen Auswirkungen von umweltpolitischen Maßnahmen im Vale do Ribeira, Brasilien. 1999. XII, 294 S., 10 Tab., 9 Karten und 1 Klappkarte.ISBN 3-923887-43-4. 23,40 €

Band 102
Stewig, Reinhard: Entstehung der Industriegesellschaft in der Türkei. Teil 3: Entwicklung seit 1980. 2000. XX, 360 S., 65 Tab., 12 Abb. und 5 Graphiken
ISBN 3-923887-44-2. 17,10 €

Band 103
*Bähr, Jürgen & Widderich, Sönke: Vom Notstand zum Normalzustand - eine Bilanz des kubanischen Transformationsprozesses. La larga marcha desde el período especial habia la normalidad – un balance de la transformación cubana. 2000. XI, 222 S., 51 Tab. und 15 Abb. ISBN 3-923887-45-0. 11,40 €

Band 104
Bähr, Jürgen & Jürgens, Ulrich: Transformationsprozesse im Südlichen Afrika – Konsequenzen für Gesellschaft und Natur. Symposium in Kiel vom 29.10.-30.10.1999. 2000. 222 S., 40 Tab., 42 Abb. und 2 Fig.
ISBN 3-923887-46-9. 13,30 €

Band 105
Gnad, Martin: Desegregation und neue Segregation in Johannesburg nach dem Ende der Apartheid. 2002. 281 S., 28 Tab. und 55 Abb.
ISBN 3-923887-47-7. 14,80 €

Band 106
*Widderich, Sönke: Die sozialen Auswirkungen des kubanischen Transformationsprozesses. 2002. 210 S., 44 Tab. und 17 Abb. ISBN 3-923887-48-5. 12,55 €

*= vergriffen

Band 107
Stewig, Reinhard: Bursa, Nordwestanatolien: 30 Jahre danach. 2003. 163 S., 16 Tab., 20 Abb. und 20 Fotos.ISBN 3-923887-49-3. 13,00 €

Band 108
Stewig, Reinhard: Proposal for Including Bursa, the Cradle City of the Ottoman Empire, in the UNESCO Wolrd Heritage Inventory. 2004. X, 75 S., 21 Abb., 16 Farbfotos und 3 Pläne. ISBN 3-923887-50-7. 18,00 €

Band 109
Rathje, Frank: Umnutzungsvorgänge in der Gutslandschaft von Schleswig-Holstein und Mecklenburg-Vorpommern. Eine Bilanz unter der besonderen Berücksichtigung des Tourismus. 2004. VI, 330 S., 56 Abb. ISBN 3-923887-51-5. 18,20 €

Band 110
Matuschewski, Anke: Regionale Verankerung der Informationswirtschaft in Deutschland. Materielle und immaterielle Beziehungen von Unternehmen der Informationswirtschaft in Dresden-Ostsachsen, Hamburg und der TechnologieRegion Karlsruhe. 2004. II, 385 S., 71 Tab. und 30 Abb. ISBN 3-923887-52-3. 18,00 €

Band 111
*Gans, Paul, Axel Priebs und Rainer Wehrhahn (Hrsg.): Kulturgeographie der Stadt. 2006. VI, 646 S., 65 Tab. und 110 Abb.
ISBN 3-923887-53-1. 34,00 €

Band 112
Plöger, Jörg: Die nachträglich abgeschotteten Nachbarschaften in Lima (Peru). Eine Analyse sozialräumlicher Kontrollmaßnahmen im Kontext zunehmender Unsicherheiten. 2006. VI, 202 S., 1 Tab. und 22 Abb. ISBN 3-923887-54-X. 14,50 €

Band 113
Stewig, Reinhard: Proposal for Including the Bosphorus, a Singularly Integrated Natural, Cultural and Historical Sea- and Landscape, in the UNESCO World Heritage Inventory. 2006. VII, 102 S., 5 Abb. und 48 Farbfotos. ISBN 3-923887-55-8. 19,50 €

Band 114
Herzig, Alexander: Entwicklung eines GIS-basierten Entscheidungsunterstützungssystems als Werkzeug nachhaltiger Landnutzungsplanung. Konzeption und Aufbau des räumlichen Landnutzungsmanagementsystems LUMASS für die ökologische Optimierung von Landnutzungsprozessen und -mustern. 2007. VI, 146 S., 21 Tab. und 46 Abb.
ISBN 978-3-923887-56-9. 12,00 €

Band 115
Galleguillos Araya-Schübelin, Myriam Ximena: Möglichkeiten zum Abbau von Segregation in Armenvierteln. Die Frage nach der sozialen und ökonomischen Nachhaltigkeit urbaner Ballungsräume am Beispiel Santiago de Chile. 2007. VIII, 226 S., 6 Tab. und 19 Abb. ISBN 978-3-923887-57-6. 15,00 €

Band 116
Sandner Le Gall, Verena: Indigenes Management mariner Ressourcen in Zentralamerika: Der Wandel von Nutzungsmustern und Institutionen in den autonomen Regionen der Kuna (Panama) und Miskito (Nicaragua). 2007. VIII, 390 S., 14 Tab. und 44 Abb.
ISBN 978-3-923887-58-3. 18,00 €

Band 117
Wehrhahn, Rainer (Hrsg.): Risiko und Vulnerabilität in Lateinamerika. 2007. II, 314 S., 13 Tab. und 50 Abb.
ISBN 978-3-923887-59-0. 16,50 €

Band 118
Klein, Ulrike: Geomedienkompetenz. Untersuchung zur Akzeptanz und Anwendung von Geomedien im Geographieunterricht unter besonderer Berücksichtigung moderner Informations- und Kommunikationstechniken. 2008. XI, 244 S., 89 Tab. und 57 Abb.
ISBN 978-3-923887-60-6. 15,50 €

*= vergriffen

Band 119
Sterr, Horst, Christoph Corves und Götz von Rohr (Hrsg.): The ToLearn Project, Learning how to Foster Sustainable Tourism in the North Sea Region 2009. III, 168 S., 6 Tab. und 23 farbige Abb.
ISBN 978-3-923887-61-3. 15,00 €

Band 120
Sandfuchs, Katrin: Wohnen in der Stadt. Bewohnerstrukturen, Nachbarschaften und Motive der Wohnstandortwahl in innenstadtnahen Neubaugebieten Hannovers. 2009. X, 282 S., 30 Tab. und 44 Abb.
ISBN 978-3-923887-62-0. 16,20 €

Band 121
Oppelt, Natascha: Monitoring of the Biophysical Status of Vegetation Using Multi-angular, Hyperspectral Remote Sensing for the Optimization of a Physically-based SVAT Model. 2010. XXII, 130 S., 34 Tab. und 62 Abb. davon 24 farbig
ISBN 978-3-923887-63-7. 14,50 €

Band 122
Mössner, Samuel: Integrierte Stadtentwicklungsprogramme – eine „Vertrauens-Konstellation". Beispiele aus Frankfurt a. M. und Mailand. 2010. X, 202 S., 5 Tab. und 6 Abb.
ISBN 978-3-923887-64-4. 14,50 €

Band 123
Sandner Le Gall, Verena und Rainer Wehrhahn (Hrsg.): Geographies of Inequality in Latin America. 2012. II, 402 S., 22 Tab. und 64 Abb.
ISBN 978-3-923887-65-1. 17,50 €

Band 124
Schlichting, Ina von: Migration, Translokalität und Doing Community. Stabilisierende Eigenschaften einer ecuadorianischen Dorfgemeinschaft in Ecuador, Deutschland und Spanien. 2013. IX, 242 S., 7 Tab. und 14 Abb.
ISBN 978-3-923887-66-8. 16,50 €

Band 125
Lukas, Michael, Neoliberale Stadtentwicklung in Santiago de Chile. Akteurskonstellationen und Machtverhältnisse in der Planung städtebaulicher Megaprojekte. 2014. IX, 244 S., 13 Tab. und 11 Abb.
ISBN 978-3-923887-67-5. 16,90 €

Band 126
Massmann, Frederick, Hochwasser in Bangkok: Verwundbarkeiten und Handlungsstrategien von Bewohnern. 2015. IX, 232 S., 4 Tab. und 53 Abb.
ISBN 978-3-923887-68-2. 16,50 €

Band 127
Maus, Gunnar, Erinnerungslandschaften: Praktiken ortsbezogenen Erinnerns am Beispiel des Kalten Krieges . 2015. IX, 293 S., 20 Tab. und 31 Abb.
ISBN 978-3-923887-69-9. 16,50 €

Band 128
Liao, Kaihuai, Debordering and Rebordering Processes in Suburban Guangzhou, China. 2016. XIV, 179 S., 9 Tab. und 35 Abb.
ISBN 978-3-923887-70-5. 15,90 €